Bourdieu

Also by Tony Schirato

Communication and Cultural Literacy
by Tony Schirato and Susan Yell (1996, 2000)

Understanding Foucault
by Tony Schirato, Geoff Danaher and Jen Webb (2000, 2012)

Understanding Bourdieu
by Jen Webb, Tony Schirato and Geoff Danaher (2002)

Get Your Message Across
by Jacqui Ewart, Gail Sedorkin and Tony Schirato (1998)

Beginning University
by Andrew Wallace, Tony Schirato and Philippa Bright (1999)

Asia
by David Birch, Tony Schirato and Sanjay Srivastava (2001)

Understanding Globalization
by Tony Schirato and Jen Webb (2003)

Reading the Visual
by Tony Schirato and Jen Webb (2004)

Understanding Sports Culture
by Tony Schirato (2008)

Understanding Judith Butler
by Anita Brady and Tony Schirato (2010)

Sports Discourse
by Tony Schirato (2015)

Bourdieu

A CRITICAL INTRODUCTION

TONY SCHIRATO WITH MARY ROBERTS

SYDNEY • MELBOURNE • AUCKLAND • LONDON

First published in 2018

Copyright © Tony Schirato and Mary Roberts 2018

All rights reserved. No part of this book may be reproduced or transmitted in any form or by any means, electronic or mechanical, including photocopying, recording or by any information storage and retrieval system, without prior permission in writing from the publisher. The Australian *Copyright Act 1968* (the Act) allows a maximum of one chapter or 10 per cent of this book, whichever is the greater, to be photocopied by any educational institution for its educational purposes provided that the educational institution (or body that administers it) has given a remuneration notice to the Copyright Agency (Australia) under the Act.

Allen & Unwin
83 Alexander Street
Crows Nest NSW 2065
Australia
Phone: (61 2) 8425 0100
Email: info@allenandunwin.com
Web: www.allenandunwin.com

A catalogue record for this book is available from the National Library of Australia

ISBN 978 1 76011 174 8

Internal design by Midland Typesetters, Australia
Set in 11/15 pt Minion LT by Midland Typesetters, Australia

10 9 8 7 6 5 4 3 2 1

*The book is dedicated to the memory of
Kay Roberts and Ron Schirato*

CONTENTS

1	Antecedents and trajectories	1
2	Scholarly trajectory	44
3	Education, socio-cultural reproduction and class	89
4	Distinction	114
5	The habitus	133
6	Cultural field	156
7	Cultural capital	174
8	Symbolic power	191
9	The logic of practice	208
Acknowledgements		241
Bibliography		243
Index		251

1
Antecedents and trajectories

Introduction

In his obituary published on *The Guardian* website in 2002, Pierre Bourdieu was described as 'for many, the leading intellectual of present-day France' (*Guardian Online* 2002). In a postscript to that obituary, Stuart Jefferies wrote:

> Last year a documentary film about Pierre Bourdieu—*Sociology is a Combat Sport*—became an unexpected hit in Paris. Its very title stressed how much of a politically engaged intellectual Bourdieu was, taking on the mantle of Emile Zola and Jean-Paul Sartre in French public life, and slugging it out with politicians because he thought that was what people like him should do. Bourdieu became 'the intellectual reference' for movements opposed to neo-liberalism and globalisation that developed in France and

> elsewhere during the 90s. 'Ours is a Darwinian world of insecurity and stress,' he wrote, 'where the permanent threat of unemployment creates a permanent state of precariousness'... Among those he actively supported was José Bové, the French small-farmers' leader, who, in 1999, gained fame overnight by leading an attack on a McDonald's outlet, regarded as a symbol of globalisation. 'For him,' Bové said about Bourdieu, 'life itself was a commitment.' Bourdieu's death deprives France of one of its great post-war intellectuals, a thinker in the same rank as Foucault, Barthes and Lacan. (*Guardian Online* 2002)

The focus in this and other accounts of Bourdieu's life and career is predominantly on his role as an intellectual who, much like Foucault, used his position and status within the French academy to intervene on a range of topics and issues, but most particularly with regard to the rights of, and the injustices suffered by, groups who remained outside mainstream networks of power (the colonized, provincial peasants, urban workers, migrants and students). What is less visible in these public testimonies is an appreciation of the scope, breadth, influence and significance of Bourdieu's scholarly and intellectual work: an argument could be made that, in terms of the extent to which his ideas have been taken up by and influenced academic and intellectual fields (education, anthropology, sociology, communication, critical and cultural theory, literature and art, to name the most obvious examples), again the only comparable contemporary figure is Foucault. As Nicholas Brown and Imre Szeman (2000) write in their Introduction to *Pierre Bourdieu: Fieldwork in Culture*, the aim of Bourdieu's academic work was not limited to 'the reinvigoration of the discipline of sociology in France': his main objective was, in his own words, nothing less than a reappropriation of 'the social unconscious' (Bourdieu 2000: 10). To achieve this, he attempted

> to produce a theory of social life drawn neither from the mental laboratories of philosophy, nor from the strict empiricism of

much of what passes for sociological research, but from a highly theoretical mode of analysis that nevertheless pays careful attention to the complex dynamics of social life itself (Brown & Szeman 2000: 1).

As Bourdieu himself (2007), along with others (Grenfell 2012; Robbins 2000) notes, his familial and social background was unusual for a highly successful French academic of the mid-twentieth century. Born in 1930, he came from a relatively poor, rural background in the southwest of France. However, academic success in the French school system led him to one of the most prestigious institutions in France, the École Normale Supérieure in Paris, in 1951 to study in one of the most academically prestigious fields: philosophy. He was an *oblat miraculé*, glossed by his translator Richard Nice as 'Bourdieu's term for a pupil who commits himself entirely to the scholastic success which gives him a "miraculous" social mobility' (Bourdieu 2007: 5). This produced

> a very strong discrepancy between high academic consecration and low social origin, in other words a cleft habitus, inhabited by tensions and contradictions. This kind of 'coincidence of contraries' no doubt helped to institute, in a lasting way, an ambivalent, contradictory relationship to the academic institution, combining rebellion and submission, rupture and expectation, which is perhaps at the root of a relation to myself that is also ambivalent and contradictory—as if the self-certainty linked to the feeling of being consecrated were undermined in its very principle by the most radical uncertainty towards the consecrating institution, a kind of bad mother, vain and deceiving. (Bourdieu 2007: 100)

After successfully completing his university studies in 1955, he taught briefly in a provincial *lycée* before being conscripted into the French army in Algeria. As he describes in *Sketch for a Self-Analysis*, he stepped off the 'very privileged route reserved for students of the École Normale' (2007: 38) and instead of completing his military service in Versailles, he was sent to Algeria as a soldier (2007: 38). Towards the end of his military service there, he took up a clerical role in the military section of the French administrative system based in Algiers. During this time, he wrote *Sociologie de l'Algérie*, which was published in 1958. After completing his military service, he taught at the University of Algiers from 1958 to 1960 (Bourdieu 2007: 38).

On his return to Paris in 1960, Bourdieu attended lectures given by Claude Lévi-Strauss and worked as an assistant to Raymond Aron (Grenfell 2012: 13), who had founded the Centre de Sociologie Européenne (CSE). Bourdieu was appointed as Secretary (Robbins 2000: 33) and eventually became the Director of the Centre in 1968 (2000: 16). Jean-Claude Passeron was also assisting Aron, and together they 'developed a research programme for the Centre which would explore the phenomenon of social mobility and analyse also the emergence of mass culture' (2000: 34). After taking a position as lecturer at the University of Lille in 1961, Bourdieu returned to Paris in 1964 to take up the positions of Director of Studies at the École Practique des Hautes Études, and lecturer at the École Normale Supérieure, which he held until 2001 and 1984 respectively (Grenfell 2012: 229).

Bourdieu's work with Passeron, which began under Aron's aegis in the 1960s, highlights an aspect of academic research that Bourdieu regarded as vital: 'his vision of research as a quintessentially collective activity whose true subject is not the individual scholar but the scientific field in toto' (Wacquant 2013: 20). Bourdieu collaborated with a wide range of scholars, and he explains the importance of the group to his work and development in a passage in *Sketch for a Self Analysis*:

> The group that I set up, based on elective affinity as much as intellectual convergence, played a decisive role in this enormous investment, with my own belief producing in others the belief capable of reinforcing and confirming my belief. Everything thus combined to favour an individual and

collective self-certainty that induced a profound detachment from the external world, its judgments and its sanctions. (Bourdieu 2007: 69–70)

The CSE enabled Bourdieu to assemble a group of fellow researchers and 'to participate in universes of thought, past or present, very distant from my own' (2007: 66). As Robbins (2000: 112) points out, some of the ideas and fields in which Bourdieu was interested were in fact researched by colleagues such as Patrick Champagne and Monique de Saint Martin. Bourdieu took up the Chair of Sociology at the Collège de France in 1982 (Bourdieu 2007), and in 1993 he accepted the 'Gold Medal of the National Center for Scientific Research' (CNRS), France's highest prize for scientific achievement (Wacquant 2013).

Bourdieu's role as a 'public intellectual' in France was accentuated when, with the 1981 election of the Socialist President Mitterand accompanied by a Socialist majority in parliament, he was asked to contribute to government policy-making. He sat on a Collège de France committee on educational reform in 1981, and later that decade chaired a government commission on education (Grenfell 2012: 230). In 1993, *La misère du monde* was published to widespread acclaim. From here, Bourdieu played an even more visible role in French public life (see Wacquant 2013), founding what was to become the association Raisons d'agir (Reasons to Act) in 1995, and the book series *Liber-Raisons d'agir*, launched in 1996 with the publication of *On Television and Journalism* (Bourdieu 1998b).

Bourdieu (2007: 100) referred to his 'ambivalent, contradictory relationship to the academic institution, combining rebellion and submission, rupture and expectation'. Wacquant (2013: 18) notes that this attitude led him to consider turning down both the chair at the Collège de France and the Gold Medal. His abhorrence of 'academic pomp' and sense of the contradictions consequent upon his 'cleft habitus' made the necessary inaugural lecture and acceptance speech a matter of extreme stress and concern to him (Bourdieu 2007: 108–10; Wacquant 2013: 18–19). In both cases he resolved the tension caused by 'the very fact of a social consecration which assaulted my self-image' (Bourdieu 2007: 109) by delivering an address that treated the occasion as an event for sociological analysis and, in the case of the Gold Medal, breaking with protocol to make political points (Wacquant 2013: 22). Gisele Sapiro (2010: xx) writes that while Bourdieu 'claimed the right to . . . speak freely on political issues . . . the autonomy of the expert is limited . . . Counterexpertise was a means of making a political use of scientific knowledge in an autonomous manner.'

In the preface to *Firing Back: Against the Tyranny of the Market 2*, a text written in the style and featuring a mode of address characteristic of his overtly interventionist later work, Bourdieu (2003: 11–12) states:

> I have come to believe that those who have the good fortune to be able to devote their lives to the study of the social world cannot stand aside, neutral and indifferent, from the struggles in which the future of that world is at stake. These struggles are, for an essential part, theoretical struggles in which the dominant can count on innumerable complicities . . . Against such power, based on the concentration and mobilization of cultural capital, the only efficacious response is a critical force of contestation backed by a similar mobilization but directed towards entirely other ends.

Two points are worth noting here. The first is Bourdieu's commitment (he 'cannot stand aside, neutral and indifferent, from the struggles in which the future of that world is at stake') to the imperative, derived from Marx's *Theses on Feuerbach*, that philosophers should not just interpret the world, but should 'change it' (Marx 1969: 15). However, both a sociological refinement and an enhancement of Marx's dictum exist and, typically for Bourdieu, these are presented—at least implicitly—as both the result of a process of reflection and duration ('I have come to believe') and as a form of work—a problem that has to be dealt with and solved in a practical manner ('the only efficacious response'). The second point relates to the claim that the future of the social world 'is at stake', and the work of salvaging the social shall be decided by 'theoretical struggles': this is a significant claim primarily because it is made by someone who is influenced by and discursively committed to Wittgenstein's (1983) meticulous care and reflexivity with regard to the use of language.

Bourdieu is not alone in claiming that the survival of the socio-cultural field is threatened by the discursive regimes, logics, values, dispositions and technologies of contemporary capitalism. The visual theorist Jonathan Crary (2013), referring to the attempts of global capitalism to make inroads into, and eventually abolish, 'the time of sleep' as non-productive and incompatible with regard to the 'allegedly irresistible forces of modernization', writes (2013: 128), 'Now there is actually only one dream, superseding all others: it is of a shared world whose fate is not terminal, a world without billionaires, which has a future other than barbarism or the post-human, and in which history can take on other forms than reified nightmares of catastrophe.'

The colonization of the social field by market economics, the catastrophic socio-cultural consequences that accompany it and the curious ideological and ethical distance that seems to separate or obfuscate the relation between its causes, actors and practices and their effects—as Maurice Blanchot (1986: 3) writes, 'The disaster is related to forgetfulness'—is a motif that Bourdieu inherited from the social economist Karl Polanyi. In *The Great Transformation* (1957) Polanyi provides an historically situated account of the coming of fascism, interpreted as a consequence of the ideological rise, hegemony and fall—the 'great transformation' of the book's title—of free market capitalism. Polanyi argues that market capitalism works to abolish the 'between us' out of which the social is constituted, facilitated and maintained; one result of this evacuation of social values and considerations in Europe in the 1920s and 1930s was that the social effected a kind of return of the repressed, in the form of a negative communal identity predicated upon disaffection, alienation and a disposition towards socio-cultural and political fascism. Capitalist economics, Polyani (1957: 258) writes, gave a false direction . . . No society is possible in . . . a market-view of society which equated economics with contractual relationships, and contractual relations with freedom . . . Vision was limited by the market which 'fragmented' life into the producers' sector that ended when his product reached the market, and the sector of consumers for whom all goods sprang from the market . . . Society as a whole remained invisible . . . Neither voters, nor owners, neither producers, nor consumers could be held responsible for such brutal restrictions of freedom as were involved in the occurrence of unemployment and destitution . . . Any decent individual . . . was unentangled in the evil of power and economic value. His lack of responsibility for them seemed so evident that he denied their reality in the name of his freedom.

In the Algerian phase of Bourdieu's work, capitalism is located, evaluated and treated as part of the French colonialist regime: the imposition of capitalist logics on Algeria is characterized as having a devastating effect on the integrity, coherence and stability of the local culture, predominantly because it replaces a way of life predicated on specific socio-cultural relations, forms of capital, identities, conventions, values and economies, and inscribed with and contextualized by local narratives, epistemological categories and meanings, with a form of market economics. While not nearly as directly interventionist as some of his later works, the anthropological writing and scholarship produced during or derived from Bourdieu's time in Algeria is characterized by an analysis and critique of the abstraction (and, by extension, the destruction) of Algerian society, culture, relationships and forms of identity by the forces and logics of colonialism and capitalism. There is a concomitant awareness that the French intellectual field of the 1950s and 1960s, and the academic disciplines and bodies of theory that dominated it—Marxism, existentialism, literary theory, phenomenology, philosophy—were complicit in this process of abstraction (Bourdieu 2007). For Bourdieu, the euphemized and depoliticized Orientalism that served as an extension of right-wing political thought during the period of the Algerian War, and that was particularly influential in the fields of ethnography and anthropology, was accompanied by leftist thought that could only conceive of Algeria and the Algerians within Marxist-oriented revolutionary narratives. Goodman and Silverstein (2009b: 10) state:

> Bourdieu sharply demarcated himself from other leading proponents of 'Algerian Algeria'—most notably, Jean-Paul Sartre and Franz Fanon. In Bourdieu's view, Sartre, Fanon, and others aligned with the Communist left were blind to the socioeconomic realities of the Algerian population ... the leftists sought to locate in the Algerian peasantry a nascent revolutionary consciousness ... Bourdieu ... found the left's utopianism 'misleading and dangerous'... The left's views were motivated, Bourdieu contended, by 'Parisian ideas' ... that ... paid little heed to the 'objective situation' of colonial Algeria.

According to Tassadit Yacine (2013: 7), Bourdieu's experiences in Algeria produced 'a profound biographical and intellectual conversion of the Paris philosopher into an anthropologist, ethnologist and sociologist' who, for the 'rest of his life', would conceive of and use the social sciences and their methodologies as 'a political weapon in the service of a social critique of forms of repression and domination'. The political and interventionist focus of Bourdieu's work was conducted and discursively situated at the level of (predominantly) scientific procedures and methodologies—in other words, it involved 'for an essential part, theoretical struggles' (2013: 12).

References to, and an analysis of, capitalism are curiously absent from Bourdieu's educational and early cultural texts that deal with more modern (and predominantly French) societies and contexts. The focus is on the role played by cultural sites, institutions, discourses and genres in the reproduction and naturalization of power differentials and class domination. In this early work, Bourdieu gradually develops and utilizes a theory of a general economy predicated upon field-specific regimes of value and the exchangeability of different forms of capital (including economic capital). What is missing from this theoretical development, according to Calhoun (1993), is an understanding and account of the role of capitalism in terms of its relations with and transformation of regimes of capital: in other words, he argues that 'what Bourdieu's approach to capital lacks ... is an idea of capitalism' (1993: 68)—or, more specifically, a theory of what John Guillory (2000: 23) refers to as 'the union of social and economic systems'.

In his body of worked devoted to the field of cultural production, Bourdieu's theory of a general economy of capital is reformulated to take into account the ways in which the state and capitalism utilize regimes of symbolic and cultural capital to naturalize and maintain their domination. Although the forms of capital that symbolic power takes under market capitalism are not precisely the same as those utilized by the state, there are methodological continuities. Bourdieu makes the point that the specific processes that have brought about the widespread economic abstraction of the socio-cultural world have affinities with the more general regime associated with the field of power and the state, whose purpose is to deny and disguise social, cultural, political and economic domination and transform it into a form of apolitical, natural and undeniable superiority:

> The ethical revolution that enabled the economy eventually to be constituted as such, in the objectivity of a separate universe, governed by its own laws (the laws of self-interested calculation and unfettered competition for profit) ... Paradoxically ... is itself inseparable from a new form of repression and denial of the economy and the economic that establishes itself with the emergence of all the fields of cultural production based on the repression of their economic and social conditions of possibility ... The emergence of these universes which, like the scholastic worlds, offer positions from which one can feel justified in apprehending the world from a lofty distance as

spectacle, and in organizing it as an entity solely intended for knowledge, goes hand in hand with the invention of a scholastic worldview that finds one of its most perfect expressions in the myth of homo economicus and in 'rational action theory'. (Bourdieu 2005c: 7)

Bourdieu's insights into the relation between symbolic capital and the facility to influence or intervene in cultural politics informed his own approach to the academic field: he understood, for instance, that work produced within or recognized as being part of the field of science enjoyed a status not usually accorded to the arts and humanities. Bourdieu's scholarly trajectory was characterized by a commitment to the procedures, imperatives and values of science, and a rigorous reflexive relation to his position and work within the field. In other parts of this book, we will deal with the claims that Bourdieu makes about, and his explanations of, the value and roles of the social sciences. It is sufficient to say here that science in its various forms has established what Bourdieu refers to as a high level of autonomy with regard to other cultural fields—most particularly the field of power—and that this relative autonomy (along with a high degree of socio-cultural prestige and its almost universal status as a positive form of cultural capital) is tied to the claims that it makes, and the evidence it provides in support of its contention that it is 'a discourse on the social' (Lefort 1986).

Claude Lefort's account of the relationship between ideology, communication and the field of science is particularly relevant by way of providing an explanation of Bourdieu's academic and intellectual strategies and orientations. Lefort argues that the notion of 'discourse on the social' is a salient aspect of the operations of what he terms 'bourgeois ideology', which claims to provide an objective, neutral and reliable account of things (the material world, social relations, human consciousness) derived from an almost ontotheological level of epistemology. The methodological rigour and neutrality of science constitute the basis of the argument that it is both distinct from and not reducible to a 'discourse of the social'. Lefort contends that the acquisition of this status also means that the value and status of science have been recognized by the field of power (constituted, at various times, by the state, capitalism and the bureaucratic field), and consequently integrated into disciplinary and normative apparatuses that operate at an ordinary and everyday level. The effect of this regime of power, according to Lefort (1986: 230),

> presupposes the representation of the scientificity of discourse . . . There was a discourse on science as well as an exploitation of science in order to produce a discourse on the social. In the context of industrial production itself, a knowledge of the rationality of work was elaborated, a knowledge which was displayed but which was also circumscribed within the limits of a ruling apparatus. Taylorism . . . eventually gave it full expression . . . This representation is that of the organization, of an organization which is not a product, a mere application of science, but one which embodies it and whose formula is not the property of the manager, but is inscribed in reality.

Within Lefort's neo-Marxist narrative, science has been appropriated, as a discourse and an apparatus, by the field of power. There are two main aspects to this process. At one level, there is a pseudo-performance of science and scientificity in the media and more generally across state institutions and bureaucracies, tied to the production of an almost limitless supply of information verified by 'the magic of objectivity' (1986: 233). At another level, the human sciences (psychology and economics are singled out here, but sociology is also referenced), by taking on the formal qualities (the models, structures and discourses) of organizational institutions, lend their 'social magic' and authority to power, allowing it to euphemize or disguise its operations within and relations to the social field. Members of the increasingly heteronomous sectors of the social sciences field can (and in fact must) commit to the notion that the employment of a technical, statistical, discursive, methodological or theoretical frame of analysis (laboratory equipment, algebraic equations, algorithms, models, maps, focus groups, content analysis, grounded theory, structuralism) delivers up the verifiable truth of a particular situation or phenomenon. However, this process—which facilitates the acquisition of cultural capital and other forms of recognition (titles, promotion, appointments) within the field—is articulated and 'produced as an extension of the field, by way of making a contribution to what Lefort (1986) calls the capitalized ideas of Progress, Modernity, Civilization and Knowledge. Here the social sciences function simultaneously as instruments of power and 'of and for themselves': because they provide the science that extends and euphemizes power, they justify themselves to, and are recognized and privileged by, power.

While Bourdieu would not share Lefort's general characterization of the relation between the sciences and the field of power, he accepts that the autonomy of the field of cultural production, within which he includes the sciences, has been infiltrated by the logics, values and discourses of capitalism, and that some areas of science function as forms of instrumental positivism. As he states (1993b: 13):

> A good number of those who describe themselves as sociologists or economists are social engineers whose function is to supply recipes to the leaders of private companies and government departments. They offer a rationalization of the practical or semi-theoretical understanding that the members of the dominant class have of the social world. The governing elite ... needs a science capable of (in both senses) rationalizing its domination, capable both of reinforcing the mechanisms that sustain it and of legitimizing it. It goes without saying that the limits of this science are set by its practical functions: neither for social engineers nor for the managers of the economy can it perform a radical questioning.

In the foreword to *Science of Science and Reflexivity*, Bourdieu (2004: vii) specifically warns that, 'The autonomy that science has gradually won against the religious, political or economic powers, and, partially at least ... the state bureaucracies which ensured the minimum conditions for its independence, has been greatly weakened'. The most serious threat is to the 'social mechanisms that were set in place' to validate and protect scientific objectivity and autonomy, such as 'the logic of peer competition'. These are now 'in danger of being subordinated to ends imposed from outside; submission to economic interests and to the seductions of the media ... undermine confidence in science and especially social science' (2004: vii). Autonomy is necessary, Bourdieu (1993b: 9) argues, if science is to continue to analyse and critique power-as-symbolic domination, and to reveal 'things that are hidden and sometimes repressed'. The sciences can carry out this function of critique because they possess an epistemological facility and value, predicated on a 'coherent system of hypotheses, concepts and methods of verification' (1993b: 9) that allows them to continue to speak as a discourse on, rather than of, the social. This is the point at stake in Bourdieu's response, in an interview collected in *Sociology in Question*, to a question about why sociological discourse needs to be scientific (1993b: 9):

> Why not say it's a science, if it is one? And then, something very important is at stake: one of the ways of disposing of awkward truths is to say that they are not scientific, which amounts to saying that they are 'political', that is, springing from 'interest', 'passion', and are therefore relative and relativizable.

An integral part of Bourdieu's commitment to science and scientific rigour, and one of the ways in which he distinguished his work from critical and theoretical work in the arts and humanities, is his insistence on the necessity of combining theoretical and empirical methodologies and approaches. He argues (Bourdieu 1996: 2) that the use of statistics in *The State Nobility* identifies 'processes such as those that lead to the differential elimination of students from different backgrounds, processes that exhibit such regularity in their complexity that one might be tempted to use mechanistic metaphors to describe them'. He further maintains that his major theoretical concepts, such as the habitus and cultural field, arose out of, and were only identifiable and recognizable in terms commensurate with, the regularities and objectivities derived from empirical studies. With regard to the question of how a cultural field could be identified, described and delimited, Bourdieu's position is that those matters had to be arrived at empirically, rather than theoretically:

> The question of the limits of the field is a very difficult one, if only because it is always at stake in the field itself . . . Participants in a field . . . constantly work to differentiate themselves from their closest rivals in order to reduce competition and to establish a monopoly over a particular subsector of the field . . . Thus the boundaries of the field can only be determined by an empirical investigation. (Bourdieu & Wacquant 1992: 100)

Bourdieu's commitment to scientific research is augmented by a strong disposition, influenced by the examples of Durkheim, Weber, Bachelard and Canguilhem, and partly a consequence of his experience in Algeria, to turn the methods by which science objectifies the world onto the contexts, presuppositions, choices, world-views and methods from and by which that objectification is derived and produced. The value of scientific work is not simply the consequence of an imitation of the 'external signs of the rigor of the most established scientific disciplines' (Bourdieu 1999: 607); nor is it necessarily guaranteed by institutional affiliations, forms of academic capital or even the process of peer review. It resides in the incorporation, at the level of the scholarly habitus, of a systematic attitude of awareness and interrogation of the researcher's relation to the regime (that is, the rules, dispositions, mechanisms and processes) of knowledge production within which the subject is located, and from which all methodological, theoretical and technical frames, ways of seeing and practices are derived. The value of the social sciences is predicated upon their reflexive relation to the everyday work of the field and the position that the researcher occupies in the field. This relation takes the most minute forms, from a Wittgenstein-like return to taken-for-granted linguistic terms that effectively make or shape (or even disappear) what they purport to deliver up or describe—as Bourdieu (2005a: 187) points out, a term such as 'underclass' does a great deal of political work by first reifying and then excluding a group of people from the social—to a questioning of what makes certain kinds of research questions possible and others unthinkable (Bourdieu 1999). Bourdieu and Wacquant (1992: 72) characterize this process as a 'discovery of the generic' and the 'shared, banal, commonplace', and argue that research into socio-cultural phenomena is always predisposed by the position and trajectory of the subject and the field from which the research emanates. In several of his earlier research projects, such as his study of families in his home area of Béarn, and of 'his own tribe' in *Homo Academicus* (1988), Bourdieu focuses on the ways in which, and the extent to which, his own habitus disposed and informed his approach to production of objects of study, and in *The Weight of the World* (1999) he develops and employs a methodological apparatus that is oriented towards trying to facilitate, on the part of the subjects of the study, relatively unmediated accounts of their experiences.

Despite this emphasis on reflexivity, Bourdieu's work has been critiqued by both scholars within the field of sociology and by academics in disciplines such as anthropology, ethnology, education, art theory and literary studies, for its determinist approach to and theorizing of socio-cultural practices. These critiques tend to fall into four main categories. First, there is the contention that his theoretical apparatus, the empirical data that it generates and the evaluations, conclusions and narratives derived from them are 'culturally specific', and therefore cannot be extrapolated to other situations and contexts (Bourdieu & Wacquant 1992). Second, and by extension, it has been argued that his major theoretical concepts (for instance, the habitus), which were developed out of specific research projects and contexts (for instance, Algeria and Béarn), are treated and deployed as if they were universal and ahistorical (Goodman & Silverstein 2009a). Third, his work has been subject to criticism from disciplinary specialists who take issue with his sociological 'colonizing' of areas outside his field of expertise (Goodman 2009). Finally, there is the charge that concepts such as the habitus and the logic of practice are mechanistic or deterministic, and under-estimate or completely deny the possibility of human agency (Jenkins 1992). We will deal with these issues in more detail in later chapters, but it is useful to provide an overview of these criticisms and the arguments that have been made in response to them.

In terms of the cultural specificity of Bourdieu's theory, methodology, data and evaluations, it is his educational texts that have attracted the most criticism. A number of scholars have argued (see the contributions to Harker et al. 1990) that the highly bureaucratized and stratified French education system is neither analogous nor comparable to education systems in countries such as the UK, Australia, Canada, New Zealand and the United States, and therefore the arguments that Bourdieu makes cannot be transferred or extrapolated outside the French context. There is also the charge that Bourdieu's theoretical concepts effectively abstracts the everyday experiences of students and teachers, much as Marxist theories of class struggle abstracted Algerian experiences of their war of independence.

In terms of the specificity (and by extension, non-transferability) of the French education system, the response that has come from Bourdieu (Bourdieu 1993b) and scholars such as Harker (1990: 98) is that while that system is idiosyncratic—'possibly the most highly bureaucratised and centralised system in the world'—it does not follow that Bourdieu's theoretical concepts and arguments cannot be used, perhaps in modified forms, to generate data, evaluations and conclusions in other educational systems. Harker (1990: 99) suggests that

> there are two tasks in front of educationalists who would seek to use Bourdieu in relation to non-French school systems. First, it is necessary to catch up with Bourdieu theoretically, by seeing his work as a method of enquiry rather than a completed theoretical edifice; and second, to work out the method in relation

to their own social space and the particular 'field' of education within it.

He argues that Bourdieu's ideas, and his general theoretical approach, are valid to the analysis of education fields and their relation to the field of power across different national contexts, but that they require specific orientations, depending on the historical and cultural dynamics of the field of analysis. This is in keeping with Bourdieu's own insistence that concepts such as field and habitus are both predicated upon and developed with regard to the scholarly task at hand, and shaped by and receptive to specific empirical data (Bourdieu & Wacquant 1992).

The second critique of Bourdieu's theorizing and analysis of the field and socio-cultural functions of education, particularly in *The Inheritors* (Bourdieu 1979b) and *Reproduction* (Bourdieu & Passeron 1990), is that he substitutes a kind of sociological grand theory and set of narratives for what are in fact micro-level relationships between the education system, forms of pedagogy and learning-as-practice. From this perspective, a text such as *Reproduction* imposes a theoretical homogeneity upon a collection of experiences that are both heterogeneous and theoretically beyond scientific or scholarly retrieval. Consider, for example, the discursive distance that separates Jacques Rancière's (2004: 175) characterization of 'the experience of the schoolchild to whom classes and bells, lessons and homework, rewards and punishments do not precisely call to mind free and disinterested exercise' from Bourdieu's (1993b: 120) explanation of school culture in *Sociology in Question*:

> The school, the site of *schole*, leisure, is the place where practices endowed with social functions and integrated into the collective calendar are converted into physical exercises . . . where one acquires a distant, neutralizing disposition towards language and the social world, the very same one which is implied in the bourgeois relation to art, language and the body . . . What is acquired in and through experience of school, a sort of retreat from the world and from real practice.

Bourdieu argues that when the cultural field, practices and processes of education are analysed, it is possible to identify objectivities of difference regarding students' educational trajectory, profile and attainments that are predicated on factors such as class position, father's profession, parents' educational capital and gender. This set of objectivities is then located within a wider socio-cultural space, where regimes of symbolic power and domination are manifested in and normalized, naturalized and maintained through the habitus-as-dispositions that is acquired, to a significant extent, within the education system. For Rancière (2004), on the other hand, the school—at least for working-class children—is an alien space, much more likely to produce indifference, boredom and resentment than ideological compliance; it is also a place where students, while understanding that the game is already heavily loaded in favour of an altogether different set of cultural literacies from those that they possess, nevertheless have the capacity to learn how to play along, simultaneously inside and outside the rules of the game. Both positions provide perfectly valid accounts of the regime of education, pedagogy and learning; however, their irreconcilability is not to be found in what happens to students, but rather in terms of what their experiences mean and, more importantly, how those experiences translate at the level of cultural politics. For Bourdieu, the argument that students resent or reject the values and world-views supposedly inculcated at school is to miss the point, which is that the production of a rejection, on their part, is precisely what school is set up to do in the first place. This rejection is part of the embodiment of a set of dispositions that ensures they remain out of, and thus help to perpetuate and naturalize, the wider socio-cultural game of symbolic power. Rancière's position is that school engenders an antagonism to the game that is carried into the socio-cultural field, and that authorized culture (and, by extension, the field of power) never accomplishes what it seems to accomplish, which is acquiescence.

With regard to the criticism that Bourdieu's theoretical apparatus is invalid or flawed because it applies supposedly synchronic and universalist concepts to situations, contexts and practices that unfold over and change in time, Bourdieu stressed that his theoretical approach, derived from sources such as Weber, Bachelard and Canguilhem, is designed to adjust to synchronic and diachronic levels of analysis.

Perhaps the best example of this tendency on Bourdieu's part to adjust and refine his theoretical apparatus to take empirical evidence, critical feedback and the specificities of the work-at-hand into account can be found in his rethinking of the relation between the field of cultural production, class and symbolic power. Whereas in his educational sociology, cultural literacy, production and consumption are effectively assigned the role of facilitating the reinscription of class differentiation and domination, during the 1980s and 1990s Bourdieu developed and provided a more nuanced account of both the dynamics of the field of cultural production and its ambivalent relation to the field of power; there are also reformulations, in the same period, of his theorizing of the mechanics of class formation, the notion of reflexivity, the strategic capabilities of the habitus, and the durability and stability of cultural fields. This refinement of his theoretical apparatus is often discussed, contextualized, worked through and explained in strongly reflexive texts such as *Sociology in Question* (1993b) and *An Invitation to Reflexive Sociology* (Bourdieu & Wacquant 1992), in the material collected in *In Other Words* (1990b) and *Language and Symbolic Power* (2005b) and in his more 'philosophical' books, most particularly *Pascalian Meditations* (2000).

Despite the incorporation of a rigorous reflexivity into his methodological and theoretical apparatus, Bourdieu's work has attracted considerable and sustained academic criticism—and, for that matter, journalistic criticism, for instance, *On Television and Journalism* (1998b)—that his theories impose a mechanistic explanation onto socio-cultural practices, and by extension deny the possibilities of human agency. As Richard Jenkins (1992: 118) summarizes it, 'The central thread which unites . . . empirical and theoretical critiques is the argument that Bourdieu's theory of cultural reproduction and social reproduction is deterministic.' The essays collected in the book *Bourdieu in Algeria* (Goodman & Silverstein 2009a) tend to follow this lead. Abdellah Hammoudi (2009: 200) suggests that by conflating tradition and the habitus, Bourdieu leaves 'little room for the study of the use of reason in social practices anterior to colonization', and that this 'not only marginalize(s) internal contradictions, but also the relative freedom that men and women in their actions exercise with regard to normative systems'.

Bourdieu has consistently denied that a notion such as the habitus is in any way mechanistic: he argues that habitus and the logic of practice were developed partly as a response to and a means of overcoming the schema of 'structures without subjects', prevalent in Levi-Strauss' anthropology, Russian Formalist literary theory and post-Saussurian linguistics, among others. The notion of habitus constitutes 'a rejection of a whole series of alternatives into which [the] social sciences ... has locked itself, that of consciousness (or of subject) and of the unconscious, that of finalism and mechanism' (Bourdieu 1985: 12). At the same time, it provides an explanation of the objective regularities of the socio-cultural world, and by extension of the way in which power, as the source of the categories of apprehension and evaluation that subjects bring to the world, is able to reproduce and maintain itself without recourse to overt forms of domination or violence. Bourdieu understands power as operating predominantly at a symbolic level: while a subject's practices and world-views are not explicable at a mechanistic level, being in the world means being inhabited by the world—or, more specifically, by certain naturalized and normalized values and categories of perception that reproduce themselves via the habitus. The habitus functions, for Bourdieu, at a level of misrecognition: the set of dispositions through which it is facilitated and manifested is acquired unconsciously, which is why 'what I am' and the 'ways I see the world' are often taken for granted, accepted as something that is innate or common sense.

Bourdieu has utilized this mode of thinking across his scholarly work on education, cultural production and the state, which he refers to as 'three stages in a single enterprise' (Bourdieu 2000: 10). To this we could add a fourth aspect: that of his later and more openly interventionist work, which utilizes techniques, discourses and forms of address taken from both traditional scholarship—*Science of Science and Reflexivity* (Bourdieu 2004), *The Social Structures of the Economy* (Bourdieu 2005c)—and the polemicist essays—*Acts of Resistance* (Bourdieu 1998a), *Firing Back* (Bourdieu 2003)—and is directed against the symbolic violence exercised by market capitalism. In this final stage of Bourdieu's career, the focus moves from an analysis and interrogation of the naturalized regime of symbolic violence associated with the 'dominant' to the imposition of a capitalist hegemony that attempts to force states 'to open up all services to the laws of free exchange and hence to make it possible to turn all service activities into commodities and sources of profit, including those responding to such fundamental rights as education and culture' (Bourdieu 2003: 77).

Antecedents

It has been noted, not least by Bourdieu himself (Bourdieu 2007), that his research was often conducted from the position of an academic outsider. This characterization can be extended to Bourdieu's status within the wider academic field:

> I ... understood retrospectively that I had entered into sociology and ethnology in part through a deep refusal of the scholastic point of view which is the principle of loftiness, a social distance, in which I could never feel at home, and to which the relationship to the social world associated with certain social origins no doubt predisposes. That posture displeased me ... and the refusal of the vision of the world associated with the academic philosophy of philosophy has no doubt contributed greatly to leading me to the social sciences, and especially to certain ways of practising them. (Bourdieu 2007: 41)

Bourdieu (2007) suggests that, as an outsider, what is denied at the level of an ease and intimate familiarity with regard to the way things are is sometimes compensated for by the absence of a disposition to see what should be or is meant to be seen—or to not take for granted what is presumed and treated as the departure point for and basis of observation, categorization and evaluation. His primary example of this tendency is the scholarly habitus: he argues that its disposition to abstract issues, situations and practices, and to remove them from the immediate context and logic of their production, is germane to academic scholarship. It is important, however, not to overplay Bourdieu's distance from the academic and intellectual fields. As he writes in *Sketch for a Self-Analysis* (2007: 102), 'How can I fail to recognize myself in Nietzsche when he says ... that he has only ever attacked things that he knew well, that he had himself experienced, and up to a point, he had himself been?'

In *Sketch* (2007: 1), Bourdieu provides an account of his uneasy relationship with(in) the French academy, and of the intellectual influences and antecedents he deemed 'pertinent from the point of view of sociology, in other words necessary for sociological explanation and understanding'. Any discussion of Bourdieu's intellectual influences and antecedents must give due weight, as Bourdieu (1988, 1993b, 2007) himself insists, to 'negative influences'—that is, those bodies of theory, methodologies or intellectual approaches from which he has differentiated himself, or that he has attempted to extend, counter or overcome. These can be divided into three main groups: philosophy, Marxism and, more broadly, the sets of theoretical approaches commonly found in but not exclusive to the social sciences, characterized by the opposition between subjectivism and objectivism. There are, of course, various other groups and sub-groups that Bourdieu critiques, such as the theories and methodologies associated with the quite antithetical approaches of cultural studies and positivism; however, the three areas above exerted a strong and continuous influence over Bourdieu's scholarly trajectory, and were the theoretical departure points for the development of concepts such as habitus, cultural field, cultural capital and reflexivity.

Bourdieu's relation to philosophy is sometimes ambivalent, but more often than not it is critical:

> If I have resolved to ask some questions that I would rather have left to philosophy, it is because it seemed to me that philosophy, for all its questioning, did not ask them; and because, especially with respect to the social sciences, it never ceased to raise questions that did not seem to me to be essential while avoiding asking itself about the reasons and above all the (often not very philosophical) causes of its questioning. (Bourdieu 2000: 1)

To accentuate this point, he adds in the next paragraph that, 'In order to justify an inquiry that hopes to open the way to truths that philosophy helps to make it hard to reach I could have invoked thinkers who are close to being seen by philosophers as enemies of philosophy', such as Wittgenstein (1983), who makes his 'prime task the dispelling of illusions, especially those that the philosophical tradition produces and reproduces' (2000: 1).

At a more contextual level, Bourdieu's critique of philosophy can be related to the academic environment that characterized his early career (Bourdieu 2007). He describes how the intellectual hegemony of the field of philosophy, to which he refers as 'a universally recognized scholastic aristocracy' (2007: 6), devalued and rendered marginal most disciplines within the social sciences, with the notable exception of anthropology. Bourdieu's intellectual sympathies and 'choices', which characteristically 'manifested themselves above all else in refusals and in intellectual antipathies that were most often barely articulated' (2007: 2), were oriented towards marginal academic figures such as Gaston Bachelard and Georges Canguilhem, whose historical and historicizing approaches contrasted markedly with that of philosophy and provided 'an antidote to the "facile" aspects of existentialism' (2007: 11). This problematical relation to philosophy, and the development of an interest in the social sciences, were accentuated by the position that various academic disciplines were to take regarding the Algerian War of Independence: Bourdieu (2007: 58) refers to the 'transformation of my vision of the world that accompanied my transition from philosophy to sociology, in which my Algerian experience is no doubt the pivotal moment'. Philosophy (both in its more traditional and Marxist versions) and anthropology tended to 'bracket off' the socio-cultural experiences of Algerians by incorporating them, for instance, into Marxist narratives that simultaneously abstracted them, or subjecting them to a euphemistic, right-wing Orientalism (2007). This contrasted sharply with Bourdieu's experiences as both a conscript and a researcher in Algeria: 'It is not easy,' he writes, 'to describe simply . . . situations and events . . . that have profoundly shaken me . . . and not only the most extreme of them' (2007: 48). This involved, among other things, informants giving him details of torture inflicted upon them by the French army, and of Bourdieu himself being the target of threats and other forms of violence (2007: 48). Bourdieu's Algerian experiences engendered 'a deep refusal of . . . the vision of the world associated with the academic philosophy of philosophy' and led him 'to the social sciences and especially to certain ways of practising them' (2007: 41).

Although sociology was regarded in the French intellectual field of the time as 'a plebeian and vulgarly materialist science of ordinary things' (2007: 17), it offered an alternative to the distanced and distancing approach of the scholarly disposition, which Bourdieu associated most particularly with philosophy. Whereas for Bourdieu philosophy treated everyday issues and problems as intellectual abstractions, sociology offered the possibility of socio-cultural intervention:

> The sociologist has the peculiarity, in no way a privilege, of being the person whose task is to tell about the things of the social world, and, as far as possible, to tell them the way they are. In itself, that is normal, even trivial. What makes his (or her) situation paradoxical, sometimes impossible, is that he is surrounded by people who either actively ignore the social world and do not talk about it—and I would be the last to criticize artists, writers or scientists for being totally absorbed in their work—or worry about it and talk about it, sometimes a lot, but without knowing much about it (there are some of

these even among recognized sociologists). It is indeed not uncommon that, when associated with ignorance, indifference or contempt, the obligation to speak that derives from suddenly acquired notoriety or the modes and models of the intellectual game inclines people to talk everywhere about the social world, but as if they were not talking about it, or as if one were talking of it to help to forget it and have it forgotten—in a word, while denying it. (Bourdieu 2000: 5)

Bourdieu's most critical account of the dispositions and attitudes he associates with philosophy is articulated in *The Political Ontology of Martin Heidegger* (1991a), but it has its antecedent in what Bourdieu refers to as his refusal of what Merleau-Ponty referred to 'in a very different sense of the common usage as "intellectualism"', which 'had long oriented my intellectual choices' (Bourdieu 2007: 77). The book on Heidegger (Bourdieu 1991a) provides a detailed account and analysis of how 'symptomatic intellectualism' functions as a form of cultural politics, while simultaneously foreclosing the possibility of its association with the political—or in fact with anything but the most distanced and non-tendentious relation to the world. This separation from the world is practised through and legitimated by the use of technical and theoretical discourses, which are irreducible to appropriation or translation—that is, they cannot be carried off to contexts or subjected to readings that don't take them on their own terms, and deal with them in their own form of discourse. Vulgar—that is, non-philosophical—readings and uses are disqualified in advance, on the grounds that they ground what cannot or should not be grounded—in other words, as both a corruption of an effectively pure discourse and an intrusion into and violation of the autonomy of the space and language of philosophy. In the Heidegger book, Bourdieu (1991a) provides an extensive analysis of the conditions, characteristics and trajectories of the philosophical cultural field and its habitus, along with a contextualizing account of precisely what is at stake (and what is to be gained) when a field separates itself from the world in order to be able to identify, discuss and pronounce upon the (abstract) truth of the world, without appearing to speak from a position mired by and within the world. Heidegger's work is shown to be available to political readings by way of its strategic and self-interested refusal to countenance any such thing. Its 'dual meaning and covert undertones' reveal

> some of the most unexpected political implications of Heidegger's philosophy, at a time when they were not recognized by historians: its condemnation of the Welfare State, hidden deep inside a theory of temporality; its anti-semitism, sublimated as a condemnation of rootlessness . . . its refusal to disavow the commitment to Nazism . . . its ultra-revolutionary conservatism, which inspired not only philosophical strategies of radical overcoming but also . . . the disappointed philosopher's break with the Hitler regime, when it failed to reward his revolutionary aspirations to the vocation of philosophical Fuhrer (1991a: viii).

Bourdieu's issues with Marxism are, to a large extent, of a different order to those identified in his critique of philosophy, and to render his relation to Marxism in the negative would be both simplistic and inaccurate. Nevertheless, Bourdieu's early academic career was characterized by a turning away from what was, in sections of the French social sciences and the area of critical theory, the domination of Marxist thought. As Bourdieu writes, 'I have always found myself on the opposite side from the models and modes dominant in the field, whether in my research or in my political position-taking' (2007: 106), a disposition that manifested itself in being 'conspicuously Weberian or Durkheimian for example when it was imperative to be Marxist' (2007: 106–7). Bourdieu's criticism of Marxist philosophy is predominantly threefold. First, he argues that with Marxism there is a tendency—implicit in its Hegelian roots—to abstraction, and to systematizing and universalizing itself. Bourdieu (1990b: 17) writes that 'Marx himself never made much use of historical criticism against Marxism itself', and he refers to his ambivalent relationship with the Frankfurt School and Althusser and their 'totalizing critique' (1990b: 19). Second, Bourdieu rejects the Marxist base-superstructure distinction, and the notion that socio-cultural reality can be reduced to, or is necessarily explicable in terms of, economic relations. Third and by extension, he is critical of the way in which Marxist theories either overlook or underplay everyday social experiences and influences: contrary to the position taken by 'mechanistic materialism' (Bourdieu 2000: 136), Bourdieu insists that the apparatuses of symbolic domination, and the ways in which they euphemize violence, are more widespread, economical and effective in disposing and naturalizing the acquiescence and acceptance of the dominated to the condition of their domination. For Bourdieu, the concepts of the habitus, cultural field and cultural capital (and relatedly, misrecognition and *illusio*) are used to identify, analyse and explain how power naturalizes and sustains itself, most particularly at a bodily and micro-level. What these concepts provide is an account and explanation of socio-cultural practices that are grounded in and derived from, but never entirely aware of, the power relations and flows that constitute the world in which practice occurs. Bourdieu (in Bourdieu & Wacquant 1992: 166–7) writes that 'under definite conditions and at a definite cost', symbolic power and violence 'can do what political and police violence can do, but more efficiently ... It is one of the great weaknesses of the Marxist tradition to have failed to make room for these "soft" forms of violence, which operate even in the economic realm.'

Bourdieu's theoretical apparatus—particularly the concepts of habitus, cultural field and cultural capital—is also designed to identify and analyse the relations between cultural practices and their socio-cultural contexts, and by extension the logic underpinning the ways in which social groups, including classes and class fractions, are formed. This perhaps constituted Bourdieu's most significant departure from Marxist theory, although it is not fully developed and integrated into his theoretical apparatus until the post-*Distinction* period of his work. In texts such as *In Other Words* (1990b), *Language and Symbolic Power* (2005b), *An Invitation to Reflexive Sociology* (Bourdieu & Wacquant

1992) and *Practical Reason* (1998c), Bourdieu argues that instead of classes having a more or less ontological reality based on, among other things, ownership of the means of production, they are instead a form of socio-cultural and political work that has to be done. Different groups of subjects within the socio-cultural field have objective affinities (the statistical likelihood of access to higher education, for instance), but also a set of values and perspectives (the habitus) that dispose them to identify with each other. In other words, because of their proximity in social space, they are potentially available to be interpellated and produced—briefly or otherwise—as a group (that is to say, class) identity. Bourdieu (2005b: 231) argues that:

> On the basis of knowledge of the space of positions, one can carve out classes in the logical sense of the word . . . sets of agents who occupy similar positions and who, being placed in similar conditions . . . have every chance of having similar dispositions and interests . . . This 'class on paper' has the theoretical existence which belongs to all theories: as the product of an explanatory classification . . . it allows one to explain and predict the practices and properties of the thing classified—including their propensity to constitute groups.

Because so much continuous and complex work is required to make and maintain classes, Bourdieu replaces the Marxist notion of ideology (and, by extension, false consciousness) with that of symbolic power. Much like Foucault's concepts of discipline, regulation and normativity, symbolic power functions to naturalize, normalize and maintain a particular regime of power ('the dominant') without seeming to exercise power. In *Masculine Domination* (2001), for instance, Bourdieu demonstrates how the extraordinarily weighty task of imposing masculine domination is carried out partly by ensuring that women are compliant with, and accept, the world-view that prescribes that certain substances (the masculine body) possess attributes (strength, forms of intelligence, an ability to behave and think in a rational manner), which in turn justifies the power differential and the socio-cultural allocation of roles and functions—for instance, across social spaces and fields such as the domestic sphere, and the cultural fields of science and the state. Whereas:

> The classical Marxist tradition emphasises the political functions of symbolic systems, and explains the connections between these systems in the interests of the dominant class, and the problem of false consciousness in the dominated classes. From Bourdieu's perspective this approach tends to reduce power relations to relations of communication. The real political function which he sees symbolic systems as fulfilling is their attempt to legitimate domination by the imposition of the 'correct' and 'legitimate' definition of the social world. The struggles between symbolic systems to impose a view of the social world defines the social space within which people construct their lives, and carry on what Bourdieu sees as the symbolic conflicts of everyday life in the use of symbolic violence of the dominant over the dominated. (Mahar, Harker & Wilkes 1990: 5)

Much like Marxist theory, subjectivism (which could be said to include existentialism and phenomenology) and objectivism (predominantly in the form of structuralism) exercised considerable influence over the French intellectual field during the 1950s and 1960s. They represented two antithetical approaches to an analysis and understanding of socio-cultural practices. Subjectivism, which was associated with existentialism and, to a lesser extent and in quite different ways, phenomenology, provides an explanation of human activity that privileged agency, free will, individual cognitive processes and what Bourdieu (2007: 11) refers to disparagingly as the exaltation of 'lived experience'. Bourdieu (Bourdieu & Wacquant 1992: 132–3) compares Sartre's 'founding myth of the uncreated creator' to the notion of the habitus, and analogizes that the former relates to the latter much as 'the myth of genesis is to the theory evolution'. He argues (Bourdieu & Wacquant 1992) that even the more rigorous forms of phenomenology posit a subject who remains relatively independent, at the level of socio-cultural identity and as a being-in-the world, from objective rules and categories.

Loïc Wacquant (in Bourdieu & Wacquant 1992) provides a useful discussion of this issue. He quotes from Merleau-Ponty's analysis of the relation between a footballer and the objective contexts (the rules of the game, the dimensions of the field, the role of the referee) as they are played out on the football field, specifically his contention that:

> It would not be sufficient to say that consciousness inhabits this milieu. At this moment consciousness is nothing other than the dialectic of milieu and action. Each maneuver undertaken by the player modifies the character of the field and establishes a new line of force in which the action in turn unfolds and is accomplished, again altering the phenomenal field. (Merleau-Ponty, quoted in Bourdieu & Wacquant 1992: 21)

Wacquant goes on to identify two points that differentiate Merleau-Ponty's approach from that of Bourdieu's work. First, he argues that while Merleau-Ponty accepts that the subject has to negotiate, and is to some extent bound by, the rules of the game, the game as a set of logics, dispositions and normalized perspectives is constitutive neither of the subject nor of the subject's apprehension of the game. In other words, Merleau-Ponty's subject, as Wacquant reads it, is both necessarily inhabited by the game (at the level both of a bodily hexis, which determines forms of physical movement, and in terms of a strategic understanding of what decisions to make and when) and somehow outside the game, to the extent that 'the soccer "field" remains a purely phenomenal form, grasped strictly from the viewpoint of the acting agent' (Bourdieu & Wacquant 1992: 22). His second point—an extension of the first—is that there is nothing in Merleau-Ponty's account that provides an explanation of the process of consciousness as a dialectic of 'world and action' and that is capable of establishing 'a solid analytical link between internal and external structures' (1992: 22).

Structuralism was associated with a diverse group of disciplines and names across the social sciences and humanities, including Levi-Strauss (anthropology), Parsons (ethnomethodology) and Barthes (literature). It dominated French anthropology during Bourdieu's time in Algeria and has been cited as an influence on his work up to and including *Outline of a Theory of Practice* (1978). Levi-Strauss' structural anthropology was particularly influential, to the extent that Bourdieu could state in *Sketch* (2007: 44) that 'I placed myself in the tradition he had created (or recreated).'

There were two aspects of Levi-Strauss' work, however, against which Bourdieu reacted: a tendency to overlook the relation between social reality and history, and a tendency to privilege the objectivities of the social at the expense of social practice (Bourdieu 2007: 45). For Bourdieu, structuralism was objectivist in the sense that it understood practice as being explicable in terms of culture frames and structures: members of a community are always inhabited by, and process the world in terms of, a set of 'meaning machines' that mirror either a specific cultural regime or the structural categories of the human mind, depending on the body of theory in question. A literary example of this idea can be found in Walter Abish's (1974) novel *Alphabetical Africa*, which is divided into chapters based on the English alphabet: the first chapter is 'A', and contains only words that begin with that letter, while 'B' contains words that begin with 'A' and 'B', and so on down to chapter 'Z', where the full complement of the alphabet is available. In the 'A' chapter, for example, notions of violence are limited to terms such as annihilation, apprehension, arson and attack; by chapter 'K', people can be killed, but they can only be murdered from chapter 'M' onwards. In Abish's novel, what is visible, and by extension what becomes meaningful, is commensurate with the cultural resources and categories at hand. Two points are being suggested here. First, subjects are always played by, and restricted in their thinking, to the world in which they live; and they cannot interrogate or step outside (that is, they cannot reflexively engage with) their cultural universe. Second, the task of the social or literary analyst is to identify the structures that produce and process practices, rather than to deal with the practices themselves. One influential example of this tendency is Saussure's division of the study of linguistics into the categories of *langue* (system) and *parole* (practices), and then exclusion of the latter from consideration because of its unruliness. Bourdieu writes that:

> Language, according to Saussure... is treated as an instrument of intellection and an object of analysis, a dead language... a self-contained system completely severed from its real uses and denuded from its practical and political functions... The illusion of autonomy of the purely 'linguistic' order which is asserted by the privilege granted to the internal logic of language, at the expense of the social conditions and correlates of its social usage, opens the way to all subsequent theories which proceed as if the theoretical mastery of the code sufficed to confer practical mastery of socially appropriate usages (Bourdieu & Wacquant 1992: 141–2).

The theoretical sources and techniques that both disposed and enabled Bourdieu to attempt to overcome the limitations of philosophical and Marxist approaches, and to bridge the gap between subjectivism and objectivism, came from a variety of areas, but perhaps the most influential and abiding of these were what we might call foundational sociological theory (represented by Durkheim and Weber), the history and philosophy of science (Bachelard and Canguilhem), and the philosophy of Pascal, Wittgenstein, and somewhat problematically and ambivalently, Nietzsche.

The influences on Bourdieu's work exercised by sociologists such as Durkheim and Weber need to be contextualized and read in two ways. The first is in terms of their transformation of sociology into a discipline and field of activity strongly informed by the rigorous approaches, methodologies and techniques associated with the sciences. The second is with regard to the challenge posed to sociology (and we might add, to its scientific status and prestige) by both popular culture and journalism ('Everyone is a sociologist'); and we could add to this the various intellectual and scholarly forces, including philosophy on the one hand (represented by the figure and work of Heidegger) and what Bourdieu terms the 'reductions and impoverishments' (Bourdieu 2007: 72) brought by positivism on the other.

Durkheim's work influenced Bourdieu's commitment to the value of a scientific approach in both underpinning scholarly work, and enabling sociology to operate as a discourse on the social. Responding to a question about the contradiction inherent in sociology's status as both an academic and a political activity, Bourdieu explains that:

> Sociology as we know it was born, in France at least, from a contradiction or misunderstanding. Durkheim was the one who did all that needed to be done to make sociology exist as a universally recognized science. When an activity is constituted as a university discipline, the question of its function and the function of those who practice it no longer arises ... Sociology is not so lucky ... the question of its *raison d'être* is asked increasingly the more it moves away from the definition of scientific practice that the founders had to accept and impose ... You know how much work Durkheim had to do to give sociology this 'pure', purely scientific, 'neutral' image ... ostentatious borrowings from the natural sciences, countless signs of a break with external functions and politics, such as preliminary definitions (Bourdieu 1993b: 27).

Durkheim provided Bourdieu with a disposition towards and an appreciation of 'theoretically grounded empirical research' (Bourdieu 2007: 73), and the methodological apparatus with which sociology could demonstrate that 'social facts "have a constant mode of being, a nature that does not depend on individual arbitrariness and from which there derive necessary relationships'" (Durkheim, quoted in Bourdieu, Chamboredon & Passeron 1991: 15).

Weber's status in this discussion is less easy to characterize, particularly given that references to his work and ideas in Bourdieu's texts are much less frequent than Durkheim citations. However, he remains influential on a number of levels: his approach is associated with scientific principles such as neutrality and objectivity, and with an identification and analysis of the minutiae of everyday socio-cultural practices inhabited by factors—such as forms of implicit or undisclosed calculation—that remain invisible to the analysis of objectivities; we can say, for instance, that 'misrecognition' and '*illusio*' are very much 'Weberian' concepts. What is also present in Weber's work, which Bourdieu identifies as comparatively lacking in his own (Bourdieu & Wacquant 1992: 93), is a sensitivity to history and historical continuities. At the same time, there are areas of ambivalence. This is apparent in Bourdieu's response to a question regarding his relation to cultural and social history in *An Invitation to Reflexive Sociology* (1992: 91–2). In his reply, Bourdieu focuses not on Weber, but on the Weberian sociologist Norbert Elias, whose work on 'the civilizing influence' is 'one which I have a great deal of intellectual sympathy, because it is . . . based on the historical psychosociology of an actual grand historical process, the continuation of a state which progressively monopolizes . . . symbolic violence' (1992: 92). Bourdieu suggests, however, that 'just like Weber before him, Elias always fails to ask who benefits and who suffers from the monopoly of the state over legitimate violence, and to raise the question . . . of the domination wielded through the state' (1992: 93). What is missing from the Weberian approach, for Bourdieu, is that it can be caught up in treating historical activities and developments as abstractions without regard to their (micro)political contexts or functions.

The influence of Bachelard and Canguilhem on Bourdieu's work was contextual as well as theoretical and methodological. On one level, they represented an alternative to the intellectual domination imposed, in the French context, by Sartre and existentialist philosophy.

Bourdieu identifies himself with those 'who sought to resist "existentialism" in its fashionable or academic forms' (Bourdieu 2007: 9), and who could draw upon

> an epistemology and a history of the sciences represented by authors such as Gaston Bachelard [and] Georges Canguilhem . . . Often of lower-class or provincial origin . . . and attached to peripheral university institutions . . . these marginal and temporally dominated authors, hidden from common perception by the celebrity of the dominant figures, offered a recourse to those who, for various reasons sought to react against the fascinating but rejected image of the total intellectual . . . Canguilhem . . . could be invoked by the occupants of opposite positions in the university field . . . as the advocate of a tradition of the history of science and epistemology, which, at the height of the triumph of existentialism, represented the heretical refuge of seriousness and rigour, he would be consecrated, with Bachelard, as the *maitre a penser* of philosophers more remote from the heart of the academic tradition. (Bourdieu 2007: 10–11)

Consistent with their role of offering the possibility of a way out from the confinement of existentialism, Bachelard and Canguilhem insist upon subjecting the knowledge-theory and methodology nexus, even in its most scientific and established manifestations, to an historicizing gaze and interrogation: 'Bachelard teaches us that epistemology is always conjunctural: its propositions and thrusts are determined by the principal threat of the moment' (Bourdieu & Wacquant 1992: 174). What fellows from the proposition that epistemology (and by extension, knowledge) is always produced with regard to the concerns emanating from a specific episteme is the notion that theoretical and methodological approaches and techniques are necessarily oriented towards some general or specific form of work, rather than being universal and trans-historical. For a variety of reasons, mostly tied to the dynamics of specific academic fields and sub-fields, theories and methodologies are often treated and deployed as if they were universally applicable, and even in the most advanced state of ossification they can continue to exert scholarly and intellectual influence—witness the hegemony still exercised over the American discipline of communication by positivist concepts, approaches and methodologies that were a product of the 1950s. However, as Bourdieu insisted throughout his career, theoretical notions such as the habitus and cultural field function as particularized or specific universals—that is, they take on inflections and orientations that are specific to the time and place both of their use and of the work at hand. We will address these issues in detail elsewhere, but one quick and relatively straightforward example to consider is that of the notion of reflexivity. If we were to trace Bourdieu's use of reflexivity, we would find that while the basic principles remained continuous, the points of focus changed over time; the concept is often deployed strategically, sometimes against a target or to defend a position, and this tendency is further accentuated by the different forms of address being used (say, an explanation of statistical analysis as opposed to an interview with a journalist). As an extension of the second point, the extent and criteria of the definitions of reflexivity often vary depending on the field or the content of its deployment so, in certain contexts, reflexivity is explicitly confined to the field of the sciences in a manner commensurate with Kuhn's (1970) formulation of paradigm shifts, while it is usually opened up where the discussion pertains to the cultural field.

Bourdieu's relation to the field and approaches of philosophy is strongly inflected by his disposition, to some extent derived from influences such as Marx and the history and philosophy of science, to see his own scholarly activity as a form of rigorous, reflexive and critical science oriented towards socio-cultural and political intervention as opposed to the 'flabby humanism' (Bourdieu 1990b: 4) of existentialism or the 'pure philosophy' (Bourdieu 1991a: 1) of Heidegger. In *Pascalian Meditations*, for instance, he identifies his position with Wittgenstein's rhetorical question: 'What is the use of studying philosophy if all that it does for you is to enable you to talk with some plausibility about some abstruse questions of logic ... and if it does not improve your thinking about the important questions of everyday life?' (2000: 42).

In an interview in *An Invitation to Reflexive Sociology* (Bourdieu & Wacquant 1992), however, Bourdieu is both more expansive and ambivalent about these relationships—for instance, his break with 'the pretensions to theoretical hauteur' (1992: 204) that came with his academic trajectory as a student of philosophy was facilitated and enabled by his 'theoretical and philosophical training' (1992: 204). When, in the same interview, he describes the work and value of sociology, he does so in terms that place both himself and the field of sociology within the Socratic philosophical tradition, while claiming the work associated with that tradition in the name of sociology:

> the sociologist is the one who goes out in the street to interview Mr. and Mrs. Anybody, listens to [them], and tries to learn from [them]. This is what Socrates used to do, but the same who celebrate Socrates today are the last to understand and to accept this sort of renunciation of the role of the philosopher-king in the face of the 'vulgar' that sociology demands. (1992: 204)

In *Pascalian Meditations*, Bourdieu (2000) repeats the claim that sociology is charged with answering the important questions, not only because philosophy fails to ask these questions, but because the scholarly attitudes and discourses of philosophy function to foreclose the possibility (and, at a level of disciplinary ethos, they stress the undesirability) of engaging with the world. There are exceptions to this characterization, and for Bourdieu the two most significant are to be found in the works of Pascal and Wittgenstein. In his Introduction to *Pascalian Meditations*, Bourdieu (2000: 1–2) justifies his title in the following way:

> In order to justify an inquiry that hopes to open the way to truths that philosophy helps to make it hard to reach, I could

> have invoked thinkers who are close to being seen by philosophers as enemies of philosophy, because, like Wittgenstein, they make its prime task the dispelling of illusions, especially those that the philosophical tradition produces and reproduces. But . . . I had various reasons for placing these reflections under the aegis of Pascal. For a long time I had adopted the habit, when asked the . . . question of my relations with Marx, of replying that . . . if I really had to affiliate myself, I would say I was more of a Pascalian. I was thinking in particular of everything that concerns symbolic power . . . But, above all, I had always been grateful to Pascal . . . for his concern, devoid of all populist naivety, for 'ordinary people' . . . and also for his determination, inseparable from that concern, always to seek the 'reason of effects', the *raison d'être* of the seemingly most illogical or derisory human behaviours.

Pascal and Wittgenstein are the two 'enemies of philosophy' that Bourdieu acknowledges most openly as influences on his work. Bourdieu (2000) claims that Pascal's work and approaches underpin his theorizing of symbolic power, particularly as it is manifested and facilitated at the level of bodily incorporation and hexis. Wittgenstein's (1983) work is seminal to his theorizing and elaboration of a theory of cultural practice in *Outline of a Theory of Practice* (Bourdieu 1978), *The Logic of Practice* (Bourdieu 1990c) and, although he is only cited once in the text, *Practical Reason* (Bourdieu 1998c). We will consider elsewhere, and in more detail, Wittgenstein's value to Bourdieu's thinking—particularly in terms of his understanding of how cultural practices are never equivalent to or explicable in terms of objectivities such as rules, formal accounts of rites and ritual, and kinship structures, but rather have their own logic of practice, which cannot be accounted for on either side of the 'antagonism between the two modes of knowledge' (Bourdieu 1990c: 25) of subjectivism and objectivism. Wittgenstein's research into the relationship between language and communication, and the forms of socio-cultural work that are done without being visible to the conventional perspectives, approaches, theories and methodologies employed by the social sciences, is germane to Bourdieu's sociology. The identification and analysis of what is necessarily repressed within socio-cultural fields—the processes of symbolic domination, the doubling of socio-cultural objectivities at the level of practices derived and embodied, at an unconscious level, via the habitus—require 'new ways of thinking' about sociological questions that are not amenable to objectivism or subjectivism:

> Getting hold of the difficulty deep down is what is hard. Because it is grasped near the surface it simply remains the difficulty it was. It has to be pulled out by the roots; and that involves our beginning to think in a new way. The change is as decisive as, for example, that from the alchemical to the chemical way of thinking. The new way of thinking is what is hard to establish. Once the new way of thinking has been established, the old problems vanish; indeed, they become hard to recapture. For they go with our way of expressing ourselves and, if we clothe ourselves in a new form of expression, the old problems are discarded along with the old garment. (Wittgenstein, quoted in Bourdieu & Wacquant 1992: 1)

It could be argued that Nietzsche should be grouped with these 'enemies of philosophy': however, for a variety of reasons, his relationship with Bourdieu's work is far more difficult to evaluate. This situation owes a great deal, in the first instance, to Bourdieu's (negative) association of Nietzsche with Heidegger, and what he refers to as an 'aesthetics of transgression' that was fashionable in French intellectual culture in the 1950s and 1960s (Bourdieu & Wacquant 1992: 154), and in the second instance to Bourdieu's very obvious lack of ease with regard to Nietzsche's 'fulgurations and fulminations'—at least concerning the extent to which they manifested his entrapment within the limitations of his position 'in social space and, more specifically, within academic space' (1992: 85).

Bourdieu's relationship with Nietzsche's work and ideas, and the extent to which that work contributed to or informed his, need to be read qualitatively rather than quantitatively, and with a due sense of care and suspicion. Going through the indexes of Bourdieu's books, and the bibliographies accompanying his chapters and articles, one is struck by the absence or infrequency of citations of Nietzsche's work: there are a handful of references in *Algeria 1960* (1979a), *The Logic of Practice* (1990c), *The Craft of Sociology* (Bourdieu, Chamboredon & Passeron 1991), *Homo Academicus* (1988), *The Field of Cultural Production* (1993a), *Distinction* (1989) and *Pascalian Meditations* (2000), and no mention at all in *Outline of a Theory of Practice* (1978), *Sociology in Question* (1993b), *The Rules of Art* (1995), *In Other Words* (1990b) and *Practical Reason* (1998c). The only extended discussions of Nietzsche or his work and ideas (and the term 'extended' is used here in a very loose sense) occur, unsurprisingly, in *The Political Ontology of Martin Heidegger* (1991a) and *Language and Symbolic Power* (2005b), and predominantly in response to specific interview questions in *An Invitation to Reflexive Sociology* (Bourdieu & Wacquant 1992). This lack of recognition is contradicted by Snook's account of Bourdieu's 'antecedents', where it is claimed first that Nietzsche is frequently acknowledged by Bourdieu (Snook 1990: 161) and second, and more reasonably, that Bourdieu's ideas regarding language and symbolic power owe a great deal to Nietzsche's theorizing of the connection between power, language and symbolic violence (Snook 1990: 161). There are a number of other examples of this claim being made: Mitchell Aboulafia (1999: 157) refers, for instance, to 'Bourdieu's Nietzschean sensibilities with regard to interest and power', and in a decidedly unsympathetic account of Bourdieu's work, Richard Jenkins (1992: 123) charges that, in terms of his failure to appreciate the forms of popular resistance to power, 'it is the shade . . . of . . . Nietzsche which lurks at Bourdieu's elbow'. However, it is difficult not to recognize the validity of Snook's (1990: 161) argument about Nietzsche's work being 'strongly influential on the development', at a technical level, of Bourdieu's understanding and theorizing of power.

Conclusion

In *An Invitation to Reflexive Sociology* (Bourdieu & Wacquant 1992), Wacquant refers to Bourdieu 'systematically developing . . . a sociological method consisting essentially in a manner of posing problems, in a . . . set of conceptual tools and procedures for constructing objects and for transferring knowledge gleaned in one area of inquiry into another' (1992: 5). Wacquant is describing an ongoing relation, extending from the period of Bourdieu's research in Algeria to his death in 2002, between the insights derived from dealing with work at hand and the development of a scholarly apparatus (knowledge, frameworks, concepts, categories, approaches, methodologies) that could be applied, with points of variation and specific emphasis, to the histories, contexts, regimes and specificities of socio-cultural politics. Bourdieu has claimed consistently that his identification of sets of empirically determined objectivities has served as the departure point for his schemes of categorization and differentiation, as well as his theorizing of the concepts of and the relation between habitus, field and practice. If the habitus exists as an entity for comprehending and explaining social phenomena, for instance, it is because for Bourdieu there are social regularities that cannot be encompassed within objectivist or subjectivist explanations of social behaviour. As he writes, 'The social game is regulated, it is the locus of certain regularities . . . I can say that all my thinking started from this point: how can behavior be regulated without being the product of an obedience to set rules?' (Bourdieu 1990b: 64–5). Concepts such as the habitus and cultural field are not just theoretical accounts of empirical data; rather, they are derivatives of an identifiable objective continuity. Bourdieu argues that the material world and its structures produce categories of thinking, apprehension and evaluation that are embodied by subjects, and that in turn remake or contribute to the maintenance of the material world, and its practices and regularities.

This book provides an account of Bourdieu's theoretical and methodological orientations, dispositions and antecedents, his scholarly trajectory and his main theoretical concepts. It discusses the ways in which Bourdieu incorporated the influence of figures such as Wittgenstein into his scholarly practices, and how those practices were to some extent informed by an attempt to move beyond established theoretical and methodological positions (structuralism, Marxism, sociological positivism). This chapter will be followed by an account of the major developments in Bourdieu's scholarly trajectory, with reference to both the content at hand (statistics about educational opportunities, the relation between Flaubert's representation of and position within the literary field) and wider strategic considerations (for instance, the claims Bourdieu was making about the range, responsibilities and methodological imperatives of the discipline of sociology).

The next chapter provides a detailed account of how this process played out across Bourdieu's scholarly trajectory, with particular regard to the development of his major theoretical concepts and methodologies, and their deployment in studies of the education system and the field of cultural production, as well as more generally with regard to the analysis of the logics underpinning cultural practices and the process of symbolic domination and violence.

2
Scholarly trajectory

Introduction

This chapter provides an account of Bourdieu's scholarly trajectory: it covers the anthropological and ethnological material produced in and about Algeria; his sociology of education period; the subsequent work on the field of cultural production; and finally his engagement with, and analysis and critique of, forms of symbolic violence associated with the state and global capitalism.

There are any number of ways of plotting Bourdieu's academic trajectory, all of which present difficulties of one kind or another. He researches and writes into, through and across a number of disciplinary fields and sub-fields, often simultaneously. The forms of work he undertakes are different, both in terms of the focus on certain subject areas (education, sociological methodology and practice, the state, the field of cultural production) and with regard to their strategic orientations, types of address and genres (scholarly books, journal articles, interviews, published lectures and talks). Moreover, Bourdieu's work needs to be contextualized, considered and evaluated not only in terms of its scholarly orientations, contributions and achievements, but also with regard to his attempts to influence and contribute to, and play the game of, the cultural politics of the academic field, which took the form, for instance, of a repeated insistence on a sociology that was scientific, historically attuned, reflexive and both theoretical and empirical. There are also theoretical and methodological trajectories to consider—not just in terms of the development and deployment of certain concepts (the habitus, reproduction, reflexivity) and methodological apparatuses—for instance, the highly specific empirical regime that characterized the research in *The Weight of the World* (1999)—but also with regard to the ways in which those theoretical concepts and methodologies sometimes reappeared in slightly altered forms, or were subject to different kinds of focus, emphasis or orientation, depending on the task at hand. Finally, there is what we can refer to as the trajectory of Bourdieu's name, and by extension the meanings, discourses and narratives associated with it: this was an aspect of which Bourdieu was clearly aware, and one that he attempted to negotiate, inflect and utilize—for instance, in terms of the activities associated with *On Television and Journalism* (1998b).

All these factors and issues are connected, and dealing with them at some level of differentiation or narrative separation is not a straightforward exercise. Bourdieu's attempts to give shape to and promote a specific type of sociology (one derived from Durkheim and Weber) were intertwined with his political imperatives, his breaks with philosophy, anthropology and ethnology, and the influence exerted over the field of sociology by the form of positivism associated with the American social sciences. If these specific factors and contexts are to be explained and understood, they need to be described, analysed and evaluated in detail—a process subject to the usual limitations of selection, focus and omission.

In his account of Bourdieu's academic trajectory, from his sociological research in the field of education to a wider engagement with and analysis of the field of cultural production, Robbins (2000) refers to Bourdieu's dictum in *Distinction* (1989: 12) that, 'There is no way out of the game of culture; and that one's only chance of objectifying the true nature of the game is to objectify as fully as possible the very operations which one is obliged to use in order to achieve that objectification.' At first glance, this citation can be taken as having a predominantly methodological orientation—that is, as referring to the reflexive disposition, acquired by way of Weber, Bachelard, Canguilhem and others, that for Bourdieu is a necessary part of a sociology that aspires to the condition and status of a (social) science. However, it also prefigures and references another set of issues pertaining to his relationship to, and place within, the specific cultural game that constitutes the academy, and by extension the ways in which he has played that game over the course of his career. This encompasses everything from the deployment of, emphasis given to and modifications of theoretical notions and concepts such as class and habitus to the more general question of Bourdieu's attempts to negotiate and explain—and, we might add, establish and authorize—how his work and theoretical concepts are understood, read and used.

There are two quite useful accounts of this issue: one in Robbins' (2000) text; the other provided by Loïc Wacquant in *An Invitation to Reflexive Sociology* (Bourdieu & Wacquant 1992), a book that contains questions posed, in interview format, by Wacquant to Bourdieu. We will consider Wacquant's version first: he begins by outlining the purpose of the book, which is 'to give access to a "mind in action" by exemplifying what Weber . . . would call "the conventional habits" of Pierre Bourdieu as "investigator and teacher in thinking in a particular way"' (1992: ix); it aims to provide 'a springboard into Bourdieu's work' and will serve 'as a tool box . . . for posing and solving sociological problems' (1992: xi). Wacquant notes that the reception of Bourdieu's work in the English-speaking world has tended to be concentrated 'around three main nodes' (1992: 4), corresponding to work carried out in the areas of education, anthropology and culture, and that, 'Each group of interpreters typically ignores the other' (1992: 5). Consequently, 'despite the recent flurry of translations and the now extensive and fast-proliferating secondary literature that has burgeoned around his writing, Bourdieu remains something of an intellectual enigma' (1992: 5). To address this situation, Wacquant proposes sketching 'in broad brushstrokes the central postulates and purposes that give Bourdieu's undertaking its overarching unity and thrust' (1992: 5). He characterizes his own task in dealing with the relation between these broad precepts, and the internal variations that occur within them, in the following way:

> Bourdieu is endlessly revising and revisiting the same Gordian knot of questions, objects and sites, as his recursive and spiraling mode of thinking unfolds over time and across analytical space. The linear technique of exposition . . . on the other hand, tends to 'freeze' this movement by artificially synchronizing formulations that correspond to different stages of Bourdieu's intellectual development . . . Though the main intentions and fault lines of Bourdieu's thought were firmly laid down as early as the mid-1960s, there are still significant shifts, turns, and breaks in his work that will be glossed over here as the internal dynamism of his theoretical structure is underplayed. (Bourdieu & Wacquant 1992: 6)

Two points are worth noting here: the first is the identification of an 'overarching' logic and set of principles that both 'undergird his scientific practice' (1992: ix) and effectively constitute an 'explanation' of his work; the second is that the connection between this abiding logic and the 'shifts, turns and breaks in his work' (1992: 6) is characterized predominantly as a technical matter. We could say that it is explicable and negotiable in terms of its own terms—that is, by way of a privileging of the techniques of reflexivity and scientific evaluation that identify and counter the forms and dispositions of the scholarly habitus. However, it is also in keeping with Bourdieu, Chamboredon & Passeron's (1991: 1) affirmation of Comte's statement that, 'Method . . . does not admit of being studied apart from the research in which it is used.'

This is both a useful and a convincing explanation of how we can contextualize, read and evaluate Bourdieu's academic trajectory; however, it requires a wider level of practical and contextual supplementation, which can be found in Robbins' *Bourdieu & Culture* (2000). After having provided a contextual and (brief) theoretical outline of Bourdieu's movement from the study of education to that of culture, Robbins (2000: xv) writes:

> It is clear that Bourdieu's analyses of culture were produced as affirmations of the approach to social scientific research outlined in (*The Craft of Sociology*) . . . Nevertheless, Bourdieu has played the 'game of culture' that he has observed. There is no more escape from that game for him than for anyone else. His productions have, therefore, been elements to his strategic position-taking—within and between fields. Like everyone else, he has been caught up in situations which have meant that his achievements have been the consequence both of his own structuring and of the structuring imposed upon him by various fields of reception and consumption.

This account and the material quoted from Wacquant are in no way incommensurate; however, there are very different points of emphasis. One obvious difference is that Robbins locates and contextualizes Bourdieu's work, and the changes to his theoretical and methodological apparatus, more strategically—in other words, we can say that Bourdieu-as-academic operates in much the same way as a player who, as a product of the dispositions and values associated with the game-as-ethos, as a participant endowed with a relevant literacy, and as a competitor capable of making and taking strategic moves and decisions, simultaneously plays and is played. So, while the unfolding of the game presents an almost infinite number of permutations and possibilities, there are certain regularities (with regard to objectivities such as rules, or durable dispositions acquired from history) that can be identified and used to situate and provide an explanation of that practice, in that situation, at that time. In this way, Robbins does no more than apply Bourdieu's precepts to Bourdieu, and he provides a quite detailed and intensive analysis of what we can term the micro-trajectories of his work, theories and name—for instance, by looking at the way in which the concept of the habitus, once it is theoretically contextualized by way of a distinction between the notions of position and situation, can move from a condition associated with determinism (and structuralism) and take on a more generative character and function.

The approaches taken by Wacquant and Robbins will be used in this and the following chapter to help organize, categorize and characterize the trajectory of Bourdieu's work. We will provide an account and analysis of the most significant characteristics of Bourdieu's work within what we have identified as the main areas and phases of his academic trajectory. By way of clarification, the term 'characteristics' will encompass features such as the content and points of focus of his scholarly work. We will also evaluate the extent to which the interaction between Bourdieu's approaches and the work being undertaken contributed to shifts in or changes to his scholarship, and how this occurred; this will involve identifying and evaluating developments in or modifications of his theoretical and methodological apparatuses. We will provide an overview and evaluation of some of the more significant ways in which Bourdieu's work in each period has been critically received both at a theoretical level and from within the relevant specific fields and sub-fields (such as anthropology and education). Finally, and following from the previous point, we will consider how those critical responses to Bourdieu's theories may have informed or inflected what we can term the 'self-presentation' of his work—in other words, we consider the kinds of discursive moves and strategies he employed in the form of explanations, justifications and clarifications of what he was doing, and why he was doing it.

The areas into which we have divided Bourdieu's scholarly trajectory often overlap, both in terms of content and chronology. In the 1960s, for instance, Bourdieu published the greater part of his ethnological and anthropological work; however, he also wrote extensively on education, as well as on aspects of the field of cultural production. The interventionist and at times polemical nature of his later work can be identified as a disposition dating from his 'entry into intellectual life, in the 1960s during the Algerian War of Independence' (Poupeau & Discepolo 2005: 64). Three of Bourdieu's major publications in the area of education, the original French versions of *The Inheritors* (Bourdieu & Passeron 1979b), *Academic Discourse* (Bourdieu, Passeron & Saint Martin 1994) and *Reproduction* (Bourdieu & Passeron 1990) were completed during this time; however there were also books, book chapters and journal articles on photography, art and museums, and sociological theory and practice. These areas of activity also overlap in terms of the coverage of socio-cultural, economic and political issues, themes and contexts. Bourdieu's interest in and awareness of the significance of the cultural field and its role in the production, maintenance and naturalization of symbolic power are germane to his educational and early cultural work; however, his understanding of the socio-cultural roles and functions of the field of cultural production undergoes a significant development in *The Field of Cultural Production* (1993a) and *Language and Symbolic Power* (2005b), and in his later, more interventionist, texts.

Bourdieu's attitude towards different areas of the academic and intellectual fields, such as ethnology, anthropology, sociology, education, linguistics, philosophy, journalism and the field of cultural production more broadly, and to theoretical approaches such as Marxism, phenomenology, gender politics, critical theory, postmodernism and speech act theory, are characterized by a mixture of continuity and discontinuity. His interest in linguistics and language theory, for instance, is relatively constant, as are his attitudes to Wittgenstein (wholly positive) and Saussure (predominantly negative). The point is that Bourdieu's interventions in critical debates, his use of specific theories and his relation to different disciplines are never straightforward or merely technical.

A final issue concerns developments and variations in how Bourdieu understands, defines, emphasizes and uses specific theoretical terms and concepts such as the habitus, cultural field, cultural capital and class. Again, we are dealing with a combination of continuities and discontinuities, informed by strategic imperatives and considerations. Bourdieu's theories are always oriented towards and to some extent inflected by specific tasks, but at the same time these theories and concepts are involved in a dialogue not just with the work at hand, but with the responses received from the various fields in which they have been deployed, or to which they have come into contact. This can be a particularly robust dialogue, such as when a theory threatens to undermine established theoretical or discursive positions (for instance, the notion of reproduction was read as a critique of 'progressive' educational theory); when it posits ideas that contradict the doxa of a field of activity (Bourdieu's notion of symbolic domination, particularly as it was outlined in *Masculine Domination* (2001), encountered strong criticism from feminist groups); and of course where a concept, idea or term is a site of struggle within a field or fields (the notion of class, as it was formulated in *Distinction* (1989) was criticized by various Marxist factions and by cultural studies scholars, often for very different reasons). Bourdieu's own explanation of his understanding of class, however, is quite different. Referring to the 'pernicious forms that lazy thinking can take in sociology' (Bourdieu & Wacquant 1992: 249), specifically the taken-for-granted deployment of Marxist notions of class, Bourdieu writes:

> To conduct surveys on social classes without any further reflection on their existence or nonexistence, on their size, and on whether they are antagonistic or not . . . is unknowingly to take as one's object the traces, within reality, of the effects wielded by Marx's theory. (1992: 249)

These criticisms do not constitute a dialogue in the conventional sense of the term—for a start, the figures are not addressing one other, and while his critics are writing very specifically about Bourdieu's theorizing of the relation between class and regimes or patterns of cultural practice and value, Bourdieu is, much more generally, responding to and criticizing the tendency of some sociologists to reify and presume class formations. Moreover, the nearest reference to *Distinction* in *An Invitation to Reflexive Sociology* (Bourdieu & Wacquant 1992), from which Bourdieu's quote is taken, occurs 22 pages before the criticism of 'lazy sociological practices'.

However, it is worth looking at what immediately precedes, and could be said to inform or contextualize, that reference. Bourdieu warns, apropos of the use and appropriateness of methodological apparatuses and practices, that 'we must be aware of all sectarian dismissals ... We must try, in every case, to mobilize all the techniques that are relevant and practically usable, given the definition of the object and the practical conditions of data collection' (Bourdieu & Wacquant 1992: 227), and he offers the example that, 'One can, for instance ... combine the most standard statistical analysis with a set of in-depth interviews or ethnographic observation, as I tried to do in *Distinction*' (1992: 227). By way of what we can term meta-theoretical clarification, he writes (1992: 228) that

> the construction of an object, at least in my personal research experience, is not something that is effected once and for all, with one stroke, through a sort of inaugural theoretical act. The program of observation and analysis through which it is effected is not a blue-print that you draw up in advance ... It is, rather, a protracted and exacting task that is accomplished little by little, through a whole series of small rectifications and amendments inspired by what is called *le metier*, the 'know-how', that is, by the set of practical principles that orients choices at once minute and decisive.

A number of things are at stake here, not least among them the issue of the process whereby objects of knowledge can be known. For Bourdieu, this process—at least as far as it plays out in his scholarly praxis—is characterized both by a willingness to apply methodological and theoretical instruments in order to see what can be seen by them, and then by taking whatever gains and insights are to be had and integrating them, at a level of accretion, into an overall understanding of the thing in question. This account, however, completely contradicts the various arguments that Frow (1995) makes regarding *Distinction*. Bourdieu's project, he writes, 'ends up like the king in medieval social taxonomy, "who, by setting himself up as the absolute subject of the classifying operation, as a principle external and superior to the classes it generated . . . assigned each group its place in the social order, and established himself as an unassailable vantage point"' (1995: 46–7).

The criticism that was directed towards *Distinction* contextualizes, to some extent, the following passage from *Practical Reason* (1998c: 10), which first appeared in French some fifteen years after the French edition of *Distinction* was published:

> To construct social space, this invisible reality that cannot be shown but which organizes agents' practices and representations, is at the same time to create the possibility of constructing theoretical classes that are as homogeneous as possible from the point of view of the two major determinants of practices and of all their attendant properties. The principle of classification thus put into play is genuinely explanatory. It is not content with describing the set of classified realities, but rather, like the good taxonomies of the natural sciences, it fixes on determinant properties which . . . allow for the prediction of other properties and which distinguish and bring together agents who are . . . as different as possible from members of other classes, whether adjacent or remote. But the validity of the classification risks encouraging a perception of theoretical classes, which are fictitious regroupings existing only on paper, through an intellectual decision by the researcher, as real classes, real groups, that are constituted as such in reality. The danger is all the greater as the research makes it appear that the divisions drawn in *Distinction* do indeed correspond to real differences in the most different, and even the most unexpected, domains of practice.

This account constitutes a major refinement of how Bourdieu articulates the relation between class and the habitus in *Distinction*. Scholarly criticism of Bourdieu's work often engendered a series of responses—for instance, in interviews and theoretical 'asides' in his books, which usually take the form of explanations and clarifications regarding the relation between the concept and the work performed. On other occasions, however, they manifest themselves as an intensification of discussions about, and modifications of, the theory or concept at the level of analytical deployment. We will consider other examples of this process, as well as of the other points of qualification, later in this chapter.

From anthropology and ethnology to sociology

The period Bourdieu spent in Algeria was the most influential of his scholarly career (Bourdieu 2007): one could almost say that, rather than forming a part of his academic trajectory, it constituted it. The most significant features of Bourdieu's work from that time on, including his abandonment of philosophy, his commitment to and development of a form of reflexive and rigorously scientific sociology and, perhaps most importantly, his disposition to regard academic and scholarly work as a form of political intervention, can be traced back to his Algerian period, and identified as incipient tendencies and dispositions that were derived from this time and its immediate scholarly aftermath. This is attested to on numerous occasions by Bourdieu (see, in particular, Bourdieu 1990c, 2000, 2007, 2012, 2013). He writes, for instance, that his break with philosophy 'no doubt owes a lot to what are called the chance events of existence, in particular a forced stay in Algeria, which one could say, without looking further, was at the origin of my "vocation" as an ethnologist and then as a sociologist' (2000: 41–2). Quite detailed technical and contextual accounts of the formative influence of his Algerian experiences can be found in *The Logic of Practice* (1990c) and in *Picturing Algeria* (2012) respectively, but perhaps more important are his references to the acquisition—or in some cases the intensification and accentuation—of certain dispositions. In the opening chapter of *Political Interventions*, Bourdieu (2008b: 4) writes:

> I wanted to be useful, by overcoming my feeling of guilt at being simply a participant observer in this disturbing war. My more or less happy integration into the intellectual field is perhaps at the root of my activities in Algeria. I could not rest content with reading the left-wing press and signing petitions, I had to do something as a scholar . . . It was absolutely indispensible for me to be at the heart of events, in order to inform public opinion, whatever the danger this might involve. To see, record, and take photographs.

In *Sketch* (2007), he provides an account of what these dangers were, and how they limited and contextualized his Algerian work. They problematized what were otherwise durable, assured and authorized scholarly attitudes, methodologies, theories and presumptions, and in the process helped him to reformulate what was at stake in, and how he should approach and conduct, his scholarly work. He makes the point, for instance, that his Algerian experiences were central to the integration of a sense of reflexivity into his academic habitus:

> To conduct sociological fieldwork in a situation of war compels one to reflect on everything, to monitor everything, and in particular all that is taken for granted in the ordinary relations between the observer and the informant, the interviewer and the interviewed: the identity of the interviewers, even the composition of the interviewing unit—one or two persons, and, if two, a man and a woman, an Algerian man and a Frenchwoman. (Bourdieu 2007: 50)

This disposition towards reflexivity was already present to some extent as a consequence of the dynamics of the French intellectual field at the time. We referred previously to the dominant position of philosophy, represented by names such as Heidegger and Sartre, with regard to the social sciences, and to the hegemony exercised by Marxist thought: neither seemed to sit well with the situation that Bourdieu encountered in Algeria. What *is* clear, however, is that as a consequence of the Algerian war and his experiences in it, Bourdieu underwent 'a transformation in his own trajectory . . . Bourdieu interrupted a career as philosopher in France and, rather than following the steep but predictable slope of philosophical theory' (Yacine 2013: 6), instead immersed himself in 'ethnographic enumeration' and the 'meticulous description of matrimonial strategies' (2013: 6).

Bourdieu points out that the position of the social sciences within the French academy and intellectual scene at this time was largely tied to the status and prestige enjoyed by the anthropological and ethnographic work of Claude Levi-Strauss (Bourdieu 2007: 40); as he explains, the social sciences, together with the history and philosophy of science, seemed to provide a more rigorous and scientific approach to doing research, along with an opportunity to 'repudiate the specious grandeurs of philosophy' (2007: 40). The kind of anthropology associated with Levi-Strauss had, for Bourdieu, four major characteristics: first, it had—or at least aspired to acquire—a quasi-scientific status, 'particularly by making reference to linguistics, which was then at its zenith' (2007: 35); second and by extension, it was strongly associated with structuralism; third, it was distinguished from other areas of the social sciences, such as sociology, by what we can call its 'aesthetic disposition' (2007: 43); finally, there was a tendency, at least on the part of Levi-Strauss, to 'hold the social world at a distance' (2007: 42). These characteristics meant that, for Bourdieu, Levi-Strauss' work had a strong tendency to produce a 'profoundly dehistoricized vision of social reality' (2007: 45).

The quasi-scientific approach of ethnology and anthropology had a strong appeal for Bourdieu while he was working in Algeria (see Bourdieu 1979a, 2007, 2012), not least because it gave him a great deal to do (interviews, observations and descriptions conducted in a cultural context regarding which the observer was largely illiterate), and it allowed for (even demanded) a close involvement with the people who were the subject of the study. He provides a number of accounts (see, in particular, Bourdieu 2007, 2008b, 2012, 2013) that capture the mix of more or less constant danger and almost hysterical scholarly activity that characterized his time in Algeria.

This differentiation carried with it something of a theoretical, but also an ethical, contradiction. On the one hand, Bourdieu was engaged in a scholarly activity that purported to be scientific and objective. On the other hand, it was apparent that this scholarship constituted a form of cultural politics, either in an interventionist sense (as a critique of colonialism) or in terms of a refusal to recognize the political dimension of an act by which the political was abstracted and rendered scientific, and the colonial relationship in effect doubled at a level of the methodological apparatus. The ethical contradiction both echoed and was not reducible to the theoretical contradiction. Bourdieu articulates and summarizes the interconnection between them, partly by way of an extended quotation from Michel Leiris, in the first chapter of *Political Interventions* (2008b: 5):

> We must recall, if only to put it to the test, the ideology according to which any research conducted in the colonial situation is supposedly affected by an essential impurity. In the words of Michel Leiris: 'It is still more evident than for other disciplines that in ethnography pure science is a myth, and we have to admit on top of this that the desire for pure scholarship weighs nothing in the case against the fact that, working in colonized countries, we ethnographers are not only metropolitans but metropolitan emissaries, since it is the state that defines our mission, so that we are less able than anyone else to wash our hands of the policy pursued by the state and its representatives towards those societies that we select for our study'... And we must add that the pure intention of doing pure science is necessarily doomed to failure.

The kinds of theoretical, methodological and ethical questions derived from the nexus of scientific aspirations and techniques associated with structuralism and, more generally, 'objectivist' theories and methodologies, and their deployment in colonial and other politicized contexts and situations, is not, as Bourdieu (2008b: 5) makes clear, something that is confined to ethnography, ethnology and anthropology. He asks, 'In what way is this original complicity different in kind from that which ties the sociologist studying his own society to his class of origin?' (2008b: 5). The cultural politics of anthropology and ethnology, however, seemed particularly problematical and pronounced in the Algerian context. Bourdieu writes that 'virtually all the works partially or totally devoted to ritual which were available when I was writing my *Sociologie de l'Algerie* seemed to me guilty, at least as regards to their objective intention and their social effects, of a particularly scandalous form of ethnocentrism', which led him to turn his 'attention in quite another direction' (Bourdieu 1990c: 3).

Bourdieu suggests, in *Sociology in Question* (1993b), that the distinction made between 'ethnology and sociology is a perfect example of a spurious frontier. As I try to show in . . . *The Logic of Practice* . . . it's a pure product of history [colonial history] that has no kind of logical justification' (1993b: 15). However, while there may be no formal distinction between them at a level of logic, in terms of their disciplinary approaches, methodologies and practices—which were strongly accentuated during the Algerian War of Independence—distinctions were clearly there, manifested in the ideological and ethical meanings that Bourdieu ascribes to certain methodological approaches and practices. The distance that ethnology insisted on maintaining with regard to its objects of study had ramifications in terms of both the methodologies it employed and, by extension, the empirical data it was able to identify and collect. The use of statistical analysis was a case in point:

> I was stupefied to discover, by the use of statistics—something that was very rarely done in ethnology—that the type of marriage

> considered to be typical in Arabo-Berber societies, namely marriage with the parallel girl cousin, accounted for about 3 to 4 per cent of cases ... This forced me to think about the notion of kinship, rule, and rules of kinship, which led me to the antipodes of the structuralist tradition. (Bourdieu 1990b: 8)

The final break with ethnology can be attributed to Bourdieu's determination to combine and refine his methodology-as-ethos. This required a commitment to a methodological approach that, in and through its attention to and deployment of the precepts of a rigorous science, could 'tell about the things of the social world, and, as far as possible, to tell them the way they are' (Bourdieu 2000: 5), while simultaneously 'submitting his own experience to the analysis that he applies to his object' (1990b: 66). The emphasis needed to be on empirical research and the identification of objectivities:

> My ... scientific enterprise is ... based on the belief that the deepest logics of the social world can be grasped only if one plunges into the particularity of an empirical reality, historically located and dated, but with the objective of constructing it as a 'special case of what is possible', as Bachelard puts it, that is, as an exemplary case in a finite world of possible configurations. (Bourdieu 1998c: 2)

What sociology seemed to offer was a scientific approach to research that, by way of the data it produced and its status as a science, enabled the researcher to break 'the enchanted circle of collective denial' (Bourdieu 2000: 5) that allowed symbolic and other forms of power and violence to naturalize and maintain themselves. It clearly provided Bourdieu with what he saw as a way out of this theoretical, methodological and ethical impasse: he refers in *Sketch* (2007: 58–9) to 'the transformation of my vision of the world that accompanied my transition from philosophy to sociology, of which my Algerian experience is no doubt the pivotal moment'.

Bourdieu's entry into the field of sociology was not without its own problems: as he explains in a number of texts (see, in particular, Bourdieu, Chamboredon & Passeron 1991; but also Bourdieu 1990b, 2007; Bourdieu & Wacquant 1992). In the 1960s, sociology in France was dominated by a form of positivism associated with Lazarsfeld, and to some extent *The Craft of Sociology*, with its attempt 'to draw up a balance-sheet of fieldwork, first in ethnology and then in sociology' (Bourdieu, Chamboredon & Passeron 1991: 247), was intended as a counter to 'the "Lazarsfeldian" invasion in France' (1991: 247). What sociology did offer was a connection with the historicizing disposition, and the methodological and scientific reflexivity and rigor, associated with Durkheim, Weber and the history and philosophy of science. Bourdieu claims that he sought to import into sociology 'a whole epistemological tradition' (Bourdieu, Chamboredon & Passeron 1991: 248), represented by names such as Bachelard and Canguilhem:

> That tradition, which cannot easily be labeled with an 'ism', has as its common basis the primacy given to construction. The fundamental scientific act is the construction of the object; you don't move to the real without a hypothesis, without instruments of construction. And when you think you are without any presuppositions, you will construct without knowing it and, in that case, almost always inadequately. In the case of sociology, this attention to construction is particularly necessary because the social world constructs itself in a sense . . . In everyday experience . . . our thinking applies instruments of knowledge which serve to construct the object when they should be taken as the object. Some of the ethnomethodologists were discovering that at about the same time, but they failed to arrive at the idea of the necessary break that is set out by Bachelard. That's why, in defining social science as a simple 'account of accounts', they ultimately remain in the positivist tradition. (1991: 248–9)

SCHOLARLY TRAJECTORY

The anthropological and ethnological approaches associated with Bourdieu's Algerian period proved to be politically and methodologically incompatible with his attempt to 'seek to restore to others the meaning of their behaviour, one of the many things that the colonial system has deprived them of' (Bourdieu 2008b: 6). Nevertheless the tension that Bourdieu observed between an objectivist account of practice and the socio-cultural realities of everyday life in colonial Algeria (and in Béarn) were extremely productive. As Yacine (2013: 6) points out, while Bourdieu did not come 'on the scene fully equipped with perfectly thought-out and established theoretical concepts (habitus, capital, field)', his theoretical apparatus developed out of and was shaped by his attempt to recover what was lost in anthropological and ethnological research practices. This involved, first, identifying the mechanisms and processes whereby subjects acquired and incorporated the dispositions that made their behaviour, at one level, predictable and amenable to objectivism and, second, being able to explain and demonstrate how the objective structures of a society and culture (rules, regulations, rituals) constituted the departure point for the strategic and tactical moves (the logic of practice as practice) that, as a form of 'resistance' to power, take 'the most unexpected forms, to the point of remaining more or less invisible to the cultivated eye' (Bourdieu 1990b: 155).

An example of how this theoretical development and refinement came about can be seen in Bourdieu's research in Béarn, which eventually gave rise to his book on bachelorhood (Bourdieu 2008a). Writing in *Sketch* about this period and the research that marked it, which he characterizes as a kind of 'experimentation on the work of reflexivity' and 'an ethnography of ethnography and ethnographers' (2007: 65), he explains that

> it was no doubt a banal remark of my mother's, which I would not even have picked up if I had not been alerted to it ('they have become very 'kith and kin' with the X's now that there's a *polytechnicien* in the family') that, at the time of my study of

bachelorhood, triggered the reflections that led me to abandon the model of the kinship rule for that of strategy.

What Bourdieu found in Béarn (and its matrimonial strategies) were insights derived from distance (from the native land) and foreignness (of culture) respectively. This emphasis on distance and foreignness produced another difference, this time in Bourdieu's own work of a sociological project transformed into a kind of ethnological study. Whereas in his work on French schools Bourdieu describes the reproduction of the objective structures (discourses, values, dispositions) of culture, with Béarn his analysis is informed by an 'ethnological style' predicated on a concern for 'minute detail' (Certeau 1988: 52). What Bourdieu discovered in the objective structures of the family in Béarn were the traces of use that obeyed logics that didn't appear to be inscribed anywhere, but that at the same time clearly constituted an ensemble of self-reflexive and flexible practices—in short, he encountered practice as a set of cultural literacies. As Certeau (1988: 53) writes:

> Genealogical tables or 'trees', surveys and geometrical plans of habitation, linear calendar cycles—these are totalizing and homogeneous productions, results of observational distance and 'neutralization' with respect to the strategies themselves that constitute as 'islands' family relations practised because they are useful, places that are distinguished by the inverted and successive movements of the body, or the periods of action carried out one after another in rhythms that are peculiar to each and mutually incommensurable. In contrast, there can be a synoptic representation, as the instrument of summation and mastery through vision, that levels and classes all the collected 'data'; it is practice that organizes discontinuities, nodes of heterogeneous operations. Matters of family relationships, space and time are thus not the same in every case.

SCHOLARLY TRAJECTORY

The strategic reading of practice that emerges from Bourdieu's analysis of the ongoing relationship between subjects, objective structures, time and place in Béarn constitutes a break with the anthropological structuralism of the 'Kabylia House' section of *Outline of a Theory of Practice* (1978), 'perhaps the last work I wrote as a blissful structuralist' (Bourdieu 1990c: 9). The situation with regard to ethnology and anthropology isn't as definite or as straightforward: *Distinction* (1989) and even *The Weight of the World* (1999), for instance, can be located within an ethnological tradition. However, the ways in which anthropological and ethnological research abstracted Algerian society and culture were read by Bourdieu as being of a similar order to Marxist interpretations of the Algerian War of Independence, and to Fanon's idealization of the Algerian peasantry (Goodman 2009: 105–6). Barnard (1990) provides a useful account of how, during the 1960s, the methodologies and perspectives of anthropology and ethnology (the bird's eye view, objectification, dehistoricization) became associated with, and in some cases indistinguishable from, the forms and institutions of colonialism, and cites the story of a cartoon, purported to be given 'prominent position in the office of a leading African nationalist', which showed 'a raised black fist in the foreground' while in the background are the figures of 'three retreating, white, pith-helmeted figures with the captions "colonial administrator", "missionary" and "anthropologist"' (Barnard 1990: 59).

The status and evaluations of Bourdieu's work on Algeria have fluctuated over the last 50 years. Generally, the relevant scholarship recognizes that it played a significant part in the development of his theoretical apparatus. The move from philosophy to ethnology and anthropology, for instance, eventually led to a form of sociology that was simultaneously historical, scientific and informed by both theoretical and empirical approaches. Scholars have argued (see Bourdieu & Wacquant 1992; Goodman & Silverstein 2009a; Harker, Mahar & Wilkes 1990; Webb, Schirato & Danaher 2002; Yacine 2013), and Bourdieu (1979a, 2007, 2013) himself has acknowledged, that the strong reflexive disposition and commitment to research-as-critique and a form of political intervention came out of the experience of working in a war zone, and of being part of an institutionalized colonialist presence. Furthermore, Bourdieu's major theoretical concepts (habitus, field, cultural capital) have at least an incipient presence in both the Algerian texts and the work on Béarn.

Other significant dispositions were also developed at this time. The decision to regard, deploy and utilize a theoretical and methodological apparatus as a set of tools both specific and subject to the task at hand may have had its full genesis in the influence of Durkheim and Weber, but it is easy to imagine that the kinds of very complex and dangerous situations in which Bourdieu found himself working also played some kind of originating role. Bourdieu's acceptance and utilization of the status of an outsider may have had its origins in his class and rural background, but researching in a culture regarding which he was, initially at least, illiterate—not to mention teaching in a university (the University of Algiers), where faculty members opposed to the war suffered torture, disappearance and execution—would have accentuated this tendency. Yacine (2013: 15) writes that 'a historian known for his commitment to Algerian independence' was 'dismissed from the university after having nearly been lynched by his own students'. Finally, Bourdieu's interest in the relationship between economic and symbolic capital, his critique of the hegemony exercised by economist logics and discourses over social and cultural fields, and his fierce criticism, in the later part of his career, of the ways in which market capitalism colonized important and influential cultural fields (such as journalism and sport) doubtlessly were derived from seeing at first hand how the introduction of capitalism into Algeria contributed to the destruction of traditional society and culture.

Bourdieu's work on Algerian society and culture has also attracted a great deal of criticism, predominantly from field-specific scholars. A good example is Goodman and Silverstein's (2009a) *Bourdieu in Algeria*. It provides various critiques of Bourdieu's work in Algeria in general, and more specifically the suitability and applicability of his theoretical concepts to the situation at hand. It also criticizes Bourdieu, in a manner that recalls Bourdieu's own criticism of Fanon, for appropriating indigenous cultural material and redeploying or configuring it within Western theoretical narratives. Many of the arguments contained in this book merely echo charges that Bourdieu has levelled at himself and his work from this period. In his Introduction to *Algeria 1960* (Bourdieu 1979a: viii) Bourdieu states, 'I had more than once felt the wish to refine and systematize the analyses, by investing in them all that subsequent work has yielded (particularly *Outline of a Theory of Practice*).'

Whatever its shortcomings and limitations, Bourdieu's Algerian work is perhaps best judged not so much in terms of what it is, but rather where it was going. The culmination of this work can be said to have been played out in the production of, and dialogue achieved between, *Outline of a Theory of Practice* (1978) and *The Logic of Practice* (1990c). The relationship between them is predicated upon the identification and development of a notion of practice that has learnt to do without and move beyond the limitations of structuralism. The major theoretical concepts are developed and refined in and across these two texts, to the point where they are recognizable in and continuous with regard to very different later texts, such as *The Rules of Art* (1995), *The State Nobility* (1996), *Practical Reason* (1998c) and *Pascalian Meditations* (2000), and it is these concepts, and their place within and relation to his wider theoretical apparatus, that help make what we know as Bourdieu's sociology possible. There is both a continuity and a development, in the work on Algeria and Béarn, from structuralism to what Bourdieu terms generative structuralism (Bourdieu & Wacquant 1992), from an analysis of cultural rituals and rules to a logic of practice, and from ethnology and anthropology to sociology. In his introduction to *Algerian Sketches*, Yacine (2013: 6) characterizes and evaluates the work undertaken in this period in the following way:

> The intent of this volume is to make available to readers the articles Bourdieu wrote while he was in Algeria, along with the interviews that he subsequently gave on this period of his scientific activity. These texts are important because, written in

extraordinary conditions, the author himself wondered how one could think of conducting research in the midst of war; they are also the symptoms of a double transformation. First of all, in the manner that Algeria and the other 'indigenous' were then conceived and represented by 'orientalists', but above all a transformation in his own trajectory, as Bourdieu interrupted a career as philosopher in France and ... opted for ethnographic enumeration, the meticulous description of matrimonial strategies, studies that involved both statistics and photography. This double about-turn would lie at the root of the invention and formation of a new way of seeing and conceiving the social world.

Education and social reproduction

Bourdieu's academic trajectory after his Algerian work was characterized by a transition from the disciplines of anthropology and ethnology to that of sociology. To a certain extent, this change is as much to do with where Bourdieu chose to speak from and what he chose to identify with—and, perhaps equally importantly, how he was named and categorized by the academic field—as it is with significant changes to or refinements of his theoretical apparatus or relation to his objects of study. Bourdieu writes, for instance, that *Distinction* 'can be read as a sort of ethnography of France' (1989: xi), and a similar characterization could be applied to texts as different as *The State Nobility* and *The Weight of the World*. However in *In Other Words* Bourdieu (1990b: 59–60) provides a more detailed explanation regarding how, where and why this disciplinary transition was played out in his own work:

> My research into marriage in the Béarn was for me the crossover point, the interface, between ethnology and sociology ... I had thought of this work on my own part of the country as a sort of epistemological experimentation: analysing, as an ethnologist,

in an environment familiar to me... the matrimonial practices that I had studied in a much more distant social environment, namely Kabyle society, was a way of giving me an opportunity to objectify the act of objectification and the objectifying subject; of objectifying the ethnologist not only as a socially situated individual but also as a scientist who professes to analyse and conceptualize the social world, and who for that reason has to withdraw from the game, whether he observes a foreign world in which he has no vested interest, or whether he observes his own world, but while standing back from the game... In short, I wanted less to observe the observer as an individual... than to observe the effects produced on the observation... by the situation of the observer... to uncover all the presuppositions inherent in the theoretical posture as an external, remote... non-involved vision.

The salient point for Bourdieu is not so much the differences inherent in analysing the strange or the familiar, as it is in socially situating the act of observation—in other words, of gaining an understanding of how and in what ways any form of socio-cultural analysis is derived from and inflected by a set of social presuppositions, both general and field-specific, and how this is to be overcome. This is sociology in the tradition of Durkheim and Weber, supplemented by a strong sense of its own contextually and historically situated perspective. It aspires to the status of a science (in its commitment to the use of theoretical and methodological apparatus capable of objectification), which is necessarily reflexive (because objectification requires a means of incorporating and objectifying the apparatus by which objectification is achieved).

The extent to and forms in which these theoretical and methodological imperatives and techniques characterize Bourdieu's work are not uniform. At different times and in different areas of work, Bourdieu's focus tended to change, depending on the nature of the tasks at hand and the contexts in which they were situated. It is possible, for instance, to trace a continuity across the educational and cultural texts produced in this period and beyond. *The Craft of Sociology*, for instance, is a kind of disciplinary overview-as-manifesto that articulated and argued for a particular form of sociology, clearly associated with Durkheim and Weber. It is both scientific and empirical in its leanings, and continuous with regard to later works such as *Distinction* and *The State Nobility*.

Bourdieu first developed and deployed his sociological scholarly apparatus in the area of education (see Grenfell 2012; Harker, Mahar & Wilkes 1990; Jenkins 1992; Webb, Schirato & Danaher 2002), most particularly in terms of theorizing the role that education played in processes of class reproduction and symbolic domination. There are three major works devoted specifically to education: *The Inheritors* (Bourdieu & Passeron 1979b), *Academic Discourse* (Bourdieu, Passeron & Saint Martin 1994) and *Reproduction* (Bourdieu & Passeron 1990). However, the scope of Bourdieu's work on the relationship between education, culture and socio-cultural reproduction is not confined to these texts: it includes *Photography* (Bourdieu et al. 1990), *The Love of Art* (Bourdieu, Darbel & Schnapper 1990), *Distinction* (1989), *Language and Symbolic Power* (2005b), *The Field of Cultural Production* (1993a), *Sociology in Question* (1993b) and *The State Nobility* (1996).

Of the three major education studies, *The Inheritors* is concerned with the relationship between cultural and symbolic capital and the French university system, specifically with regard to the extent to which universities privilege class-based cultural literacies; *Academic Discourse*, as the title suggests, deals with the kinds of discourse used and valued in French higher education, and how this dominant discursive regime is implicated in the exclusion of students from certain backgrounds; and *Reproduction* is a study of symbolic power, manifested as forms of symbolic violence played out and reproduced through the French education system. The notion of social reproduction informs all three texts, although how this process is understood, and the theorizing of the relationship between culture, cultural capital and educational attainments and the progress that underpins it, varies considerably.

SCHOLARLY TRAJECTORY

Bourdieu's research into French university life and culture in *The Inheritors* identifies the numerous cultural threads (based on gender, class, regional affiliations, educational background, familial situation and other factors) that, when woven together, ensure that the literacies, experiences and dispositions associated with certain backgrounds constitute and are recognized as cultural capital; this means that the game of university education continues to be played out long after the results are determined and known. Entering university or choosing certain academic paths is always a loaded game, and players can only adapt to 'rules' or conventions that are, simultaneously, everywhere and nowhere. By way of example, and in a manner that he takes up much later in *Masculine Domination*, Bourdieu (1979b: 62) argues that while the female university students in his study perform a discursive commitment to the values of academic education, this engagement is always recuperated and reformulated in terms that are commensurate with the perceived role of women as being academic outsiders:

> In short, because their present is dominated by the image of a future which belies or questions it, female students cannot unconditionally espouse the values of the intelligentsia and are less successful than men in concealing from themselves the unreality of their present by acting as if the future were unreal. And if scholastic docility offers itself to them as the least bad way of managing to do so, this is perhaps because it constitutes a felicitous interpretation of the traditional model of female dependence which ... perfectly matches the expectations of a higher education system that has remained traditional (and male-oriented) in its spirit (and its teaching staff).

The significance of what is referred to in *Academic Discourse* as 'linguistic misunderstanding in higher education and the determining role of linguistic inheritance in academic success' (Bourdieu, Passeron & Saint Martin 1994: 37) is taken up and developed, in a broader and more systematic way, in *Reproduction*. The elements of this development will be discussed in detail in Chapter 3. We can, however, make two general points about the issues covered, the arguments made and the theories employed in that text. First, Bourdieu, Passeron and Saint Martin take the position that 'it is the culture of the dominant group ... the group (or groups) that control ... economic, social and political resources which is embodied in the schools, and that it is this "embodiment" that works as a reproduction strategy for the dominant group' (Harker 1990: 87). Second, they argue that the process of reproduction is facilitated by way of and through a web of relationships involving the concepts of cultural (in this case, predominantly linguistic) capital, the habitus and the cultural field. The concept of cultural capital is identified as the mechanism—or, perhaps more correctly, the system—whereby forms of domination are practised, maintained and reproduced in a manner that never draws attention to itself as a form of violence, and this differential seems to be, for both the person who acts and the person who is acted upon, something normal and natural. In this regard, cultural capital is closely associated with and largely a derivative of the habitus, in the sense that forms of capital are sought after and acquired, and also embodied and performed, by way of a bodily hexis and a style (a superior ease) of relating to things and people. The habitus and cultural capital are always subject to the influences and dynamics of cultural fields: one of the points that Bourdieu, Passeron and Saint Martin make in *Reproduction* is that there is inevitably a mismatch between the habitus of students from the lower classes and that which is more or less institutionalized within the education system; one of the consequences of this mismatch is that lower-class students disqualify themselves in advance as not being the 'right kind of people' (Bourdieu & Passeron 1990).

Bourdieu's work on education was highly influential, but it was also subjected to considerable criticism, both from field-specific sources (Harker, Mahar & Wilkes 1990) and, more generally, from cultural theorists who argued or implied that it was deterministic, and effectively foreclosed the possibility of human agency and, by extension, of cultural change or non-reproduction (Certeau 1988; Jenkins 1992;

Rancière 2004; Reed-Danahay 2005). In his educational texts, Bourdieu delimits the role of strategy, literacy and calculation with regard to the production and enactment of socio-cultural practices, particularly on the part of students and teachers, who necessarily misrecognize the meaning of their actions. In *The Inheritors* and *Reproduction* (and, for that matter, in *Distinction*), Bourdieu is theoretically committed to the proposition that, at least within educational sites and contexts, cultural forms and practices are largely explicable in terms of the processes and regimes of symbolic domination. Bourdieu's work in this period was marked by a set of significant developments, both with regard to his theoretical apparatus and in terms of variations in his scholarly and disciplinary orientation, but also by changes to how his name and his work were identified, categorized, produced, represented and made meaningful. He continued to undertake empirical and scientific projects similar to his educational work, but they were often focused on the field of cultural production.

The cultural turn

To some extent, it is misleading to talk about Bourdieu's work or academic trajectory taking a 'cultural turn' in the 1980s, given that his educational sociology incorporated cultural material and data into his empirical studies (Harker, Mahar & Wilkes 1990; Robbins 2000). However, it is also possible to argue, as Robbins does, that in the 1970s Bourdieu 'was laying the foundations for establishing a sociology of culture that could be independent of the sociology of education' (2000: xv). Robbins is referring to the way in which *Distinction* (1989) presaged a set of texts (*The Field of Cultural Production* (1993a), *The Rules of Art* (1995), *Free Exchange* (Bourdieu & Haacke 1995), *On Television and Journalism* (1998b)) that either dealt with, or were specifically oriented towards analysing and theorizing, cultural activities as belonging to a separate cultural field (the field of cultural production)—a field with its own discourses, forms of capital and socio-cultural functions. In the

1980s, Bourdieu started to take a much greater interest in the processes and dynamics by which the field of cultural production—partly as a consequence of its relatively autonomous status, and partly because it constituted a set of sites characterized, to some extent, by a reflexive attitude to the workings of discourse and the field of power—played something other than a reproductive role in the game of symbolic power and domination. This last issue was complicated further by Bourdieu's recognition of the increasing tendency of the field of power, and in particular the state and neo-liberal capitalism, to colonize and alienate what had been relatively inalienable cultural forms and spaces (the situation of the field of journalism is a case in point here).

These developments were characterized by both continuities and significant changes in and across Bourdieu's theoretical and methodological apparatus. The theoretical developments that began to take shape in *Outline of a Theory of Practice* (1978) were reconsidered, refined and reformulated not just in the cultural texts mentioned above, but also in two books about the academic field and its discourses—*Homo Academicus* (1988) and *The Political Ontology of Martin Heidegger* (1991a)—in more general texts on sociological and cultural theory (*The Logic of Practice* (1990c), *Sociology in Question* (1993b), *In Other Words* (1990b), *An Invitation to Reflexive Sociology* (Bourdieu & Wacquant 1992), *Practical Reason* (1998c) and *Pascalian Meditations* (2000)—and in two studies of symbolic power and violence—*Language and Symbolic Power* (2005b) and *The Weight of the World* (1999). Bourdieu's move to a sociology of culture, and more specifically his research in and about the field of cultural production, was integral to—and indeed can be said to have necessitated—the theoretical and methodological development of a number of his concepts. The main changes were, first, with regard to the dynamics and characteristics of cultural fields, and the role played by cultural capital within those fields; second, in terms of the forms, techniques, processes and logics of symbolic power and violence that were enacted within and by way of the internal dynamics of, and the relationship between, cultural fields; and finally, and in a more general sense, regarding the relation between the habitus, cultural fields and the logic of practice.

In some ways, the work done in *Distinction* marks both the limitations of and the departure point for Bourdieu's understanding and theorizing of culture and cultural politics. A number of critics (Calhoun 1993; Frow 1995; Jenkins 1992) have suggested that *Distinction* suffers from the same problems that they see as characterizing Bourdieu's educational work, specifically a tendency to impose a theoretical system upon a set of cultural relations and practices without leaving any room for an understanding of practice as anything but a form of reproduction and, by extension, for failing to allow for the possibility of anything but homogeneity within particular socio-cultural or class positions. Frow (1995: 44–5) makes the point, for instance, that Bourdieu's theorizing and evaluation of the role of intellectuals and the intelligentsia in the game of power are vitiated by a decidedly unscientific tendency to dismiss or disregard evidence that doesn't fit in with his preconceived schema:

> Bourdieu's unification at the level of capital-equivalence of a 'dominant class' leads him to neglect the potential for contradiction in the role of the intelligentsia. The coincidence between the voting patterns of intellectuals and the working class seems to him 'paradoxical' . . . and contradictions in political ideology are read as a sign of bad faith . . . The disparity between 'ethos' and 'discourse' is taken as an index of hypocrisy, and Bourdieu (cites) . . . the 'nuances' of expression—evident only in the interview situation and too subtle to be reproduced in his text—which subvert the reality or genuineness of these opinions.

The same criticism is directed at Bourdieu's account of the working class and the employment of a rigid (and non-historicized) dominated/dominant dichotomy to characterize the relation between class and cultural formations:

> this dominance of the dominant values—which is never really given a historical and national specificity—then seems to become something absolute, and the working class to be inevitably and inexorably entrapped within the cultural limits imposed on it . . . The totalizing grip of the 'dominant norms', understood as a unitary set of values, allows for no possibility of critique and social transformation. (Frow 1995: 45–6)

A further problem with Bourdieu's approach in both the educational texts, and in his transition to cultural analysis in *Distinction*, is that there is little evidence of any incorporation, on a practical level, of techniques of reflexivity. As early as the manifesto that was *The Craft of Sociology* (Bourdieu, Chamboredon & Passeron 1991), Bourdieu and his co-authors could write about the necessity of subjecting 'scientific practice to a reflection' (1991: 8) and, more tellingly, that:

> an exclusive concern with the atemporal relationships between abstract propositions, at the expense of the processes through which each proposition or concept has been established and has given rise to others, can be of no help to those who are involved in the drama of scientific work, because all the action takes place behind the scenes and only the denouement is brought on to the stage.

This warning sits uneasily with the circularity of much of the thinking and reasoning that characterizes *Distinction*, which for Frow (1995: 46) seems to be written 'from an impossible perspective, a point that transcends the social space'.

We made the point that *Distinction* can also be read as a departure point for Bourdieu's later work on culture and cultural politics. This is something that Frow implicitly acknowledges when he writes (1995: 45) that Bourdieu's 'rigid dichotomization is modified somewhat in later sections of the book'. Robbins is more explicit, pointing to a chapter in *Distinction* titled 'Culture and Politics', which signalled a change in how Bourdieu approached and understood the socio-political role and function of culture:

> Whereas, in the 1960s, Bourdieu had argued that the state-controlled education system was an instrument for imposing a dominant culture and of excluding the many functionally satisfactory, but dominated, cultures existing within society, by the 1980s he was more inclined to regard the political system and its associated political discourse as more powerful instruments of domination . . . The 'autonomisation' of cultural studies is a political phenomenon which, in Bourdieu's view, had to be analysed as such sociologically. (Robbins 2000: xix)

Unlike the earlier sections of *Distinction*, 'Culture and Politics' is marked by acknowledgements of and references to cultural difference, non-compliance, complexity and the difficulty of identifying a logic of practice within practices. One example is Bourdieu's analysis of the relationship between class, political dispositions, newspaper consumption, newspapers as genre and the processes and techniques of reading and textual production:

> To endeavour to specify the relationship between the social classes and the political opinions socially constituted at a given moment, one may be tempted to examine, on the basis of statistics available, how the different classes and class fractions distribute their choices among the different politically marked newspapers and magazines. However, the inherent fallacies of such a procedure cannot be avoided unless one starts by considering what 'reading a newspaper' means for the different categories of readers, since it may have nothing in common with the functions commonly attributed to it or with those assigned to it by the producers or their backers. (Bourdieu 1989: 440–1)

There is also the highly significant recognition, noted by Robbins, that what Bourdieu calls 'the field of ideological production' is a 'relatively autonomous universe in which amidst competition and conflict, the instruments for thinking the social world are created and where, through this process, the field of the politically thinkable... is defined' (Bourdieu 1989: 399), and of the 'paradoxical coincidence' between intellectuals and the dominated classes, and their political dispositions. This pointed, among other things, to the need to refine the relationships between the habitus, cultural trajectories, the position of classes and class fractions with regard to the field of power, and position-taking across the wider socio-political field.

Distinction was followed by two lengthy studies of the cultural field of literature, essays collected as *The Field of Cultural Production* (1993a) and *The Rules of Art* (1995), a co-authored text with Hans Haacke, *Free Exchange* (1995), which was concerned with the socio-cultural functions and status of the field of art, and a book on journalism and its relation to the field of the media, *On Television and Journalism* (1998b). To provide some idea of the difference between the theoretical apparatuses operating in *Distinction* and *The Field of Cultural Production*, it is worth dealing briefly with an aspect of Bourdieu's theoretical development that is not found in the earlier book: the frame that contextualizes and helps to explicate whether a work is confirmed as being 'of the field' and consecrated as literature. The literary field is identified as having a character that is the antithesis of heteronomous fields and the field of power. This is, however, only part of the story, since a cultural field—even a relatively 'pure' field—is never entirely itself: both literature and the field of cultural production more generally are divided into sectors that tend to be more autonomous or heteronomous, and that are differentiated by different forms of cultural capital, discourses, identities, genres and perspectives. For a 'literary' novel to be recognized and verified as having literary value, for instance, it must correspond, in a variety of ways, with the values and narratives of the autonomous pole of the field of cultural production. In part, this is about being confirmed by the right kind of people, but it can be just as important or useful, in some ways, to be dismissed by the wrong kind of people. And there is no necessary homology between forms of capital recognized by and accepted across most cultural fields and confirmed by the field of power, and the kind of capital that leads to or facilitates literary consecration: to have an award conferred by a venerable institution that has immense standing with the field of power can constitute a kiss of death to certain kinds of literary ambitions, and the same can be true of a work attaining commercial success.

The essays collected in *The Field of Cultural Production* (1993a) are divided into three sections, the second of which is titled 'Flaubert and the French Literary Field'. The choice of Flaubert as the focus of this part of the study was probably based on a number of factors, one of which, discussed in some detail by Robbins (2000: 74), was connected to Sartre's existentialist appropriation of Flaubert as someone who lived 'always in "bad faith"—always to condemn the bourgeoisie without ever ceasing to be bourgeois'. There was also the desire to critique the 'romantic view of the artist as creator' that makes the literary field 'particularly resistant to a sociological approach' (2000: 75). Perhaps more important, however, was the homology that Bourdieu drew between the sociologist trying to locate and explain Flaubert's trajectory (his career and textual history, and his name understood as a signifier within the literary field and the wider field of cultural production), and Flaubert's work, read as a form of socio-cultural analysis of the world (and in particular the field of power) and Flaubert's place in it. Bourdieu (1993a: 145) writes of *Sentimental Education* that it 'contains an analysis of the social space in which the author was himself located and thus gives us the instruments we need for an analysis of him. Flaubert the sociologist gives us a sociological insight on Flaubert the man.'

Bourdieu extends his analysis of Flaubert's literary trajectory and practices in *The Rules of Art*. After a careful and very detailed description and evaluation—punctuated by citations from Flaubert's correspondence and from critics within the field—of Flaubert's relation to and reception within the field, and of his stylistic changes and orientations, particularly his use of realism and, by extension, his transformation of the 'definition of the novel' (Bourdieu 1995: 89), Bourdieu writes that, 'The space of position-takings that that analysis reconstitutes does not present itself as such to the writer's consciousness; that would oblige us to interpret his choices as conscious strategies of distinction' (1995: 93).

Under consideration in both these books is the status of the relation between a cultural field and the habitus. In other words, what needs to be understood and explained on Bourdieu's part is the extent to which everyday practices are informed and oriented by the dynamic relation between a cultural field, which is always caught up in diachronic flows and interactions, and is therefore never exactly 'itself', and a habitus, which takes its lead from, and is itself constituted through, the discourses, values and imperatives that stand in for (and discursively constitute) the field-as-community. Bourdieu insists that the field in which Flaubert finds himself, and to which he commits himself, is constituted both as a relatively stable and continuous discursive identity and set of objectivities in which every subject-of-the-field is immersed and positioned. In an interview with Wacquant in *An Invitation to Reflexive Sociology*, Bourdieu (Bourdieu & Wacquant 1992: 97) defines a cultural field and its relation to the subjects who inhabit it in predominantly objective and objectifying terms. In this account, the notion of cultural field is explained as:

> a network, or a configuration, of objective relations between positions. These positions are objectively defined, in their existence and in the determinations they impose upon their occupants, agents or institutions, by the present and potential situations ... in the structure of the distribution of the species of power (or capital) whose possession commands access to the specific profits that are at stake in the field, as well as by their objective relation to other positions ... domination, subordination, homology.

What is achieved in the complexity and detail of these analyses of the interactions between subjects and field is an enhanced and developed theoretical comprehension and account of the factors that constitute and maintain a field; the internal dynamics of fields; the relationship between the formative influence of the habitus and the imperatives associated with belief in and membership of a field; the pedagogical function of field-specific discourses; the role of bodily hexis and the embodiment of field-specific values in the process of differentiating and distinguishing fields; the imbrication of cultural capital and cultural literacy, and how this plays out in the development of a 'feel for the game' that allows subjects to anticipate the trajectory of a field; and the relation between specific fields and the field of power, and the extent to which this informs and inflects the trajectory and nature of fields and their membership, forms of identity, categories, cultural capital, practices, values, logics and discourses.

Bourdieu uses the literary field and its texts, logics and imperatives against the field in order to put forward an account and explanation of literary practice free from the dominant (and circular) romantic notion of genius. What is perhaps more important is that, first, Bourdieu's approach and theoretical apparatus (particularly habitus, field and capital) provide a way of 'thinking about transformations as well as the internal dialectics of positions', and explain 'how we think and how we act as cultural beings, and how these modes of thought and conduct change' (Danto 1999: 218); and second, they enable us not just to understand and explain how and why fields undergo transformation, but to situate them historically in terms of how their internal relations, dynamics and changes are informed by wider developments in the socio-cultural field and the field of power. What is still missing from these texts, however, is an appreciation of the way in which the acquisition of forms of cultural literacy, changes to the discourses and forms of capital within a field and, more specifically, the opening up of a gap between how different members of a field understand and relate to a field, might enable subjects to acquire a more reflexive relation to the field in which they operate.

These issues are also dealt with in the set of theoretical texts produced over a fifteen-year period, starting with *The Logic of Practice*

(1990c) and including *Language and Symbolic Power* (2005b), *Sociology in Question* (1993b), *In Other Words* (1990b), *An Invitation to Reflexive Sociology* (Bourdieu & Wacquant 1992), *Practical Reason* (1998c) and *Pascalian Meditations* (2000). They are also considered, but to a lesser extent and with a very different set of foci, in the other two studies of the field of cultural production, *Free Exchange* (Bourdieu & Haacke 1995) and *On Television and Journalism* (1998b). *The Logic of Practice* is usually read as a continuation and refinement of the project begun in *Outline of a Theory of Practice* (1978). Perhaps the best way to summarize the work that it undertakes is to suggest that it uses a set of ideas taken from Wittgenstein (1983) in an attempt to overcome 'the most fundamental, and the most ruinous' of the 'oppositions that artificially divide social science', that between 'subjectivism and objectivism' (Bourdieu 1990c: 25). This involves thinking with Wittgenstein in order to arrive at a logic of cultural practice defined as a practical understanding that is to be distinguished 'from the interpretations which one can only arrive at by placing oneself outside the practice' (1990c: 18). *Sociology in Question* (1993b) and *An Invitation to Reflexive Sociology* (Bourdieu & Wacquant 1992) can be read as sociological manifestos: both contain sets of interviews in which Bourdieu takes the opportunity to explain and defend his work. The former also contains essays on the field of cultural production (music, art, journalism, sport), while the latter is the place where Bourdieu most comprehensively articulates and explains the role of reflexivity in sociological analysis. The essays collected in *In Other Words* also contain interviews, and deal with many of the theoretical and methodological issues covered in *An Invitation to Reflexive Sociology*. As with *Sociology in Question*, there are essays on culture (sport, literature, journalism), but also on the academic and intellectual fields.

We can point to three interesting aspects of this body of work. First, the inclusion of interviews makes a difference to both the language and the form of address that Bourdieu adopts to respond to questions and explain technical points. This is not uniformly the case: the 'stage-managed' interviews and responses of *An Invitation to Reflexive Sociology* allow Bourdieu to maintain a certain distance from, and use language that isn't reducible to, the 'informality' that characterizes most of the other interviews. However, even in that text Bourdieu often resorts to relatively non-technical language to deal with technical questions. In some ways, the tone, self-presentation and narrative patterns presented in the interviews are not entirely dissimilar to that which characterizes Foucault's 'Collège de France' lecture series: the genres (the interview, the lecture) are very different, but in both sets of texts there is seemingly less at stake (reputation, status, the notion of rigor); less time to organize, manage and protect material, which is presented in a discursive and at times digressive manner; and processes of thought that are less smooth and complete (they are marked by the expression of qualifications, doubts, clarifications, asides, and unexpected references to antecedents and citations). Bourdieu's own lecture series at the Collège de France from 1989 to 1992, collected in *On the State* (2014), is similarly discursive and informal, incorporates questions and takes into account the different literacy levels of the audience (2014: 278); the content also tends to be oriented towards the historical and theoretical, rather than the empirical or statistical.

A second point of interest is that the style of the writing and the analytical approach in some sections of *In Other Words* (1990b), and more consistently in *Language and Symbolic Power* (2005b), *Practical Reason* (1998c) and *Pascalian Meditations* (2000), are much closer to that of critical theory than to empirical sociology. Parts of *Pascalian Meditations*, for instance—particularly, and not surprisingly, those dealing with bodily knowledge and the historicity of reason—are not far removed from the work and thought of Foucault. Part of the explanation is all of these texts deal, to a lesser or greater extent, with symbolic power, and it is from the field of philosophy—and particularly from the work of Pascal, Nietzsche and Wittgenstein—that Bourdieu derives the theoretical underpinnings of his investigation into the relation between symbolic power and violence, and the logics that inform cultural practice.

Finally, we can say that there is considerable theoretical continuity across the texts produced in this and the following period. The issues dealt with in *Pascalian Meditations* are developed from work carried out in *Language and Symbolic Power* (2005b), *In Other Words* (1990b), *Masculine Domination* (2001), *The Weight of the World* (1999) and *Practical Reason* (1998c); the notion of epistemological reflexivity (and, by extension, the capacity for objectifying forms of socio-cultural production) that is central to both *Pascalian Meditations* and *Science of Science and Reflexivity* is addressed in *The Logic of Practice, Language and Symbolic Power, Sociology in Question, In Other Words, An Invitation to Reflexive Sociology, The Field of Cultural Production, The Rules of Art* and *Free Exchange*, and precursors to *On Television and Journalism* include a number of essays devoted to the disciplinary and commercial functions undertaken by or increasingly associated with the cultural field of sport.

The state, neo-liberalism and symbolic power

The collection of texts referred to above, and in particular the studies of the field of cultural production, constitute a change of direction from Bourdieu's work in the sociology of education; they are oriented towards a reconsideration of the function and status of the cultural field, and characterized by a wider refinement of his theories of cultural field and the relation between habitus and socio-cultural practices, and between culture and symbolic power and violence. The major theoretical, and more conventionally scholarly, studies produced in the later stage of Bourdieu's academic trajectory, specifically *Pascalian Meditations, Science of Science and Reflexivity, The Social Structures of the Economy* and *On Television and Journalism,* are all continuous with regard to, but also reorient, this theoretical apparatus. Bourdieu's concern with the relation between symbolic power and cultural practices is developed and elaborated upon in *Pascalian Meditations*. The diminution of the autonomy of the scientific field by the state and capitalism, and the consequences of this development, is the focus of *Science of Science and Reflexivity* (2004), and the manner in which the economic field and its discourses naturalize forms of economism (neo-liberalism, the free market) as arbiters of value that inform the formulation of socio-cultural policies and practices, while simultaneously abstracting socio-cultural factors, elements and issues, is a central concern of *The Social Structures of the Economy* (2005c).

The main points of focus of Bourdieu's work in the final stage of his academic trajectory were the colonisation of the field of cultural production, and by extension of everyday life, by the logics, values, economies and discourses of capitalism; the censorship imposed upon it, in various forms, by the state and its functionaries; and the infiltration into the political field and public sphere culture of the logics associated with the media-as-spectacle. Bourdieu's approach to these issues took a number of forms, the most obvious of which were the overtly polemical texts such as *Acts of Resistance* (1998a) and *Firing Back* (2003). There were also numerous essays, interviews and lectures collected in books such as *Political Interventions* (2008b) and *Sociology is a Martial Art* (2010), which, for instance, use non-scholarly forms of address and language to warn against and draw attention to the consequences for civil society of the imbrication of commercial media and the field of politics:

> Television has probably contributed as much as bribery to the degradation of civic virtue. It has invited and projected on to the political and intellectual stage a set of self-promoting personalities concerned above all to get themselves noticed and admired, in total contradiction with the values of unspectacular devotion to the collective interest which once characterized the civil servant or the activist. It is the same self-serving attention seeking ... which explains why 'headline grabbing' has become such a common practice. For many ministers ... a measure is only valid if it can be announced and regarded as achieved as soon as it has been made public. (Bourdieu 1998a: 4)

The topics and targets of Bourdieu's interventionist works were identified and initially focused upon during the period of his cultural turn: the difference in the last stage of his work is in both the form and intensity of the address that is utilized. By way of example, consider the Introduction to *Acts of Resistance*:

> The texts that follow were written or spoken as contributions to movements and moments of resistance, and it is because I believe that the dangers that provoked them are neither isolated nor occasional that I decided to bring them together for publication. Although they are more exposed than methodologically controlled texts to the inconsistencies stemming from the diversity of circumstances, I hope that they can still provide useful weapons to all those who are striving to resist the scourge of neo-liberalism. I do not have much inclination for prophetic interventions and I have always been wary of occasions to which the situation or a sense of solidarity could lead me to overstep the limits of my competence. So I would not have engaged in public position-taking if I had not, each time, had the—perhaps illusory—sense of being forced into it by a kind of legitimate rage, sometimes closer to something like a sense of duty . . . And if, to be effective, I have sometimes had to commit myself in my own person and my own name, I have always done it in the hope—if not of triggering a mobilization, or even one of those debates without object or subject which arise periodically in the world of the media—at least of breaking the appearance of unanimity which is the greater part of the symbolic force of the dominant discourse. (Bourdieu 1998a: vii–viii)

Gisèle Sapiro (2010: ix), in her Introduction to the essays and interviews collected in *Sociology is a Martial Art*, initially situates this practice and tactic within the French tradition of the public intellectual:

The texts collected in this volume were conceived by Pierre Bourdieu as 'interventions'. Having achieved high academic recognition, Bourdieu decided to put his symbolic capital at the service of a cause, thus embodying—after Voltaire, Zola, Sartre, and Foucault—the French traditional figure of the public intellectual who engages in political and social matters. According to this model, an intellectual, a scholar, should not remain in an ivory tower; it is his or her duty to be involved in current affairs. His role is to offer a critical perspective and not to serve the political, economic, or religious powers. He must keep autonomous from political organizations and economic interests.

Sapiro (2010: ix) describes how Bourdieu reformulated his position in terms that both cited and developed Foucault's notion of the specific intellectual:

> Critical of the figure of the media intellectual that emerged in the late 1970s . . . Bourdieu went one step further in seriously considering the division of scientific labor. He suggested the notion of the 'collective intellectual', whose political stands are based on scientific knowledge and the result of individual or collective research. Like Foucault's 'specific individual', Bourdieu's 'collective intellectual' . . . stands in contradistinction to the figure of the expert called on by the political and economic forces to provide 'neutral' scientific knowledge in order to legitimize policies he has not elaborated or answer problems he has not defined by himself.

The forms of address and discourse that characterize this piece of writing are still relatively formal, and retain a connection with the status, identity and performances associated with the academic field—nowhere more obviously than in the technical observation, occupying a position simultaneously inside and outside the terms of the Introduction, that works of this kind 'are more exposed than methodologically controlled texts to the inconsistencies stemming from the diversity of circumstances' (Bourdieu 1998a: vii). However, the form of address isn't really commensurate with academic distance; instead, it demands from the reader some level of understanding of and engagement with the seriousness, gravity and urgency of the situation—nowhere more apparent than in Bourdieu's (1998a: vii) confessional utterance that recourse to this kind of approach, on the part of one for whom methodological control and rigor are professional, intellectual and ethical considerations, testifies to the extent to which the 'dangers that provoked' their production and publication 'are neither isolated nor occasional'. The discourse is also both overtly political and frequently affective: it includes references to 'resistance', 'dangers', 'weapons', 'scourge', 'solidarity', 'public position-taking', 'rage', 'duty', 'commit myself' and 'mobilization'. That this is not a performance entirely given over to polemicizing, nor separated off from Bourdieu's professional status and identity, is partly a case of the impossibility of escaping the field. As Bourdieu (2000) observes in *Pascalian Meditations*, to be in the world necessarily involves incorporating the world at the level of both mental dispositions and bodily hexis; and writing is a product of both these factors. However, strategic considerations are also relevant here: when Bourdieu commits himself in his own person and name, he is effectively deploying and utilizing the cultural capital that accompanies that name, and by extension the symbolic capital that—certainly in France but also within a European context and to some extent more globally—is activated when the Chair of Sociology at the Collège de France chooses to speak.

What Bourdieu recognizes, and what his work increasingly draws attention to—most particularly in the final stage of his academic trajectory— is what Brown and Szeman (2000: 5) characterize as 'the threat posed by contemporary "neoliberalism"' and the 'unique danger of the present moment of capitalism' that 'threatens to forestall or eliminate discussions about social, political, and economic alternatives' (2000: 5). Within this context, Bourdieu's work 'constitutes both an assessment of the dangers of the present moment for various cultural fields and a call to intellectuals to respond to the threat that the market poses to contemporary cultural and intellectual production' (2000: 6).

Conclusion

The contention that Bourdieu's scholarly apparatus develops out of, and is oriented towards and modified by, the forms of work at hand is nowhere better demonstrated and exemplified than with regard to the case of the habitus, a 'system of models for the production of practices and a system of models for the perception and appreciation of practices' (Bourdieu 1990b: 131). As with the concepts of cultural field and the logic of practice, the set of theoretical and methodological problems towards which the habitus is directed concerns what we can call the epistemology of the relation between, continuity across and conditions that are constitutive of subjectivity, identity and sociocultural practice. Bourdieu (2000: 138) maintains that this facility of the habitus 'to generate appropriate and endlessly renewed strategies' is delimited by 'the structural constraints of which they are the product and which define them'. However, from the period of his cultural turn, there are variations on and refinements of this dictum, specifically with regard, first, to his account of the habitus associated with the field of cultural production; and second, and by extension, to his theorizing of the relation between the habitus, cultural field and cultural capital.

Bourdieu developed the notion of cultural capital within his sociology of education work to account for the relation between evaluative regimes, power and symbolic violence. In *The Inheritors* (Bourdieu & Passeron 1979b), *Academic Discourse* (Bourdieu, Passeron & Saint Martin 1994) and *Reproduction* (Bourdieu & Passeron 1990), Bourdieu identifies, analyses and theorizes key issues that inform the relationship between the education system and the process of sociocultural reproduction, including the nature and function of selection in the education system; the hidden nature of the relationship between educational structures and social structures; the systemic nature of teaching; the role of language in school and teaching; the need to focus on the socio-cultural trajectory of students, both in the family and through school; and the impossibility of a rational pedagogy. In *Reproduction*, these ideas come together in the form of an argument that education systems exist to reproduce the culture of the dominant group/s in any society. In the following chapter, we will provide an account of Bourdieu's argument about how the education system, by explicitly valorizing the epistemological structures, discourses and values of the dominant, and by ignoring or explicitly devaluing those of the dominated, facilitates processes of socio-cultural reproduction.

3
Education, socio-cultural reproduction and class

Introduction

Bourdieu first came to the notice of the Anglophone academy as a sociologist of education. His three major works in this area (all co-authored) appeared in French in a relatively tight timeframe of just six years (1964–70). They represent a program of research that was undertaken over a decade, with most of the fieldwork being carried out in the first few years. This body of research helped to develop a theoretical apparatus that culminated in *Reproduction in Education, Society and Culture* (1990, first published in French in 1970).

Within this relatively constrained timeframe, Bourdieu conducted an extensive sociological inquiry into the French education system, which he knew as a successful insider—albeit as a 'wonder boy' (Bourdieu & Passeron 1990: 161) whose success was, in class background terms, statistically unlikely. He refers to his work in *The Inheritors* as 'only the beginning' (Bourdieu & Passeron 1979a: vii), and describes *Reproduction* as a 'work of youth' (Bourdieu & Passeron 1990: x). Despite these qualifications, the three main works on education are significant because they not only show the working processes behind some of the main components of Bourdieu's theoretical apparatus, but they also made an influential contribution to the sociology of education, particularly during the 1970s and 1980s. However, as Harker (1990: 86) points out, if we confine ourselves to these three books when using Bourdieu's theoretical approach to think about education, we will be missing the point: they represent only a part of Bourdieu's sociology of education work. Although he was not to publish another book specifically on education—*Homo Academicus* (1988) is more concerned with reflexivity than university education—texts such as *Distinction* (1989) and *The State Nobility* (1996) are derived from and closely follow Bourdieu's sociology of education work. This chapter deals mainly with issues of cultural reproduction and symbolic power as addressed in the three 'education' books; later developments in these areas are taken up in other chapters.

Bourdieu approached his research on education as an inquiry into social structures and relations of power. Weber and Durkheim both preceded him in this inquiry, and Durkheim in particular influenced his thinking, if only by failing to extend his analysis of the French education system, which Bourdieu otherwise admired (Bourdieu & Passeron 1990: 195–8), by underplaying the issue of power. In *Reproduction*, Bourdieu and Passeron (1990: 198) note that Durkheim fails to realize that not all school systems exist purely to conserve the culture inherited from the past, and that 'pedagogic conservatism', where it occurs, is the ally of 'social and political conservatism', and thus 'contributes . . . to the maintenance of "the social order"'. Conservatism, for Bourdieu, is a common but not universal result of the key function of maintaining social order. This link between education and the maintenance of social order was to be reformulated in his work in terms of the way in which symbolic power is utilized by the education system to exercise symbolic violence that upholds and sustains the cultural arbitrary of the dominant classes.

The Inheritors (Bourdieu & Passeron 1979b, first French publication 1964) and the works that make up *Academic Discourse* (Bourdieu, Passeron & Saint Martin 1994, first French publication 1965) were written while Bourdieu was in the process of developing the theoretical framework and concepts that characterized his later work. In his preface to the American edition of *The Inheritors* (1979b: vii), Bourdieu explains that the research was 'intended to mark a break with the prevailing tradition in the sociology of education', and that it was to do this by 'outlin[ing] a program for a sociology of cultural reproduction as a dimension of social reproduction'. The 'chief virtue' of the book, he writes, is 'the effort it makes to hold together aspects of the social world which the traditions and divisions of social science tended to keep apart' (1979b: vii).

One of Bourdieu and Passeron's key concerns in *The Inheritors* is the relationship between social origin and academic achievement within the educational system in France. In the prefatory note to the 1964 edition, the authors justify the focus of the book on 'an analysis of cultural privilege' as a 'risk that had to be taken, in order to grasp the fundamental problem which the ritual problematic in this area almost always manages to conceal' (Bourdieu & Passeron 1979b: ix). They argue that an important aspect of academic success is the sense of social 'ease' that membership of a dominant class confers: 'thus ironic casualness, mannered elegance, or the statutory assurance which lends ease or the affectation of ease are almost always the mark of students from the upper classes, where such manners signal membership in the elite' (1979b: 20). They also contend that 'the most privileged students derive from their background of origin habits, skills and attitudes which serve them directly in their scholastic tasks' and that their studies also profit from their inherited 'knowledge and know-how, tastes, and . . . "good taste"' (1979b: 17), which enables them to transform 'social privilege into individual gifts or merits' (1979b: 27). Bourdieu and Passeron's analysis of this process, which is outlined in both *The Inheritors* and *Academic Discourse* (Bourdieu, Passeron & Saint Martin 1994) is extended, with greater theoretical nuance, in *Reproduction* (Bourdieu

& Passeron 1990), where they recast the discussion in terms of symbolic violence, power and domination.

Two related issues that are important to Bourdieu's analysis of the field of education are the processes that determine the selection of students for progression through the educational system, and the necessary blindness on the part of participants to the function of school as a system of socio-cultural reproduction. In all three of the sociology of education books, Bourdieu and his co-researchers emphasize the effects of selection. In *The Inheritors*, they claim that 'the educational system objectively effects an elimination which is steadily more thorough, the less privileged the social class', and point out that it is not just a matter of less privileged students being ejected from the educational system. There are 'other, more hidden forms of educational inequality . . . such as the relegation of working class or lower-middle-class students to certain disciplines, or the fact that they fall behind and mark time in their progress through school' (Bourdieu & Passeron 1979b: 2). The possibility of undertaking higher education, for instance, is predicated upon 'a selection process which, throughout the school system, is applied with very unequal severity, depending on the student's social origin. In fact, for the most disadvantaged classes, it is purely and simply a matter of *elimination*' (1979b: 2). This argument is extended in *Academic Discourse*. Bourdieu, Passeron and Saint Martin (1994: 41) claim that working-class children are both eliminated from the system more frequently and, if they do 'reach higher education . . . [they] have . . . necessarily undergone greater selection than other groups' (1994: 41). They point out that, as well as class, gender also influences the chances of selection, noting that in both cases the individuals who do get through the system have often had to do better than most of the other students in their subject area: girls who studied Greek, for instance, tended to score very highly on the tests administered by the research team (1994: 45).

In *Reproduction* (1990), Bourdieu and Passeron refine and develop their argument regarding the process of selection. They note (1990: 71) that, 'When we first started our research, we began with the intention of treating the pedagogic relation as a simple relation of communication and measuring its efficiency.' However, they came to realize that, in order to understand how and why some students succeed in the education system and others do not, it was not enough to understand the processes of communication in the classroom or the figures of student retention throughout the various levels of education. In order to grasp what was happening, it was necessary to recognize the 'systematic relationship' that existed between 'the two systems of relations subsumed under the two concepts *linguistic capital* and *degree of selection*' (1990: 72–3). Bourdieu and Passeron (1990: 87) explain that:

> It is the system of factors, acting as a system, which exerts the indivisible action of a *structural causality* on behavior and attitudes and hence on success and elimination, so that it would be absurd to try to isolate the influence of any one factor . . . at the different moments of the process or in the different structures of factors.

This reformulates the argument first made in *Academic Discourse* (Bourdieu, Passeron & Saint Martin 1994: 40–1, 51) that there is no point in measuring, at any given point in time, a feature such as participation in the education system in terms of gender or class. Bourdieu and Passeron argue that such measurements are always meaningless, in that they never tell us about the subjects' trajectories through time in relation to a given set of social structures or contexts. Sociologists, according to Bourdieu and Passeron, are 'liable to forget that, unlike strictly logical structures, the structures sociology deals with are the product of transformations which, unfolding in time, cannot be considered as reversible . . . since they express the successive states of a process that is aetiologically irreversible' (1990: 88). This focus on selection, first identified as an aspect of class privilege in *The Inheritors*, contributed to Bourdieu's recognition of the importance of the nature of social structures and their interconnection over time, and to the development of the concepts of cultural field (with its focus on the intersections of specific social forces) and habitus. And it also reinforced Bourdieu's growing commitment to the importance of exercising a high degree of reflexivity in the construction of the research object.

For Bourdieu the process of selection throughout each student's school trajectory is a function of the educational system's role in serving the interests of the dominant classes in society, and he and his co-authors use a range of metaphors, such as blindness, secrecy, masks, veils and hiddenness, in characterizing this phenomenon. In *The Inheritors*, Bourdieu and Passeron (1979b: 67–8) argue that what is hidden is the advantage that class confers in the educational system:

> Blindness to social inequalities both obliges and allows one to explain all inequalities, particularly those in educational achievement, as natural inequalities, unequal giftedness. Such an attitude is part of the logic of a system which is based on the postulate of the formal equality of all pupils, as a precondition of its operation, and cannot recognize any inequalities other than those arising from individual gifts. . . . [Those who argue that] the *concours* gives everyone an equal opportunity . . . forget that the formal equality provided by the *concours* merely transforms privilege into merit, since it allows the influence of social origin to operate, though through more secret channels.

One of the things that is hidden—or, to use Bourdieu's later terminology, misrecognized—in this process is the role that education plays in valorizing and naturalizing privilege: 'What might be called the charisma ideology . . . supplies the privileged classes with a legitimation of their cultural privileges . . . transmuted from a social heritage into individual grace or a personal merit. Behind this mask, "class racism" can be flaunted without ever being seen for what it is' (1979b: 69–70). Bourdieu, Passeron and Saint Martin (1994: 21) return to this theme in *Academic Discourse*: 'the ability to manipulate academic language remains the principal factor in success at examinations. Here we encounter one of the most important, though most hidden, mediations between the social origins of children [and] their scholastic fates.'

However, in *Academic Discourse* another layer is added to the analysis of the relationship between education systems and the social structures in which they are situated. The relationship is no longer portrayed simply as one where members of the privileged classes are able to assume that they are intellectually gifted, but rather one where the education system works to inculcate and buttress the structures that support privilege: 'Traditional teaching uses words to seduce. Through a process of osmosis it promotes the transmission of an already confirmed and legitimate culture, and secures commitment to the values which this contains' (Bourdieu, Passeron & Saint Martin 1994: 20).

Academic Discourse was published in French in 1965, but it did not appear in a complete form in an English translation until 1994. It comprises a collection of essays focusing on research conducted by Bourdieu and colleagues over several years prior to 1965, with a focus on the use of language in the education system (at the secondary and tertiary levels). Although it is not stated explicitly, it seems that the research initially was undertaken in the hope that the insights gained would lead to 'rationalizing the uses of language in teaching [which] could constitute a decisive step forward in democratizing the academic universe' (Bourdieu, Passeron & Saint Martin 1994: 22). In certain ways, this overlaps with work being carried out by the educational linguist Basil Bernstein. Both Bourdieu and Bernstein were interested in the role of education in the process of social reproduction, along with the related issues of the role of language in educational achievement and the relationships between language, education and class. The affinities and differences between their research have been noted by writers such as Archer (1983), Cause (2010), Collins (2000) and Harker and May (1993) and, to a lesser extent, by Bernstein and Bourdieu themselves. Archer (1983: 196) suggests that, 'The work of Basil Bernstein and Pierre Bourdieu is often seen as the beginning of a new synthesis in the sociology of education which will lead to a theoretical reunification of large scale structural analysis with the study of more immediate processes of interaction'. Harker and May (1993: 171) take a different position, arguing that despite the similarities in the object of their research, Bernstein's insistence on separating 'the underlying, regulative structures (codes) from their surface realisations' gives his work a more structuralist orientation, whereas Bourdieu's theoretical developments allow him to successfully articulate micro- and macro-level analyses of social practice (1993: 176).

The work on language gathered together in *Academic Discourse* is important because it constituted a major step in developing Bourdieu's understanding of the systemic nature of the relation between the field of education and the processes and mechanisms of symbolic domination. Bourdieu, Passeron and Saint Martin (1994: 3) state, 'There can be no prospect of achieving real change until it is recognized that teaching is a system . . . research into the causes of linguistic misunderstanding which characterizes the teaching relationship must extend to the functions which this failure serves in perpetuating the system.' Initially, the researchers' 'concern was to understand and to explain the nature of communication between university teachers and their students—a social phenomenon marked by specific institutional constraints and traditions' (1994: 35). However, they soon came to see that constraints and traditions were derived from outside the education system. Bourdieu, Passeron and Saint Martin (1994: 55–6) argue that class experience (and, by extension, family history and experience) is integral to understanding the way in which meanings are derived from a complex system of relationships, and that, 'The real experiences described by these abstractions assume concrete, unitary and meaningful form only thanks to the fact that they are constituted by the class situation, the point from which every possible view unfolds and upon which no single point of view is possible'. For Bourdieu, language—important though it initially appears to be in the success or failure of university students—is not in fact the key. Much more important are the social contexts in which language skills are both transmitted and ascribed a particular value within the market for linguistic capital.

The other important idea developed in *Academic Discourse* and then extended in *Reproduction* is the notion of a complicity between teachers and students in maintaining a system that both groups can see is not actually working as it should, or as it claims to:

> What makes this complicity possible, as the intersection of the complicity of each partner with himself, is the fact that the ideological relationship of student and teacher to their own practices operates with reference to the same objective end. They are products of a traditional system, which focuses on maximizing security. (Bourdieu, Passeron and Saint Martin 1994: 23–4)

In his 1990 preface to the English edition of *Reproduction*, Bourdieu (1990a: ix–x) rephrased these ideas, aligning them more directly with the theoretical framework that was used in his later work:

> In [*Academic Discourse*], we examined the social construction of the multilevel social relation of classroom understanding in and through misunderstanding to reveal the process whereby students and teachers come to agree, by a sort of tacit transaction tacitly guided by the concern to minimize costs and risks in a situation that neither controls fully, on a minimal working definition of the situation of communication. [Against a 1960s/70s background of visions of mobility, the end of class and similar notions] *Reproduction* sought to propose a model of the social mediations and processes which tend, behind the back of the agents engaged in the school system—teachers, students and their parents—and often *against their will*, to ensure the transmission of cultural capital across generations and to stamp pre-existing differences in inherited cultural capital with a meritocratic seal of academic consecration by virtue of the special symbolic potency of the *title* (credential).

In *Reproduction*, Bourdieu utilizes a different and more developed theoretical framework than was the case in his previous educational texts—one designed specifically to objectivize the object of research. As Bottomore (1990: xiv) points out in his foreword to the book, theory and empiricism 'are very closely connected, the theoretical propositions arising on one side from the needs of research, and on the other side being constructed or elaborated in order to make possible empirical testing'. *Reproduction* brings together insights derived from Bourdieu's research in Algeria, Béarn and in the French education system to formulate an argument about the nature of cultural reproduction:

> Every power to exert symbolic violence, i.e. every power which manages to impose meanings and to impose them as legitimate by concealing the power relations which are at the basis of its force, adds its own specifically symbolic force to those power relations ... this axiom [is] a principle of the theory of sociological knowledge. (Bourdieu & Passeron 1990: 4)

Education and socio-cultural reproduction

In his sociology of education books, Bourdieu argues that the types of education enacted in the family and at school constitute a form of symbolic violence, because they involve the selection and imposition of specific cultural forms that tend to legitimize pre-existing power relations. At the same time, 'every PA [pedagogic action] requires as the condition of its exercise the social misrecognition of the objective truth of [pedagogic action]' (Bourdieu & Passeron 1990: 12). That is, for pedagogic action to be completely successful in legitimating a given set of power relations, it should never be apparent to the transmitter or receiver of the pedagogic action that education reinforces social hierarchies and power differentials. For Bourdieu, the dominated are complicit in their domination and this complicity is partly made possible by the hidden nature of the violence to which they are subjected. As Bourdieu argues, symbolic violence enacted through and by way of the education system is often more effective and easier to sustain than regimes of power that rely upon threats of physical violence: 'The School is better able than ever . . . in the only way conceivable in a society wedded to democratic ideologies, to contribute to the reproduction of the established order, since it succeeds better than ever in concealing the function it performs' (Bourdieu & Passeron 1990: 167). The salient point of pedagogic action, from this perspective, is to authorize and valorize without appearing to do so, and to create and maintain a situation that it purports to be describing. In *Reproduction*, the notion of symbolic violence is utilized to address the question of how socio-cultural domination reproduces itself, both over time and at an everyday level. Language, as the key medium of symbolic domination, is a central aspect of this process.

In *The Inheritors* and *Academic Discourse*, Bourdieu emphasizes the importance of a diachronic analysis of familial and social processes to an understanding of how the education system 'does its work'. This theme is continued in *Reproduction* (Bourdieu & Passeron 1990: ix, 73), and is extended to include the concepts of the habitus and cultural capital. Bourdieu and Passeron (1990: 30) explicitly identify the 'earliest phase of upbringing' as a key stage in the inculcation of a cultural arbitrary and its relation to evaluative regimes of cultural capital. They characterize cultural capital as:

> The cultural goods transmitted by the different family [pedagogic actions], whose value qua cultural capital varies with the distance between the cultural arbitrary imposed by the dominant [pedagogic action] and the cultural arbitrary inculcated by the family [pedagogic action] within the different groups or classes.

They also argue that the process of pedagogic action has to be carried out, by pedagogic work, over a sufficiently long period of time to create the durable, transposable and exhaustive habitus (1990: 34), and:

> Insofar is it is a prolonged process of inculcation producing internalization of the principles of a cultural arbitrary in the form of a durable, transposable habitus, capable of generating practices conforming with those principles outside of and beyond any express regulation or any explicit reminding of the rule [pedagogic work] enables the group or class which delegates its authority to [pedagogic action] to produce and reproduce its intellectual and moral integration without resorting to external repression or, in particular, physical coercion. (1990: 36)

The value and significance of this theoretical work is immediately obvious. In the previous two books Bourdieu had difficulty articulating the links between class, educational success, and the apparent necessity of dissimulating the links between these two factors. Habitus and cultural capital allowed him to demonstrate how class relations defined 'the primordial conditions of production of the differences between habitus' (1990: 203). Schools align their teaching to the already acquired habitus of the dominant classes, thus ignoring the needs of students who arrive with a different habitus (1990: 128). What is in play and activated in this process, and what works to ensure its efficacy, is the complicity of the habitus of teachers, students and the field of education more generally:

> More profoundly, only an adequate theory of the habitus, as the site of the internalization of externality and the externalizations of internality, can fully bring to light the social conditions of performance of the function of legitimating the social order, doubtless the best concealed of all the functions of the School. (1990: 205)

A specific form of cultural capital—of particular interest in the context of education—is linguistic capital. Language is, in the first instance, transmitted in the family context and is part of the cultural capital that the child brings to school. In a later work on the economy of linguistic exchanges, Bourdieu (2005b: 82) describes how this capital is formed within the family context, and how the subjects come to have a sense of the value of the 'linguistic products' offered on the market in exchange for cultural capital:

> We have not learned to speak simply by hearing a certain kind of speech spoken but also by speaking, thus by offering a determinate form of speech on a determinate market. This occurs through exchanges within a family occupying a particular position in social space and thus presenting the child's imitative propensity with models and sanctions that diverge more or less from legitimate usage. And we have learned the value that the products offered on this primary market, together with the authority which it provides, receive on other markets (like that of the school). The system of successive reinforcements or refutations has thus constituted in each one of us a certain sense of the social value of linguistic usages and of the relation between the different usages and the different markets, which organizes all subsequent perceptions of linguistic products, tending to endow it with considerable stability.

Bourdieu and Passeron (1990: 73) argue that the closer the alignment is between the child's linguistic capital and the language used and legitimated within the school, the more advantaged the child will be: 'The influence of linguistic capital, particularly manifest in the first years of schooling when the understanding and use of language are the major points of leverage for teachers' assessments, never ceases to be felt: style is always taken into account.'

In *The Inheritors*, Bourdieu and Passeron (1979b: 22) identify language as one of a collection of markers of privilege and 'class cultural habits' (1979b: 22), and in *Academic Discourse* they extend their thinking to take into consideration the links between language, class privilege and education, and more specifically the point that 'what we inherit from our social origins is not only a language, but—inseparably—a relationship to language ... and [its] value' (Bourdieu, Passeron & Saint Martin 1994: 21). Bourdieu, Passeron and Saint Martin (1994: 51) argue that 'language ability' is:

> the expression not of a series of partial connections, but of a structure in which it is the complex system of relationships which determines the meaning of any particular association ... Indeed, it is through all the components of a *school career* as a whole—choice of curriculum stream or of programme, type of school attended, and previous success—that the direct influence of family background is relayed by being translated into a properly scholastic logic.

This linkage of language to educational outcomes is made explicit in *Reproduction*. Only through the framework of a

> theoretical model such as one which interrelates the two systems of relations subsumed under the two concepts *linguistic capital* and *degree of selection* is capable of bringing to light the system of facts which it constructs as such by setting up a systematic relationship between them ... language is not simply an instrument of communication: it also provides ... a more or less complex system of categories, so that the capacity to decipher and manipulate complex structures ... depends partly on the complexity of the language transmitted by the family (Bourdieu & Passeron 1990: 72–3).

Interestingly, in this passage Bourdieu and Passeron seem to accept the idea that the language of the dominant classes is a more complex system, and thus confers superior abilities to 'manipulate complex structures', rather than suggesting that complexity is only identified and valorized in certain privileged forms of discourse. However, regardless of whether the language of the dominant classes is in some objective way more complex and thus more fitted for educational work, the evaluative regime that privileges that language still continues to be applied at every stage of students' linguistic careers, and plays a part in determining their chances for continuation and success in, or elimination from, the education system. Thus the students most likely to succeed and least likely to be eliminated are those whose own cultural and linguistic capital is derived from family backgrounds of the dominant classes: they bring to school the forms of capital that the school system recognizes as legitimate. The students who are most likely to be high achievers are those who can recognize, imitate, acquire and assimilate the forms of linguistic and cultural capital valued by the school system. This process does not entail the complete elimination of students from dominated classes: it is not only acceptable, but desirable, that some students from the dominated classes succeed, because it gives the impression and maintains the doxa that the system is open to everyone, regardless of class background. The occasional success of these students facilitates the notion that success at school is merit based, rather than being a game loaded in favour of the dominant.

Bourdieu's work on education, and specifically the habitus, has often been charged with being deterministic—a contention he has consistently denied (Bourdieu 1990b: 116–18). However, one area in which he does imply that there is no possibility of change is in the nature of the education system as a system of cultural reproduction that supports the dominant classes in society. He argues that it is not that the education system cannot change its practices; rather, it cannot change the function of those practices. In all three of his sociology of education books, Bourdieu discusses the impossibility of introducing a 'rational pedagogy'. In *The Inheritors,* he and Passeron (1979b: 73) explicitly state that 'nothing is further from our minds than an appeal to so-called scientific pedagogy'. Such a pedagogy, by the nature of the social system within which it functioned, would fail to acknowledge the crucial role of social differences in educational engagement and success, and thus 'would allow real inequalities to weigh more heavily than ever, with more justifications than ever' (1979b: 74). Under the prevailing conditions, 'A truly rational pedagogy . . . would . . . not be able to become a reality unless all the conditions for a true democratization of the recruitment of teachers and pupils were fulfilled, the first of which would be the setting up of a rational pedagogy' (1979b: 76).

In *Academic Discourse*, Bourdieu, Passeron and Saint Martin return to the idea of a rational pedagogy, only to dismiss the idea as impossible to implement: 'The whole of our previous analysis suggests that the propositions aimed at a rational teaching practice which flow from [our analysis] remain strictly utopian under present conditions' (Bourdieu, Passeron & Saint Martin 1994: 23). They take much the same position in *Reproduction*: their argument is that while 'Pedagogic work expressly guided by the methodical pursuit of maximum efficiency would thus tend consciously to reduce the gap between the level of transmission and level of reception' (Bourdieu & Passeron 1990: 126), a maximally efficient pedagogy would require a completely different education system and society. Only an educational field 'serving another system of external functions and, correlatively, another state of the balance of power between the classes could make such a pedagogic action possible' (1990: 127). In their discussion of rational pedagogy in *The Inheritors*, Bourdieu and Passeron (1979b: 57–8) recognize that it would lead to a very different kind of teaching, one that would, in all probability, devalue the role of the teacher in their own eyes:

> If ever the student formed a rational and realistic image of his position, the professor would find himself confronted with demands which relegate him to the role of a teaching auxiliary. The professor's occupational task would then become merely an aspect of an occupational project of which he is no longer the master and whose full significance lies beyond him.

Bourdieu claims that a rational pedagogy is impossible because it would subvert the key function of any educational system, which is the conservation of the social order. If the aim of a rational pedagogy was to ensure that all students benefited from the schooling process as fully as their intellectual and personal abilities allowed and if, in order to achieve that aim, schools had to teach in a way that legitimated the cultures of the dominated, then the current social order would be threatened. For teachers, whose position within the education system is tied to social hierarchies, a rational pedagogy of the sort Bourdieu and Passeron (1990: 152–3) envisage would devalue their status in both fields.

When the first two books were written, Bourdieu and his collaborators were focusing on a French education system that was conservative and largely unchanged from their own childhoods, although enrolment rates at university had increased for students from all class backgrounds in France in the 1960s (Bourdieu & Passeron 1990: 91). By 1970, when *Reproduction* was published, Bourdieu and Passeron could see that at least one change was taking place in the French education system, and it was modelled on the US university system, 'which provides for the institutional resolution of the tensions resulting from the disparity between the aspirations it helps to instil and the social means of realizing them' (1990: 218, n 36). Regarding the changes being carried out within the French system, they state:

> If educational systems are nowadays increasingly resorting to the 'soft approach' to eliminate the classes most distant from school culture, despite its greater cost in time and material, the reason is that, as an institution of symbolic government condemned to disappoint in some the aspirations it encourages in all, the educational system must give itself the means of obtaining recognition of the legitimacy of its sanctions and their social effects, so that machinery and techniques for organized, explicit manipulation cannot fail to make their appearance when exclusion no longer suffices per se to impose internalization of the legitimacy of exclusion. (Bourdieu & Passeron 1990: 209–10)

These ideas are extended and made more specific in the epilogue to *The Inheritors,* published in the US edition in 1979:

> Whereas the old system with its strongly marked boundaries led to the internalizing of scholastic divisions clearly corresponding to social divisions, the new system with its fuzzy classifications and blurred edges encourages and entertains ... aspirations that are themselves blurred and fuzzy. Aspiration levels are now adjusted to scholastic hurdles and standards in a less strict and also less harsh manner than under the old system, which was characterized by the remorseless rigor of the national competitive examination. It is true that the new system fobs off a good number of its users with devalued qualifications ... However it does not force them into such abrupt 'disinvestment' as the old system. (Bourdieu & Passeron 1979a: 91–2)

These comments are essentially asides to the main arguments developed in *Reproduction*. However, they reinforce the argument that the function of the educational system is essentially impervious to change: their position is that more open educational systems perform in much the same way as rigorous and overtly hierarchical systems. Bourdieu and Passeron argue that more open systems no longer work to ensure that the dispossessed internalize their unsuitability for the academic world, but rather that they are never forced to confront it in any serious way, instead being fobbed off with 'devalued qualifications'. With remarkable prescience, given that the book was written in 1970, Bourdieu and Passeron ask us to consider 'the limiting case, [in which] one imagines universities which ... would equip themselves with all the institutionalized instruments ... and specialized personnel ... required for the discreet, friendly manipulation of those whom the institution condemns, excludes or relegates' (Bourdieu & Passeron 1990: 218–19).

In most contemporary English-speaking universities, Bourdieu and Passeron's limiting case is now the norm, particularly in terms of the growth in the last four decades of student learning and counselling services, and specialist support resources for targeted groups (women, ethnic minorities, migrants, refugees, LGBTQI students). In the 1990 preface to *Reproduction*, Bourdieu (1990a: x–xi) points out that this book, first published twenty years earlier, had 'contributed' to a 'change of perspective', which led to 'a range of works that have emerged since and have entirely renewed our knowledge and understanding of the school, in both the United States and Great Britain'. It is certainly arguable that, in its turn, this research on the school system in the United States and the United Kingdom contributed to the changes in educational policy that Bourdieu characterizes as a 'blurred and fuzzy' move away from the 'harshness' and 'rigor' of the old systems. Some of this work focused on making visible the connection between privilege and educational success, which Bourdieu in his earliest analyses noted was so invisible. Researchers may have hoped that, once it became visible, policy efforts would focus on severing the connection. In fact, whether by design or because of the nature of misrecognition and illusion, the connection, rather than being severed, has been hidden more thoroughly by being hidden more 'kindly'; the onus has been lifted from the unsuccessful student, and the student's lack of success has, where possible, been hidden from view.

In *The Logic of Practice*, Bourdieu (1990c: 15) writes that 'the principle of a more rigorous definition, less dependent on individual dispositions, of the proper relation to the object . . . is one of the most decisive conditions of truly scientific practice in the social sciences'. *Reproduction* is the first of the education books in which this idea is specifically set out. According to Bourdieu and Passeron (1990: 101), if the object of observation had been constituted as a 'student population defined independently of its relation to the population eliminated', then it would not have been possible to provide a systemic explanation of the empirical variations, and they and their fellow researchers would have observed 'only a population of survivors'. In order to avoid this trap, they needed to be careful and deliberate about what they took as their object of educational research, and in fact in their case 'the true object of research' was 'the principles by which the school system selects a population whose pertinent properties, as it moves through the system, are increasingly the effect of the system's own action of training, channelling and eliminating' (1990: 101).

This statement incorporates two other important methodological issues that are explored in *Reproduction*: the relation between time and structure and the necessity of accounting for the role of time in the development of any given set of social relationships or outcomes, and of understanding the interconnected set of social structures in which those relationships and outcomes developed. Bourdieu and Passeron (1990: 88) suggest that the techniques used by most sociologists are 'implicitly ... analytical and instantaneist', and that multivariate analysis fails to show us how 'the ensemble of synchronic relations it is dealing with' came to that specific conjuncture (1990: 88). As they point out, there is little point in simply studying the population of student 'survivors' of the education system's elimination processes if the aim is to understand educational outcomes in France. What is needed is a diachronic account of how the eliminated students came to be eliminated, and how that elimination relates to both school and social structures. Ultimately, it is 'the system of factors, acting as a system, which exerts the indivisible action of a *structural causality* on behaviour and attitudes and hence on success and elimination, so that it would be absurd to try to isolate the influence of any one factor ... at the different moments of the process or in the different structures of factors' (1990: 87).

These systems of factors are 'established only through the mediation of class membership' (Bourdieu & Passeron 1990: 204). It is one of the weaknesses of the argument in *Reproduction* that the concept of class is made to do so much work without ever being very thoroughly defined. However, Bourdieu and Passeron's point here is that if the relationship is not anchored in class membership, then it is random and the systems can be linked up in any way—or, even worse, for the analyst they can take on a kind of fictive agency (1990: 204):

> The effort to catalogue the external functions of the educational system [i.e.] the objective relations between this system and the other sub-systems, for example the economic system or value system, remains fictitious whenever the relations thereby established are not brought into relationship with the structure

of the relations prevailing at a given moment between the social classes. (1990: 178)

Time and structure are also key elements in the theoretical concepts of habitus and field, and class plays a role in both. Bourdieu's concern about the methodological importance of acknowledging the role played by time in the creation of social relationships and outcomes certainly influenced his decision to adopt and reanimate the scholastic notion of habitus (Bourdieu 1985: 13). The habitus is necessarily the product of time, of history (Bourdieu 1990b: 116; 1990c: 56), and thus when using the concept of habitus, the analyst necessarily also introduces the concept of the passage of time into the analysis. Similarly, the concept of cultural field helps to integrate a schematic representation of the interconnection of social systems and sub-systems. Throughout *Reproduction*, Bourdieu and Passeron stress the methodological necessity of recognizing the interplay of multiple social systems. They argue (1990: 101) that it is pointless to look at only one system because such a conceptualization of social interaction will inevitably lead to an uninformative analysis:

> Analysis of the social and academic characteristics of the receivers of a pedagogic message is therefore meaningful only if it leads to the construction of the system of relations between, on the one side, the school system conceived as an institution for the reproduction of legitimate culture, determining inter alia the legitimate mode of imposition and inculcation of academic culture, and, on the other side, the social classes, characterized, with respect to the efficiency of pedagogic communication, by unequal distances from academic culture and different dispositions to recognize and acquire it. There would be no end to an enumeration of the impeccable and irreproachable omissions to which the sociology of education is condemned when it studies separately the school population and the organization of the institution and its system of values, as if it were dealing

with two substantial realities whose characteristics pre-existed their interrelation.

They also point out that if researchers were to do this, they would inevitably commit errors such as focusing on notions such as 'student aspirations' and 'parental motivation':

> Only by constructing the system of relations between the educational system and the structure of the relations between the social classes can one genuinely escape these reifying abstractions and produce relational concepts, such as probability of enrolment, disposition towards school, distance from academic culture, or degree of selection, which integrate into the unity of an explanatory theory properties linked to class membership ... and pertinent properties of school organization. (1990: 102)

Although Bourdieu and Passeron do not use the term 'cultural field' very often in *Reproduction*, they recognize that the ways in which different social systems interact are a necessary part of any sociological analysis. They describe the 'structure of class relations' as 'a field of forces' which 'defines the primordial conditions of the differences between habitus' (1990: 203). The habitus, formed within the shaping context of class membership, mediates the interactions of subjects in 'different areas of activity' (1990: 204). The account of the mediating capacity of the habitus provides a way out of the 'fashionable, fictitious dilemma' (1990: 203) of a completely determining structuralism or the total creative freedom of the subject-as-individual. By positing a theoretical structure in which subjects are endowed with a habitus, created by practices generated by the (class) structure in which their family was situated, and which inevitably affects their interactions within an interrelated series of social systems, Bourdieu and Passeron provide a framework that recognizes the generative functions of structures, practices and habitus. This relational method does not—and does not claim to—produce a comprehensive description of any given set of social interactions and outcomes. As Bourdieu and Passeron (1990: 102) point out regarding this example, it deals with 'the school system treated *only* as a system of communication', and thus over-simplifies the relationship between social class and education, presenting it primarily as a matter of communication. However, it is a necessary methodological abstraction if the research aim is to understand the consequences of relations between systems that power tends to keep hidden, such as the cultural politics that determines the homology between the habitus of the dominant classes and the habitus privileged in the school system.

Bourdieu and Passeron (1990: 179–85) argue that what they call the technocratic, culturalist or configurationalist, and the radical analyses of the education system, each has its own approach to research, focusing on 'productivity' (1990: 179–85), culture and national characteristics (1990: 188–90) and 'generic alienations' (1990: 193–4) respectively. However, all these approaches fail to realize the importance of focusing on systems and systemic relationships, differentiation and the crucial role played by the level of autonomy of the school system. '[T]he relative autonomy of the educational system', despite 'its dependence on the structure of class relations' (1990: 194), is an important factor in Bourdieu's educational work. It is the autonomy of the educational system that allows it to exercise symbolic violence: because it is seen as autonomous in relation to the dominant classes, it is able to reinforce the legitimacy of the dominant culture. Thus a failure to take into account the relationship of the school system to the class system and the differentiated nature of the class experience (ideas that would later be expressed more clearly in the concepts of field and habitus) leads to an inability to recognize the all important 'deniability' that is facilitated by the relative autonomy of the school.

Bourdieu's sociology of education is informed by what, in *Reproduction*, he and Passeron refer to as 'comparative' method of analysis (Bourdieu & Passeron 1990: 141). Comparative method, as they use the term, compares specific social objects of research across cultures and/or time. The aim is to establish what is inherent to a social object in any situation, and how this is related to the social systems in which that object exists or has developed. For Bourdieu and Passeron (1990: 144),

> there is no alternative to using the comparative method when one wants to separate out what derives from external demands and what derives from the way they are responded to, or what, in the case of a given system, derives from the generic tendencies every educational system owes to its essential function of inculcation, to the particular traditions of a university history, and to its social functions, which are never completely reducible to the technical function of communication and producing skills.

They use the 'comparative method' with regard to Koran schools, the Sophists and Zen masters (1990: 190) in order to identify and demonstrate the 'characteristic tendency of every education system . . . to reinterpret and retranslate external demands in accordance with its essential function . . . [and to resist external demands by] invoking the traditions of autonomy bequeathed by a relatively autonomous history' (1990: 191). Bourdieu and Passeron argue that this method is more useful than both culturalist analysis, where 'The presumption that a leap of pure intuition can take one straight to the very principle of the cultural system is particularly ineffectual in the case of class societies, where it dispenses one from preliminary analysis of the different types or levels of practice and the different classes' differential relations to those practices' (1990: 188), and 'the vicious circles of thematic analysis' (1990: 189), which lead only to 'commonplaces' (1990: 189). Their position is that if research is not informed by a thoroughly worked-out theoretical framework for the analysis of social data, and a theory of class relations and the way that relates to social systems, then it is condemned to making guesses that can only be based on a non-scientific understanding of the evidence. This is an argument and position to which, many years later, Bourdieu returns in the most methodologically complex and reflexive of his empirical studies, *The Weight of the World* (1999):

In fact, it is precisely by leaving things alone, abstaining from any intervention and all construction that one falls into error: the terrain is then free for preconstructions or for the automatic effects of social mechanisms at work in even the most elementary scientific operations (conception and formulation of questions, definitions of categories for coding, etc.). Only active denunciation of the tacit presuppositions of common sense can counter the effects of all the representations of social reality to which both interviewers and interviewees are continually exposed. (1999: 620)

Conclusion

Bourdieu's sociology of education period overlaps with his development and refinement of a theory of the relationship between regimes of cultural distinction and class formation. At the same time as he was developing his theory of educational reproduction, he was analysing various forms of cultural consumption—as demonstrated in *Photography* (Bourdieu et al. 1990, first French publication 1965) and *The Love of Art* (Bourdieu, Darbel & Schnapper 1990, first French publication 1966)—within the wider theoretical context of processes of symbolic power and domination, culminating in the lengthy empirical study that was *Distinction* (1989). In the next chapter, we will provide an account of this stage of Bourdieu's work, focusing on the relationship between the culture, symbolic power, and the production and reproduction of class formations.

4
Distinction

Introduction

In his preface to the English-language edition of *Distinction*, Bourdieu (1989: xiii–xiv) writes that he is undertaking a task that 'transgresses one of the fundamental taboos of the intellectual world, in relating intellectual products and producers to their social conditions of existence'. Moreover, and paradoxically, it is a task that has to be carried out with a singular regard for and compliance with intellectual propriety, 'which condemn[s] as barbarous any attempt to treat culture, that present incarnation of the sacred, as an object of science'. The 'immoderate ambition' of *Distinction* is to provide

> a scientific answer to the old questions of Kant's critique of judgement, by seeking in the structure of the social classes the basis of the systems of classification which structure perception

of the social world and designates the objects of aesthetic enjoyment.

The taboo to which Bourdieu refers is the attempt to locate, contextualize, analyse and explain high cultural texts and practices (art, literature, ballet) in terms of the logics, discourses and socio-cultural politics of the everyday world. More specifically, and much as he does with his book on Heidegger (Bourdieu 1991a), Bourdieu seeks to demonstrate how the claim to autonomy emanating from a discursive regime always and necessarily enacts and constitutes the opposite of that claim: the point is to endow the subject's (the artist, the philosopher, the field of art) position, work and practices with a particular value within the socio-cultural world.

The efficacy of art-as-culture is tied, at least from the perspective of Kantian aesthetics, to its 'disinterestedness', which 'to Kant means the lack of interference from desire . . . undisturbed, uninterfered with . . . by immediate utilitarian ends' (Wellek 1981: 229–30). However, Bourdieu argues that this claim to disinterestedness is demonstrably 'interested'—or, as Frow characterizes it, 'socially functional' (Frow 1995: 29). This functionality is an integral aspect of the operations that Bourdieu describes and analyses in his educational work (particularly Bourdieu 2013). In an earlier chapter, we dealt in detail with the relationship that he posits between pedagogical practices, the privileging and naturalizing of forms of culture as capital and the reproductive processes of symbolic power and domination. In *Distinction*, Bourdieu gives this study another point of focus, which involves identifying, analysing and explaining how regimes of cultural production, consumption and literacy dispose subjects to understand and view the world, and their place in it, in a manner that is commensurate with, and follows on from, the dictates and interests of the dominant. Rather than being separated off from the world and its mechanisms of alienation (various forms of economic relations) and power struggles (class conflicts, the naturalization and universalization of the arbitrary, the privileging of certain forms of cultural literacy), Bourdieu argues that, in actuality, art-as-culture turns away from the world in order to better intervene in it. Aesthetic culture and values

> do not obey an autonomous aesthetic logic; they dispose distinctions of class into distinctions of taste, and thereby strengthen the boundaries between classes. But they also assert the right of the ruling class to legitimate domination over other classes. Bourdieu argues this through an economic metaphor: competence in cultural codes constitutes a 'cultural capital' which is unequally distributed among social classes (although it has the appearance of an innate talent, a 'natural gift'). (Frow 1995: 29–30)

Bourdieu's account of the field of high or 'legitimate' culture, understood as an embodiment of Kantian aesthetics, has four main points. First, the field-as-discourse is characterized by a set of values and dispositions informed by the imperatives, struggles and proclivities of time and place (classical versus romantic art) and across different activities (establishing a brand identity for the wines of Château Margaux). Second, as a discursive formation, it makes the world over in its own image, rather than simply describing it (by way of a preference for abstract rather than representational art, or stream-of-consciousness writing over didactic narratives). Third, it reproduces and naturalizes an aesthetic disposition-as-habitus manifested in objective practices (attendance at museums and art galleries). Finally, and following on from the previous two points, the aesthetic disposition functions as an apparatus-as-ethos (taste, disinterestedness) that facilitates, naturalizes, justifies and sustains power and symbolic domination.

For Bourdieu, the process begins with an interrogation of what is meant, or has been made to mean, by the word 'culture'. In the Introduction to *Distinction* (1989), he proposes to subject the notion of culture as an aristocratic and privileged domain to a socio-cultural analysis. Culture-as-value and ethos is to be reconsidered in light of the concept, germane to anthropology and sociology, of culture as a set of categories, relations and codes whereby the natural and social worlds are imagined into existence and experienced as an interrelated set of meaningful entities. What Bourdieu proposes, in effect, is simultaneously to bring high culture and its activities and practices within the purview of the social sciences, and to extend the scientific understanding of culture and cultural practices by introducing into scientific analysis a recognition of the discursive effects of dominant modes of culture:

> Sociology endeavours to establish the conditions in which the consumers of cultural goods, and their taste for them, are produced, and at the same time to describe the different ways of appropriating such of these objects as are regarded at a particular moment as works of art, and the social conditions of the constitution of the mode of appropriation that is considered legitimate. But one cannot fully understand cultural practices unless 'culture', in the restricted, normative sense of ordinary usage, is brought back into 'culture' in the anthropological sense. (1989: 1)

Prior to *Distinction*, Bourdieu—along with a number of collaborators—produced two studies (Bourdieu et al. 1990; Bourdieu, Chamboredon & Passeron 1991) of cultural values, codes, practices and forms of consumption using empirical methodologies associated with sociology. The first of these, *Photography: A Middle-brow Art*, uses study groups, questionnaires, surveys and statistics to uncover how, with regard to photography, 'each group or class regulates and organizes the individual practice by conferring upon it functions attuned to their own interests', so that 'the meaning and function conferred upon photography are directly related to the structure of the group' (1990: 8). The empirical evidence leads the authors to several conclusions: first, that there are a number of aesthetic codes that dispose subjects to understand what photography means to them, and what its legitimate or relevant functions are; second, that this experience and understanding of photography are linked to class positions; third, that for working-class groups photography is categorized and contextualized in terms of its use value; and finally, that the code that informs the function of photography also determines what constitutes legitimate and illegitimate photographic objects. These different aesthetic codes not only correspond to different class positions, but also mark out the limits or parameters of a particular class literacy and epistemology. A photograph that depicts a family wedding, or provides information about a news story, is explicable and legitimate within a working-class aesthetic partly because it corresponds with or is produced through familiar and naturalized categories of perception and perspective. Bourdieu argues that photographic practices and objects that are the product of a high cultural aesthetic—that is, for which there is no obvious point or utility, and which approach or render their subject in an indirect or less than literal manner—do not make sense to a working class demographic. He refers in *Distinction* (1989: 43) to the:

> Refusal of the meaningless . . . image, which has neither sense nor interest, or of the ambiguous image means refusing to treat it as a finality without purpose, as an image signifying itself, and therefore having no other referent than itself. The value of photography is measured by the interest of the information it conveys, and by the clarity with which it fulfils this informative function, in short, its legibility, which itself varies with the legibility of its intention or function, the judgement it provokes being more or less favourable depending on the expressive adequacy of the signifier to the signified.

In *The Love of Art* (Bourdieu, Darbel & Schnapper 1990), Bourdieu and his co-authors extended their empirical research into the area of museum attendance, undertaking 'a systematic survey of the European museum-going public' in order to identify 'its social and educational characteristics, its attitude to museums and its artistic preferences' (1990: 5). The main theoretical issue at stake is the validity or otherwise of the proposition that, because high culture constitutes a form of value that is neither arbitrary nor reducible to specific temporal, spatial, social or demographic considerations, then it follows, first, that there is a natural and universally translational—if relatively rare—literacy regarding, and appreciation of, culture-as-art; and second, that possession of this facility marks out the subject as a member of an elite, elect and privileged community. The dictum that underpins *Distinction*, which is that 'Taste classifies, and it classifies the classifier' (Bourdieu 1989: 6), is largely derived from and predicated upon the critique of the notion of a specific cultural literacy-as-universal value undertaken and accomplished in *The Love of Art*. It is extended in *Distinction* to take into account a range of cultural forms, not just those valorized and appreciated by the 'self-legitimating imagination of the "happy few"' (Bourdieu 1989: 31). *Distinction* both complements and extends Bourdieu's educational and early cultural work through its analysis of the relation between symbolic power, class and cultural consumption, with specific regard to the concept of 'taste'. The 'happy few' are distinguished by their 'taste', which can be defined as a recognized and recognizable disposition and literacy played out in practices of cultural evaluation and consumption. Whereas a text such as *Reproduction* (Bourdieu & Passeron 1990) emphasizes how forms of knowledge and styles of self-presentation differentiate those who belong in the education system from those who don't, in *Distinction* Bourdieu shows, by way of a lengthy empirical study, how the habitus associated with dominant groups or class positions produces dispositions that orient subjects towards the 'right kinds' of cultural literacy, appreciation, categorization and consumption.

Distinction follows on from, and develops, the work of *Photography* and *The Love of Art* in terms of the approach, breadth, complexity and ambition of its methodological and theoretical apparatus, which provides the empirical data that facilitates the mapping of social space in terms of the volume, forms and qualities of subjects' cultural capital. This is not, as Bourdieu explains in *Language and Symbolic Power* (2005b) merely a question of establishing a correspondence between capital and social space, although it does allow for the construction of 'a simplified model of the social field as a whole, a model which allows one to plot each agent's position in all possible spaces of the game' (2005b: 230). A number of other complicating factors need to be taken into account, such as the relationship between dynamics of the field of power and the individual cultural fields-as-games, each with its own discourses, logics, regimes of capital, and forms and categories of identity. More generally, there is also the question of the relation between cultural capital, class, and social factors and identity categories, including ethnicity, social geography and most particularly gender. Bourdieu claims, in *Distinction* (1989: 107), that 'a class is defined in an essential respect by the place and value it gives to the two sexes and to their socially constituted dispositions'. Nevertheless:

> On the basis of the knowledge of the space of positions, one can carve out *classes* in the logical sense of the word ... sets of agents who occupy similar positions and who, being placed in similar conditions and submitted to similar types of conditioning, have every chance of having similar dispositions and interests, and thus of producing similar practices and adopting similar stances. This 'class on paper' has the *theoretical* existence which belongs to all theories: as the product of an explanatory classification, one which is altogether similar to that of zoologists or botanists, it allows one to *explain* and predict the practices and properties of the things classified—including their propensity to constitute groups. It is not really a class, an actual class, in the sense of being a group, a group mobilized for struggle; at most one could say that it is a *probable class*, insofar as it is a set of agents which will place fewer objective obstacles in the way of efforts of mobilization than any other set of agents. (Bourdieu 2005b: 231–2).

For Bourdieu, classes are derived from the same empirical-theoretical nexus—and consequently have a similar objective status—as that of the habitus and cultural fields: the empirical methodology that Bourdieu employs in *Distinction* (and even more comprehensively in *The State Nobility* (1996)) is, as the above references to zoology and botany indicate, strongly mathematical, statistical and, by extension, scientific. The specific statistical technique that drives and organizes the analysis of data in *Distinction* is termed 'multiple correspondence analysis' (MCA), which is similar to factor analysis but more suitable for 'categorical variables' in that it 'allows us to take a relatively high number of non-numerical variables and to derive from them a small number of numerical variables' (Crossley 2008: 91). It allows the researcher, 'using the level of . . . association between each variable and the other' (2008: 92), to proceed from quantitative information derived from responses given in a questionnaire about forms and volumes of capital to qualitative and evaluative associations that are meaningful and predictive above and beyond the numerical status of those responses:

> We might find, for example, that 'having a degree' is very strongly associated with the other cultural variables on our survey, achieving a score that is three times higher than 'owning fifty or more books'. In that case, to simplify somewhat, survey respondents would score three points on our cultural capital scale for having a degree but only one point for owning fifty or more books. We might also find that some variables which we had assumed to be facets of cultural capital have very little positive association with others, such that we are persuaded to exclude them from our measure. (2008: 92)

The MCA maps and other methodological techniques that Bourdieu uses to identify socio-cultural objectivities are sophisticated, but 'like many other statistical techniques' are based upon 'decisions and manipulations that affect outcomes . . . Bourdieu does not just 'discover' that social space consists of two key dimensions (volume and composition of capital) . . . This 'discovery' . . . depends upon interpretation' (Crossley 2008: 92).

This problematical aspect of the methodology carries over into the complex question of the relationship between different regimes of capital (economic, cultural, social, symbolic) and Bourdieu's account of the extent to and circumstances in which they are equivalent, commensurate, exchangeable or transferrable. John Frow (1995) argues, for instance, that Bourdieu's failure to adequately theorize the relation between cultural and economic capital undermines his proposition that the dominant class is constituted of symbiotic groups that share socio-political functions (the naturalization of power, the furthering of their own interests), given that no explanation is advanced as to how and why, and on what evidence or basis, such symbiosis is effected and sustained. Intellectuals, for instance, are characterized as the dominated faction of the dominant because they are rich in cultural capital (but poor in economic capital). Their membership of the dominant class is predicated on a recognition (on the part of the field of power and the holders of economic capital) of the validity of their cultural capital, so that while 'the structure of the distribution of economic capital is symmetrical and opposite to that of cultural capital' (Bourdieu 1989: 120), and the 'two forms of capital are mutually exclusive' (Frow 1995: 39), they are somehow 'mutually convertible' (1995: 40). However:

> In the last instance symbolic and real capital are not equivalent, and this means that there is a real question about the class location of intellectuals . . . Bourdieu posits that possessors of economic and cultural capital constitute two asymmetrical (dominant/dominated) faction of the 'same' class. It is difficult, however—given that class is not defined in terms of *functional* identity—to know what establishes this sameness other than the assumed equivalence of the two forms of capital. Its effect is to bring about a systematically misleading conflation of the intelligentsia and its culture with the bourgeoisie and its culture—a conflation that is entirely the consequence of the initial methodological decision. (1995: 40)

These and other similar critiques were productive in the sense that, while Bourdieu frequently complained about the extent to which his critics had missed the point—'Here I open a parenthesis,' he writes in *Practical Reason*, 'in order to dispel a frequent, yet disastrous, misunderstanding about the title *Distinction*' (Bourdieu 1998c: 9)—they doubtlessly helped to bring about a reappraisal and reconsideration, in works such as *In Other Words* (Bourdieu 1990b) and *An Invitation to Reflexive Sociology* (Bourdieu & Wacquant 1992), of important questions regarding the socio-political functions of the field of culture, the role of the field of power in determining and transforming regimes of capital, and the relationship between different forms of cultural literacy and the operations and mechanisms of symbolic power. They also led to the development of enhanced accounts of the field of cultural production (Bourdieu 1993a; 1996), of the nature and extent of intellectual and scientific reflexivity (Bourdieu 2004) and of the relationship between economic and cultural capital (Bourdieu 2005b). Finally, in *Masculine Domination*, Bourdieu extends his theorizing of the relationship between gender, class and distinction to take into account the relationship between gender-inflected fields and the field of power (2001: 105) and the role played by women, often within specific cultural fields such as fashion and art, in 'the conversion of economic capital into symbolic capital within the domestic unit' (2001: 101).

Distinction

In his introduction to *Distinction*, Bourdieu (1989: 2) claims that, 'The definition of cultural nobility is the stake in a struggle which has gone on unceasingly, from the seventeenth century to the present day, between groups differing in their ideas of culture and to works of art.' He argues that this struggle, which is in the first instance about what constitutes culture—or, more specifically, culture-as-universal value—is an integral part of the wider operations and mechanisms of symbolic power and domination, which are played out at the levels of class (broadly, dominant/dominated), gender relations, sexuality, race, ethnicity, age and social geography (in a French context, Paris as opposed to the provinces). The field of cultural production is the set of sites and spaces charged with producing, inflecting, organizing, disseminating, valorizing and explicating socio-cultural narratives, representations, discourses and meanings. Its main function, as characterized in Bourdieu's work from the period of his educational sociology, up to and including the three cultural case studies (*Photography*, *The Love of Art* and *Distinction*), is to naturalize its own status, value and regime of capital *vis-à-vis* the field of power and the wider social field, while facilitating the operations of symbolic power and the right to rule of the dominant class (of which it is a dominated faction). In short, high culture attests to the aristocracies of socio-political class and aesthetic taste, twin 'essentialisms' that 'set no intrinsic value on the deeds and misdeeds enrolled in the records and registries of bureaucratic memory' (Bourdieu 1989: 24).

This continuity between cultural valorization and social reproduction and domination is played out, within social networks and relations, in the tacit but authorized presumption of a 'pre-established harmony . . . between goods and taste' (Bourdieu 1993b: 108). Taste is not simply a matter of knowing which cultural names, forms and genres to privilege; rather, it manifests as a naturalized ease and certainty in moving through cultural spaces, activities and performances, and knowing how and when to behave in specific contexts (polite applause during a break in a ballet performance, standing and clapping enthusiastically when the conductor motions the orchestra to rise at the end of an opera, observing a thoughtful and quasi-reverential silence standing in front of a Rothko painting). The 'correct' judgements, categorizations, responses, discourses and interests (opera over Canto-pop, tennis rather than rugby) constitute the elaboration of a code of symbolic belonging to which the key is having an aesthetic sympathy and disposition, manifested as a privileging of disinterestedness over enthusiasm, form over content and canonical rather than popular valorization:

> tastes ... emerge as choices among practices ... and properties ... through which taste, in the sense of the principles underlying these choices, manifests itself. In order for there to be tastes, there have to be goods that are classified, as being in 'good' or 'bad' taste, 'distinguished' or 'vulgar'—classified and thereby classifying, hierarchized and hierarchizing—and people endowed with principles of classification, taste, that enable them to identify, among those goods, those that suit them, that are 'to their taste'. In fact there can be taste without goods ... in the sense of a principle of classification, a principle of division, a capacity for distinction ... and goods without taste. (1993b: 108)

Distinction-as-taste, a recognizable and more or less universally valid form of cultural capital, attracts other forms of capital (professional positions, connections), and by extension helps to smooth the path of the subject through school and university, and across social, bureaucratic and business fields. By and through this process and regime of cultural performativity, like recognizes like, and the dominant reprise their domination. On the other side of the symbolic coin, the dominated disqualify themselves in a variety of ways, such as their bodily hexis, clothes, choice of sports and lack of discernment regarding fine wine and food, and are then disposed to treat their exclusion as a case of 'not having the right stuff'. In *The State Nobility*, a lengthy and empirically driven study of the French class system, Bourdieu extends this analysis to the nameless and invisible 'aristocratic club' that dominates French socio-cultural, educational, political, bureaucratic and business life, without any explicit discursive articulation or demonstration of power, purpose or privilege (Bourdieu 1996). The first principle in Bourdieu's study of the logic of social domination

> is the vexing yet obdurate relationship of collision and collusion, autonomy and complicity, distance and dependence, between material and symbolic power. As Weber noted well, in every structure of domination, 'those privileged through existing

political, social and economic orders' are never content to wield their power unvarnished, and to impose their prerogatives naked. (Wacquant 1996: ix)

Bourdieu argues that this symbiotic (or, perhaps more correctly, parasitic) relationship has largely been consummated and consecrated, since the second part of the nineteenth century (Bourdieu 1989: 93), within the pedagogical regimes and practices of the cultural field of education. This complex of forces has been, and continues to be, subject to the dynamics of and shifts in the field of power. The struggles between the various factions of the dominant class to define, within educational contexts, the relation between culture, value and subjectivity constitute one of the complicating factors in attempts to analyse the dynamic of economic, educational and cultural capital. As Bourdieu writes, 'It is . . . clear that the difficulty of analysis was due to the fact that what the very tools of analysis . . . educational level and social origin . . . designate is being fought out in struggles which have the objects of analysis . . . as their prize in reality itself' (1989: 92). He argues that the contemporary game of culture is played out

> between those who are identified with the scholastic definition of culture and the scholastic mode of acquisition, and those who defend a 'non-institutional' culture and relation to culture. The latter, though mainly recruited from the oldest sector of the bourgeoisie, receive unquestioned support from writers and artists and from the charismatic conception of the production and consumption of art, of which they are the inventors and guarantors. Battles over authors and schools, which hold the limelight of the literary or artistic stage, conceal more important struggles, such as those which opposed teachers (from whose ranks, throughout the nineteenth century, critics were often recruited) and writers, who tend to be more closely linked, by origin and 'connections', to the dominant faction of the dominant class; or the endless struggles between the

dominated factions as a whole and the dominant faction over the definition of the accomplished man and the education designed to produce him. (1989: 92)

By way of example, in England in the mid-nineteenth century, the public school emphasis on high culture (predominantly classical literature and aesthetics) gradually gave way to an increasing preoccupation with team games and physical pursuits such as football and rugby, which served as a means of accommodating and developing a notion of the subject and the body that had little in common with Greek athletics or the Renaissance courtly tradition of formal and technical exercises, both of which were widely associated with the effete pursuits of physical beauty, the harmonious configuration of body and spirit, and intellectual refinement. The point was to develop a form of character broadly understood as an amalgam of self-reliance, loyalty, endurance, teamwork and self-sacrifice. Games-as-sport supposedly equipped boys with a set of transferable skills and strengths that could be applied to important socio-political spheres such as government, business or colonial administration.

At one level, this was explicable in terms of the fairly conventional notion of the body being trained and learning to endure and overcome physical and psychological stress and pain for the greater benefit of the team. This neatly encapsulated the apparent contradiction that public school sport developed leadership by fostering a culture of self-abnegation. Victorian public school students embodied the strengths and virtues of the dominant class faction, and provided these leaders-in-waiting with a set of durable beliefs, dispositions, attitudes and a bodily hexis—a habitus—that served as a marker of socio-cultural distinction and reinforced, valorized and justified power differentials at the level of class, race, ethnicity, social geography, gender and sexuality. Boys would leave a public school secure in the belief, first, that they were English gentlemen and, second, that there was a necessary articulation between that identity and moral, physical and cultural superiority— and, further down the track, military, social, political and economic success. Immersion in this culture generated a series of performances that were strictly scripted, choreographed, assured and foreclosed. Moreover, practices weren't judged on their results so much as their form: like a rugby player who tackles, chases and struggles long after the game has gone, the right kind of failure was heroic and especially laudable. This partly accounts for the strong anti-intellectual culture in public schools: determination, action, strength and endurance defined masculinity, while boys were taught that 'most material forms of intelligence were slightly effeminate' (Mangan 1981: 106).

Similar kinds of struggles are played out, in terms of the privileging or otherwise of values, discourses, lifestyles and regimes of capital, between different factions of the field of cultural production. This praxis effectively functions as an economy without economics, and as an inversion of the logics of classical capitalism: Bourdieu refers to the 'competition for rare goods and practices, whose particularity no doubt owes more to the logic of supply . . . the specific forms of competition between the producers, than to the logic of demand and taste' (Bourdieu 1989: 99–100). This set of relations is further complicated by factors such as the socio-cultural trajectories and literacies of subjects, the extent to which cultural capital is valorized within schools and academic institutions, the levels of symbolic capital associated with those institutions (manifested in the connections, accent, sense of aristocratic ease and the universality of capital that distinguishes an Oxbridge education from one acquired in a provincial university) and, following on from the previous points, the relation between and relative value of acquired and inherited cultural capital. As Bourdieu (1989: 80–1) explains, by way of a reflection on the difficulty of integrating these and other associated factors into the methodological and analytical apparatus utilized in *Distinction*:

> the differences which the relationship to educational capital leaves unexplained, and which mainly appear in the relationship with social origin, may be due to the differences in the mode of acquisition of the cultural capital now possessed. But

they may also be due to differences in the degree to which this capital is recognized and guaranteed by academic qualifications: a certain proportion of the capital actually owned may not have received academic sanction, when it has been directly inherited and even when it has been acquired in school ... If the same volume of educational capital ... may correspond to different volumes of socially profitable cultural capital, this is first because although the educational system ... governs the conversion of inherited capital into educational capital, it does not have a monopoly on the production of cultural capital. It gives its sanction to inherited capital to a greater or lesser extent ... because, at different moments ... levels and in different sectors, what it demands is more or less identical to what the 'inheritors' bring in, and because it acknowledges ... value in other forms of embodied capital ... such as docility towards the institution itself.

The question of the relationship between educational regimes and institutions, and the valorization or otherwise of embodied capital is usually played out as a recognition of *what* is recognized: in other words, in terms of the privileging of specific forms of embodied capital such as the performance of a sense of natural aristocratic ease, or a literacy with regard to and demonstrated appreciation of obscure artists, canonical texts, cultural genres and aesthetic values, which are treated by schools and universities as markers of 'belonging'. This continuity extends into and across other cultural fields and practices of cultural consumption, where it is accentuated and manifested as taste: in the first instance, as an ability to differentiate and distinguish between 'the taste of sense' and the 'taste of reflection', and second as a disposition for 'pure pleasure, pleasure purified of pleasure' as opposed to 'facile pleasure ... a pleasure of the senses' (Bourdieu 1989: 6). The observation that, 'Taste classifies, and it classifies the classifier' (1989: 6) incorporates both aspects of the reciprocal (and circular) process whereby literacy with regard to what constitutes 'the right kind' of culture and cultural consumption and appreciation turns back to valorize the subject as a 'truly human man' (1989: 6), marked by 'moral excellence and a measure of the capacity for sublimation' (1989: 6). It is through this process that the capacity for and disposition with regard to disinterestedness take on a theological dimension: as Bourdieu writes, 'The culture which results from this magical division is sacred' (1989: 6).

Bourdieu makes reference to two related cases that demonstrate how taste-as-disinterestedness is played out at a discursive level. 'Proof enough' is found in two separate reviews, both published in *Le Monde*, which deal with nakedness on the ballet stage and in the musical production of *Hair*, and which 'might almost have been written for the delight of the sociologist' (1989: 6):

> What struck me most is this: nothing could be obscene on the stage of our premier theatre, and the ballerinas of the Opera, even as naked dancers, sylphs, sprites or Bachae, retain an inviolate purity.
>
> There are obscene postures, the stimulated [sic] intercourse which offends the eye . . . As for the nude scenes, what can one say . . . I will not say it as chaste or innocent, for nothing commercial can be so described . . . In *Hair*, the nakedness fails to be symbolic.

There are a number of discursive markers across both texts that reinforce the distinction between the body as a predominantly corporeal and sexual entity and as an aestheticized object. These are overlaid on a further distinction that is implied in the first account and stated in the second, which is that the intrusion of commercial logics and imperatives alienates both the body-as-object of the gaze, and potentially the gaze itself. While the description of the naked bodies in *Hair* as being 'neither chaste or innocent' seems to discursively reprise the reference to 'obscenity' (in the first account), and what presumably should have been translated as 'simulated intercourse' (in the second), and to damn the musical for bringing sexuality into a public place, what is perhaps more at stake is that the bodies in *Hair* have, in Arjun Appadurai's (1988) terms, entered the commodity phase of their cultural lives. The two sets of bodies have passed in the opposite ontological direction: one is consecrated as pure value-of-itself, while the other is turned into things to be bought and sold in the market. The ballerinas are inviolate with regard to coarse meaning, while the dancers are stripped of any possibility of redemption-through-meaning ('the nakedness fails to be symbolic').

This denial, on the part of aesthetic culture, of the legitimacy of both the corporeal and the commercial gazes, and the imperatives and forms of enjoyment associated with them, 'implies an affirmation of the superiority of those who can be satisfied ... with the ... distinguished pleasures forever closed to the profane ... and this is why art and cultural consumption ... fulfil a social function of legitimating social difference' (Bourdieu 1989: 7). Bourdieu argues that a sense of distinction simultaneously constitutes a regime of difference-as-value and a form of symbolic power that is put to work to naturalize the domination of classes and class factions. We will discuss the wider processes, forms, techniques and mechanisms of symbolic power in more detail in a later chapter; however, the singularly most significant and influential facet of symbolic domination and reproduction is the habitus. It can be characterized as a regime of naturalized values, categories and perspectives that both sees through subjects by way of the classificatory grids and categories that make the world explicable and meaningful, and that provides the basis of all calculations-as-extensions of the subject's epistemological relation to and immersion in the world, particularly with regard to potential socio cultural trajectories and lifestyles.

Conclusion

In the transition that Bourdieu makes from *Outline of a Theory of Practice* (1978) to *The Logic of Practice* (1990c), he focuses on the relation between the habitus and socio-cultural practices, and by extension the issues and problems attendant upon attempts to theorize, identify, objectify and explain the logics that inform or animate those practices. These problems are of an epistemological order: 'The logic of practice,' he writes, 'can only be grasped through constructions which destroy it as such' (1990c: 11). Consequently, these constructions 'are only valid as long as they are taken for . . . logical models giving an account of the observed facts in the most coherent and economical way; and they become false and dangerous as soon as they are treated as the real principle of practices' (1990c: 11). Bourdieu's theory of the logic of practice insists that 'the objects of knowledge are constructed, not passively recorded, and . . . that the principle of this construction is the system of structured, structuring dispositions, the habitus' (1990c: 52). In the next chapter, we will provide an account of Bourdieu's development and formulation of the notion of the habitus, and its relation and significance with regard to the production and naturalization of cultural values and practices.

5
The habitus

Introduction

The habitus can be characterized as the forgetting of history that determines the present—that is, as a naturalization of dispositions acquired, at the level of accretion, across a subject's socio-cultural trajectory, but understood as 'the way things are and the way I am'. As Bourdieu's critics point out (Jenkins 1992), there is little room for subjectivist notions of agency within this schema. Bourdieu rejects the idea of a knowing, transcendental consciousness (along the lines of the Cartesian *cogito*) that is separated from and independent of history, social trajectories and cultural frameworks. All activity and knowledge—and this includes both disinterested scientific or scholarly work, and the most tacit (and therefore virtually unconscious) physical movements or personal dispositions—are always informed by a relationship between the agent's history and how this history has been incorporated on the one hand, and their context or circumstances (both in a general sense and 'of the moment') on the other. A subject's practices are always the result of a coming together of the habitus and the specific cultural fields and contexts in which agents 'find themselves', in both senses of the expression, and it is in this conjunction that the habitus appears. The habitus 'reveals itself only with reference to a situation . . . it is in a relationship to a certain situation that habitus produces something' (Bourdieu & Chartier 2015: 57).

In the previous chapter, we referred to how Bourdieu's work in the immediate post-Algerian period attempted to address the limitations of the two dominant approaches within the social sciences, namely objectivism (largely in the form of anthropological and Marxist versions of structuralism) and subjectivism (which was associated with existentialism and phenomenology). Bourdieu (1978: 2) makes his position clear in *Outline of a Theory of Practice*:

> It is significant that 'culture' is sometimes described as a map; it is the analogy which occurs to an outsider who has to find his way around a foreign landscape and who compensates for his lack of practical mastery, the prerogative of the native, by the use of a model of all possible routes.

In order to avoid falling into this epistemological trap, he states that it is necessary 'to abandon all theories which explicitly or implicitly treat practice as a mechanical reaction, directly determined by the antecedent conditions and entirely reducible to the mechanical functioning of pre-established assemblies, "models" or "roles"' (1978: 73). However, he is equally insistent that

> rejection of mechanistic theories in no way implies that . . . we should bestow on some creative free will the free and wilful power to constitute, on the instant, the meaning of the situation by projecting the ends aiming at its transformation, and that we should reduce the objective intentions . . . of actions . . . to the conscious and deliberate intentions of their authors (1978: 73).

In *Outline*, and in subsequent texts such as *In Other Words* (1990b), *The Logic of Practice* (1990c), *An Invitation to Reflexive Sociology* (Bourdieu & Wacquant 1992), *Practical Reason* (1998c) and *Pascalian Meditations* (2000), Bourdieu argues that one of the most significant deficiencies with any objectivist theory of practice is that it functions as a convenient framework whereby academic scholarship can both produce, and then organize and formalize, the results of empirical research and fieldwork. This process can produce a detailed account of socio-cultural identity as an authorized or conventionalized schema, but without being able to demonstrate, at an empirical level, that there is a continuity between that schema and cultural practices. From this perspective, objectivism effectively replicates Saussure's privileging of the rules and systems of language over its uses and practices, while overlooking the regularities of practice that are not in any way commensurate with the notion of the rule. Subjectivism, on the other hand, can only put forward, as an explanation for these objective regularities of practice, an abstract sense of calculation that is belied by the identifiable affiliations and continuations between those objectivities and the socio-cultural contexts and spaces (class, educational, linguistic, gender and age demographics, for instance). In other words, in the domain of socio-cultural practice, there are regularities 'which do not appear to be explicable in a satisfactory manner either by the invocation of the rules ... or in terms of brute causality' (Bouveresse 1999: 49).

The theoretical problem is that practices are carried out by subjects who are clearly involved in and oriented by the world, without being in any way mechanistically reproductive of the objective rules of the world. The notion of the habitus, however,

> seems effectively indispensable for a satisfactory account of regularities of a certain type: regularities which have as part of their essence a certain amount of variability, plasticity, indetermination, and imply all sorts of adaptations, innovations and exceptions ... the sort of regularity in short which

characterizes the domain of the practical, of practical reason and the logic of practice. (Bouveresse 1999: 62)

A second, and related, set of theoretical tasks that Bourdieu sets himself is to identify and explain, first, how and why socio-cultural contexts are able to affiliate themselves, consistently and continuously, with subjects; second, the techniques whereby this affiliation of the world and the subject is developed and maintained; and third, the processes by which the subject's immersion in the world generates practices that are both compliant with regard to, but also capable of negotiating, the different temporal and spatial conjunctions of the world. The great value of the habitus is that it addresses all these issues in a manner that both explains and is commensurate with regard to the objectivities of practice. The key element is the formulation of the habitus as the means by which the world and its categories of perception and evaluation are incorporated, at the level of bodily hexis, as a form of belief that never knows itself as such. The habitus is not in any sense aligned with notions of the subject as a reasonable, rational and self-knowing entity, able and disposed to calculate moves and actions in terms of competing options or probabilities of profit or interest: it is animated not by the things of logic, but by the logic of things, and the theoretical source and antecedent that underpins it is not Descartes, but Pascal. Bourdieu (2000: 12) writes in *Pascalian Meditations* that:

> To speak of a decision to commit oneself to ... any ... of the fundamental investments of life—vocation, passion, devotion ... is, as Pascal himself was well aware, almost as absurd as evoking a decision to believe, as he does, with few illusions, in the argument of the wager. To hope that the unbeliever can be persuaded to decide to believe because he has been shown by cogent reasons that he who gambles on the existence of God risks a finite investment to win infinite profit, one would have to believe him disposed to believe sufficiently in reason to be sensitive to the reasons of that demonstration. But as

Pascal himself very well puts it, 'we are as much automatic as intellectual; and hence it comes that the instrument by which conviction is attained is not demonstration alone. How few things are demonstrated! Proofs only convince the mind. Custom is the source of our strongest and most believed proofs. It inclines the automaton, which persuades the mind without thinking about the matter.

There are a number of influences upon which Bourdieu draws in his formulation of the concept of the habitus, including 'authors as different as Hegel, Husserl, Weber, Durkheim and Mauss, all of whom used it in a more or less methodical way' (Bourdieu 1990b: 12). He emphasizes two interrelated features that he acquired from these antecedents: the habitus is explicable only with regard to the socio-cultural conditions and contexts from which it was derived, but it also functions as an extension rather than a simple reproduction of socio-cultural frameworks and contexts. He states (1990b: 12–13), 'I wanted to insist on the generative capacity of dispositions, it being understood that these are acquired, socially constituted dispositions.' The habitus provides subjects with an epistemological facility that enables them to grasp and negotiate the world in a manner that is commensurate with the world, but not as a set of rules or formulae. The situations in which subjects find themselves are rarely negotiable in terms of rules or practices derived from algorithms. On the contrary, and as Bourdieu (2005c) points out, social exchanges and relations are invariably informed by, or subject to, regimes of authority (symbolic power) that operate both without disclosure and not in accordance with the objective rules, conventions, explanations and discourses of a society. The habitus does not have to function at a level that is conscious of the actualities of symbolic power in order to be literate, at a tacit level, with the practical and pragmatic conditions and consequences of decision-making: if the subject is embarked by the habitus, it is always with a capacity that facilitates a practical choice among choices. The notion of the habitus as a set of dispositions rather than rules means that it retains a predictive function (there will be a correlation between the objectivities of the socio-cultural context with which the habitus is associated and the logic of practice of the subject) and enables the subject's relative ease within the world, while allowing for a certain flexibility in the face of 'of the moment' demands and requirements, variations (both temporal and spatial) in and across cultural fields, and the difficulties encountered through changes in its socio-cultural trajectory:

> The habitus, as the system of dispositions . . . is an objective basis for regular modes of behaviour, and thus for the regularity of modes of practice, and if practices can be predicted . . . this is because the effect of the habitus is that agents who are equipped with it will behave in a certain way in certain circumstances. That being said, this tendency to act in a regular manner which, when its principle is explicitly constituted, can act as the basis of a forecast . . . is not based on an explicit rule or law. This means that the modes of behaviour created by the habitus do not have the fine regularity of the modes of behaviour deduced from a legislative principle: the habitus goes hand in hand with vagueness and indeterminacy. As a generative spontaneity which asserts itself in an improvised confrontation with ever-renewed situations, it obeys a practical logic, that of vagueness, of the more-or-less, which defines one's ordinary relation to the world. (Bourdieu 1990b: 77–8)

Another direct influence on Bourdieu's development of the notion of habitus was Panofsky's work, specifically 'two articles by Panofsky which up to that point had never been looked at together; one on Gothic architecture where the word habitus was used as an "indigenous" concept, to explain the effect of scholastic thinking in the area of architecture, the other article on the Abbot Suger' (Bourdieu 1985: 13). These texts helped Bourdieu to develop his theory of how the scholarly point of view-as-habitus informed and helped produce the objects of scholarly research. As well as enabling Bourdieu to account for the connection between French colonialism and scholarship in Algeria, it also led to him undertaking specific research projects—his Béarn work, *Homo Academicus* (1988)—in which he could study the theoretical and methodological consequences of his own personal and professional habitus. From here, the concept of the habitus served as the cornerstone of his research into and theorizing of the ways in which students' educational status and experiences facilitated the reproduction of symbolic power and domination, and produced class affiliations and patterns of cultural consumption and evaluation. It also explained how and why cultural fields were imagined into existence, how they interpellated and inculcated their members, and why they were able to naturalize their epistemological regimes and forms of cultural capital, and maintain their consistency and durability.

The concept of the habitus underwent major refinements from the time of being detailed in *Outline* (1978) through to Bourdieu's redevelopment of the notion of the embodied habitus in *Pascalian Meditations* (2000). The most significant issue involved whether and to what extent the habitus might be said to have a strategic orientation or dimension. Bourdieu's earlier treatment of the issues—for instance, in *Outline* and his earlier educational texts—emphasizes that the habitus is the source of a 'series of moves which are objectively organized as strategies without being the product of a genuinely strategic intention' (Bourdieu 1978: 73), and where practices show signs of being consequent on the calculation of possible benefits and prospects, 'one strategy among other possible strategies' (1978: 73) recognized and considered as an option is produced by and through the epistemological categories of the habitus. Other possibilities that might seem perfectly natural or normal to subjects whose habitus has been formed in very different trajectories or fields are simply foreclosed: they are either unthinkable, or the subject, intuiting that the chances of success are slender or impossible, will reject the rejection as 'not being for me'. To paraphrase Derrida (1976), there is, from this perspective, nothing outside the habitus:

It is, of course, never ruled out that the responses of the habitus may be accompanied by a strategic calculation tending to perform in a conscious mode the operation that the habitus performs quite differently, namely an estimation of chances presupposing transformation of the past effect into an expected objective. But these responses are first defined, without any calculation, in relation to objective potentialities, immediately inscribed in the present, things to do or not to do, things to say or not to say, in relation to a probable, 'upcoming' future ... which ... puts itself forward with an urgency and a claim to existence that excludes all deliberation. Stimuli do not exist for practice in their objective truth, as conditional, conventional triggers, acting only on condition that they encounter agents conditioned to recognize them. The practical world that is constituted in the relationship with the habitus, acting as a system of cognitive and motivating structures, is a world of already realized ends—procedures to follow, paths to take—and of objects endowed with a 'permanent teleological character' ... This is because the regularities inherent in an arbitrary condition ... tend to appear as necessary, even natural, since they are the basis of the schemes of perception and appreciation through which they are apprehended. (Bourdieu 1990c: 53–4)

This position was subject to reconsideration during the period of Bourdieu's cultural turn. While there is a continued insistence and re-emphasis on, and a technical development of, the idea and process of the unconscious bodily incorporation and naturalization of the habitus—see, in particular, *Language and Symbolic Power* (2005b), *Practical Reason* (1998c) and *Pascalian Meditations* (2000)—there is also a gradual recognition that playing the game of the field has the potential to increase the subject's levels of cultural literacy, and by extension to produce what Bourdieu refers to as an enhanced 'feel for the game'. In the first essay of *The Field of Cultural Production* (1993a), titled 'Is the Structure of *Sentimental Education* an Instance of Social Self-analysis?', Bourdieu provides an analytical account of the relation between Flaubert's literary habitus and his knowledge of and literacy with regard to the field-as-game by way of his fictional characters and narratives, which are read and interpreted as either surrogates of himself and other subject-positions within, or as symptomatic of the culture of, the literary field. While Flaubert is not exactly allowed the same kind of epistemological or theoretical understanding or status of the sociologist, he is credited with the ability to analyse, comprehend and articulate the cultural politics of the field in which he is immersed in a way that, while never openly contradicting or questioning his own *illusio*-as-habitus, is certainly something other and more than a simple reproduction of literary doxa. Bourdieu (1993a: 158) argues that there are discursive, technical and epistemological orientations, germane to both cultural fields, that effectively differentiate Flaubert's literary literacy from reflexive sociology:

> For the sociologist lays bare a truth that the literary text will reveal only in veiled terms, that is to say only in such a manner as to leave unsaid, by a means of negation, of *verneinung*, as Freud used the term . . . The way of withholding things which is characteristic of the literary view of life is the thing which, above and beyond the aesthetic function it fulfils, enables an author to reveal truths that would otherwise be unbearable.

Bourdieu (1993a: 158) asks about the extent to which Flaubert 'knowingly construct the model' of the literary field that Bourdieu identifies in *Sentimental Education* and other texts. His response is that, in a sense, Flaubert cannot know—or if he can, he can't say he knows—because he is bound, via the interaction-as-interdiction that characterizes the writing and reading of his realist novels, in a kind of complicity of silence with his bourgeoisie readers, and possibly with himself: the 'appearance of reality which satisfies the need to know is in fact achieved by that semblance of reality which allows the reader to ignore the real state of things, to refuse to see things as they really are' (1993a: 158). Into this game comes sociology, which 'breaks the spell' by revealing the 'relationship of negation with regard to the reality indicated in the text' (1993a: 158). Bourdieu makes clear, in a very muddled way, that the truth of sociology is not the same as the truth of the novel. Bourdieu's sociological reading,

> although it reveals a truth that the text says, but in such a way as to not say it, does not reveal the text's own truth; and it would be completely erroneous if it claimed to give the entire truth contained in a text which owes its specificity precisely to the fact that it does not say what it says in a way a scientific text would say it. It is doubtless the form, the literary form in which objectification takes place, which enables the most deeply buried and the most safely hidden truth to emerge: indeed the form constitutes the veil that allows author and reader to hide from themselves . . . this repressed truth . . . in this case, the structure of the field of power. (1993a: 159)

This explains how and why literature is able to reveal 'truths which social sciences . . . cannot quite grasp' (1993a: 159). However, this capacity to represent truth is predicated, first, on literature's tendency to deal with 'serious matters without asking to be taken completely seriously' (1993a: 159); and second, on the necessity of subscribing, at some level or another but at least partly unconsciously, to a form of *illusio*, which facilitates, 'The smooth running of all social mechanisms, whether in the literary field or in the field of power' (1993a: 159).

This epistemological facility is implicitly posited as a form of reflexivity, which Bourdieu had formerly associated, more or less exclusively, with the scientific habitus and field. The key element in this development is Bourdieu's reappraisal of the notion of disinterestedness. In his sociology of education work, he argues that in scholarly culture, disinterestedness enables and enacts a distancing from and an abstraction of the object of study. Within the educational system, disinterestedness is read as a component and manifestation of the embodiment, on the part of the dominant class, of a naturalized, aristocratic ease. However, in *The Field of Cultural Production* (1993a) and *The Rules of Art* (1995), disinterestedness is cast in an altogether different and more generative form: it is reconsidered as potentially facilitating the production of alternative sets of perspectives and accounts of the socio-cultural world that are not necessarily compliant with the meanings and narratives associated with symbolic power. In *Practical Reason* (1998c), for instance, disinterestedness is associated with the disposition of the scientific field and the autonomous pole of the field of cultural production to take a critical and reflexive position with regard to both their own discourses and those of the field of power. This applies to all forms of critical social analysis, which, in a scholarly, literary, artistic, political or journalistic text, successfully draw attention to or denaturalize the hidden systems, processes and effects of symbolic power, and by doing so are capable of influencing, changing or transforming the habitus. Bourdieu argues, for instance, that:

> When you apply reflexive sociology to yourself, you open up the possibility of identifying true sites of freedom, and thus of building small-scale, modest, practical morals in keeping with the scope of human freedom which, in my opinion, is not that large. Social fields are universes where things continually move and are never completely predetermined. (Bourdieu & Wacquant 1992: 199–200)

The relationship between disinterestedness and the acquisition of a critical socio-cultural disposition is a matter of the logics and imperatives of the cultural field, and how this plays out at the level of the habitus. Bourdieu (1998c: 88) writes that, 'If disinterestedness is sociologically possible', it can only be brought about

> through the encounter between the habitus predisposed to disinterestedness and the universes in which disinterestedness

is rewarded. Among these universes, the most typical are . . . the different fields of cultural production . . . [and] the scientific field, microcosms which are constituted on the basis of an inversion of the fundamental law of the economic world and in which the law of economic interest is suspended . . . this does not mean that they do not know other forms of interest: the sociology of art or literature unveils . . . and analyzes the specific interests which are constituted by the field's functioning . . . and for which one is ready to die.

The habitus

Bourdieu (1978: 78) defines the habitus as 'the durably installed generative principle of regulated improvisations . . . [that produces] practices', but he emphasizes that although the habitus is durable, circumstances and contexts are not necessarily receptive to or in tune with it. The inevitable misfit between habitus and field constitutes the basis of the various negotiations and improvisations that subjects are forced into if they are to function effectively within or across different fields. Such negotiations and improvisations serve to bring about change in the habitus itself by sidestepping its automatic responses in the interests of a more competent navigation of a particular context; they determine the extent to which subjects can attain knowledge of, and negotiate, various cultural fields.

If this sounds like an overly restrictive and mechanistic explanation of practice, it should be pointed out that for Bourdieu the habitus is extraordinarily productive and adaptive. In an analysis of Bourdieu's supposed 'determinism', Jacques Bouveresse (1999) explores what is at stake, theoretically and practically, in the use of terms such as freedom, free will and spontaneity, and how these terms (and the meanings associated with them) fit with the notion of the habitus. His essay makes two main points. The first is that freedom and free will are not concepts that subjects come to without considerable affective baggage, and that they often function as empty signifiers that different groups claim association with, and 'fill in' in an arbitrary but motivated way. Regardless of the content, however, the significance of freedom, as an affective catalyst, is that it is something whose loss is dreaded:

> If we are more or less terrified of the idea that we might not be free, it is because we have a certain idea of the appalling fate that would be our own if we were not free . . . literature on this point provides us with a multitude of analogies each more worrying than the last: 'not having free will would be somewhat like being in prison, or being hypnotised, or being paralysed, or being a puppet'. (1999: 48)

His second point is that there is nothing inherent in Bourdieu's concept of the habitus that militates against or forecloses the notion of practice resulting from or based on spontaneity. He approaches the question via Wittgenstein's (1983) theorizing of the relation between and continuity across socio-cultural rules, practices, cultural literacy and consciousness:

> As Wittgenstein often remarked, the learning of a game can quite easily involve the explicit formulation and acquisition of the rules which govern it. But one can equally acquire the sort of regular behavior equivalent to a complete mastery of the game without the explicit statement of the rules ever intervening in the process at all. (1999: 51–2)

The habitus, as an acquired and generative set of dispositions, is consistent with Wittgenstein's (1983) formulation of the status of cultural literacy: it is both productive of and informed by a level of deliberation; and it is often characterized by a level of spontaneity, such as when certain options are dismissed because they might eventually leave the subject ill-at-ease, a 'fish out of water'. For Bouveresse (1999: 47), 'what free will . . . adds to spontaneity is the idea of a decision based on a process of deliberation. Free will can be defined as "spontaneity coupled with deliberation". From this perspective, it matters little whether deliberation runs into and stops short of what are effectively self-imposed limits. To take a path that is bound to lead to 'rejection' because certain objective requirements cannot be met is a perverse form of freedom, just as it is unreasonable to characterize a refusal to take an option that is foreclosed as a form of reproduction or mechanistic behaviour. He argues that just because forms of behaviour derive from the habitus, this is:

> not a threat to the spontaneity of his action, as the action is not the result of an external constraint, but of a disposition whose seat is in the agent himself. But insofar as the exercise of free will includes deliberation, a good part of our actions, and in particular those which are the result of the habitus, are simply spontaneous and not strictly speaking free. But neither can it be said that they are truly constrained. (1999: 47)

For Bourdieu, the logic of practice is characterized by considerable varieties of movement within, but not outside, the parameters of the field-as-habitus. He argues that the habitus is acquired, first, at an early age; second, across the socio-cultural trajectory-as-history of the subject; third, in an unconscious and naturalizing manner; and fourth, as an embodiment of a series of dispositions that are commensurate with the central discourses, perspectives, values and epistemological categories of the field or context in question. The earliest experiences of the habitus are the most influential and durable, both because they are constitutive of and strongly associated with the subject's identity and personal orientation (as daughter, student, churchgoer) and because they engage the subject for a relatively long and crucially formative period (in childhood and adolescence). The family, along with educational, socio-cultural and religious institutions (primary and secondary school, sporting teams, church) and socio-cultural texts (television, film, comics, toys, games, the internet), provides the basis of the habitus-as-dispositions which are likely to persist, in some form, into old age and across various cultural fields.

The acquisition of these dispositions allows for a relative predictability with regard to the practices of the subject, without in any way producing a mechanistic reproduction of the rules and conventions of the field, or a conscious adherence to matching or applying the field-as-rule to the situation at hand. The bodily incorporation of the habitus-as-dispositions means that, in most cases, little thought or consideration is required whenever the subject is presented with a set of options: the body learns and the subject follows. As children move through and are immersed in the rituals, conventions and genres of family life, school, church, sport and social activities, along with the media in all its increasingly ubiquitous forms, the habitus is gradually constituted at the level of a bodily hexis, in the form of ways of walking, hand gestures and mannerisms, facial expressions, and levels and styles of activity: 'It is in the dialectical relationship between the body and a space . . . that one finds . . . the structural apprenticeship which leads to the em-bodying of the structures of the world, that is, the appropriating by the world of a body thus enabled to appropriate the world' (Bourdieu 1978: 89).

Dispositions acquired from childhood (family, school) will continue to constitute and orient the subject throughout the transition across socio-cultural identities (as daughter, Roman Catholic, university student, girlfriend, leftist, feminist, academic) and fields (religion, academe, politics, the social field), generally with only minor adjustments and variations:

> The habitus, a product of history, produces individual and collective practices—more history—in accordance with the schemes generated by history. It ensures the active presence of past experiences, which, deposited in each organism in the form of schemes of perception, thought and action, tend to guarantee the 'correctness' of practices and their constancy over time, more reliably than all formal rules and

explicit norms. This system of dispositions—a present past that tends to perpetuate itself into the future by reactivation in similarly structured practices ... is constantly exerted—is the principle of the continuity and regularity which objectivism sees in social practices without being able to account for it; and also of the regulated transformations that cannot be explained either by the extrinsic, instantaneous determinism of mechanistic sociologism or by the purely internal but equally instantaneous determination of spontaneous subjectivism. (Bourdieu 1990c: 58)

There is a continuity between Bourdieu's idea of the embodied habitus and Foucault's notion of the subject as being disciplined, normalized and regulated into existence, and shaped, oriented and maintained in this form by the process of socio-cultural and self-surveillance—a similarity that, for all its obviousness, was only really acknowledged by Bourdieu late in his career (Bourdieu 2000: 141). If there is a significant difference between their approaches, it is that Foucault emphasizes the institutional sites of discipline, regulation and normalization, while Bourdieu is more interested in how 'the pressure or opposition, continuous and often unnoticed, of the ordinary order of things, the conditionings imposed by the material conditions of existence' (2000: 141) shape and sustain forms of subjectivity and identity. What also connects these two sets of theories of the subject-as-embodiment (of the habitus; of templates and performances of normalization), however, is that they both tend to underplay the extent to which the media (and various socio-cultural forms and genres), and in particular the capitalist media and its discourses, narratives, imperatives and logics (the privileging of the body as a form of self-commoditization, for instance), constitute one of the most pervasive influences on subject formation and deformation.

The commercial media offer up a storehouse of templates of identity (specific to gender, age, class, ethnicity and profession) that are recognizably both 'normal' and desirable, and played out in shorter (advertisements, music videos) and longer (films, television sit-coms and dramas) narrative forms, often attached to various processes of commoditization as self-commoditization (the clothes that both 'stand in' for and guarantee a particular style of identity, the sexualized body that functions as cultural capital). Moreover, the increasing ubiquity of media texts, driven by technology that is now eminently portable and multi-platformed, effectively hystericizes the processes of self-surveillance and self-commoditization. This ensures that the habitus is continually subject, at an everyday level (in the gym, walking home, accessing internet dating sites) to an entirely new level of influence of the 'continuous and often unnoticed... the ordinary order of things, the conditionings imposed by the material conditions of existence' (Bourdieu 2000: 141). While early experiences provide the template of the subject, the habitus-as-bodily hexis continues to undergo changes and refinements commensurate with its socio-cultural trajectory (the development of the gym-shaped body, the acquisition of a fashion-oriented style of self-presentation) and its immersion in the media-dominated world. For Bourdieu, the habitus is the body and the body is its history: 'we are disposed,' he writes, 'because we are exposed' (2000: 140).

Despite the speeding up of the usually 'glacial' rate of change of the habitus (Appadurai 1997) through contact with the global media, the trajectory of the subject-as-habitus is likely to be consistent with the original acquisition and form of the habitus, because that trajectory is disposed by and usually consistent with regard to—that is to say, is constituted from—the habitus itself. A subject's perspectives, values and practices are commensurate and consistent with the habitus because it speaks, feels and sees through the subject. As Bourdieu (1978: 18) states, 'If agents are possessed by their habitus more than they possess it, this is because it acts within them as the organizing principle of their actions.'

As an organizing and organizational principle, the habitus has a productive and dynamic relationship with the world: it both makes what it finds and experiences through a recognition-as-designation of things, people, spaces and situations via its various incorporated categories, genres, discourses and narratives (which produce regularities and objectivities of practice), while simultaneously leaving enough room for navigation through and negotiation of differences that resist integration into the habitus-as-schema. While certain levels or intensities of differences, and the options that they entail, will be foreclosed, this is entirely for pragmatic reasons, derived from and defined by a general economy of practice: either they take the form of the rejection that must be rejected in advance, for the simple reason that to aspire to what is objectively unattainable is, in the end, a form of wasted energy; or they are not taken up because they constitute a destabilizing threat to the habitus-as-field, which is built upon a level of socio-cultural, temporal and psychological commitment that militates against drastic change.

The space that is opened up for dealing with difference and otherness is consequent on the habitus functioning not as the embodiment of certain rules and laws, but rather as a set of dispositions. This aspect is central to Bourdieu's most detailed and worked through early account of the habitus in *Outline*:

> The structures constitutive of a particular type of environment ... produce habitus, systems of durable, transposable dispositions, structured structures predisposed to function as structuring structures, that is, as principles of the generation and structuring of practices and representations which can be objectively 'regulated' and 'regular' without in any way being the product of obedience to rules, objectively adapted to their goals without presupposing a conscious aiming at ends ... collectively orchestrated without being the product of the orchestrating action of a conductor. (1978: 72)

One way of showing what is at stake in the difference between the habitus-as-rule and the habitus-as-disposition is to consider how inauthentic or inappropriate performances of identity-as-field are read, in Schopenhauer's terms, as 'pedantically comical', and elicit laughter 'provoked by a character when he produces an action that is not inscribed within the limits of the concept which defines him' (Bourdieu 2005b: 124). The subject who can only apply the discourses, categories, values and narratives of the field-as-habitus to the wider social field, without the ability to adjust to infelicitous or anomalous circumstances, or to recognize that the world is not the field, is potentially a figure of fun and an object of laughter. The best literary example is Don Quixote: what makes him a ludicrous and satirical figure is not so much that he consistently gets things wrong, mistakes windmills for dragons, or employs an anachronistic order of discourse; above all else, he never learns, never comes to understand that his habitus-as-perspective is fundamentally incommensurate with the everyday discourses and categories of perception of the society through which he moves. One of the consequences of a subject or character becoming irredeemably comic is that they are, potentially at least, also irredeemably alienated from the social field: as long as Quixote remains in the world, it will only offer him symbolic or physical violence, and the only recourse he has is to retreat into a society-of-one.

Immersion in a field, particularly over longer duration, gives rise to an ease of movement through the field-as-world. The experience of a prolonged positive correlation between the doxa of a field and its objectivities means that subjects more or less always and automatically 'know where they stand'—know what to think and feel and do—because the world is perceived as stable, ordered and naturally meaningful. This produces what Bourdieu (1990c: 58) refers to as a 'common-sense' understanding of and approach to the world:

> Insofar ... as habitus are the incorporation of the same history, or more concretely, of the same history objectified in habitus and structures, the practices they generate are mutually intelligible and immediately adjusted to the structures ... and endowed with an objective meaning that is at once unitary

and systematic, transcending subjective intentions ... One of the fundamental effects of the harmony between the practical sense and objectified meanings ... is the production of a common-sense world.

At the same time the diachronic field presents a problem to the habitus because it is different from the synchronic field—which is the form that the field usually articulates and represents 'as itself', both to its members and to other fields and the field of power. While the habitus is incorporated by the subject at a bodily level, activated in the various practices of recognizing, seeing, organizing, categorizing, narrating and evaluating the world, and is constitutive of the subject in the world, the fact of being in the world means that there is a constant tension, and something of a dynamic relationship, between the durability of the habitus and the inconstancy and vicissitudes of the subject's sociocultural trajectory.

Being admitted into or consistently being exposed to a new cultural field constitutes an important and ongoing aspect of the development and deformation of the habitus. However, because the habitus is incorporated and functions at an unconscious level, it remains—much like Kuhn's (1970) scientific paradigms—'always itself', at least at a formal discursive level, until internal dynamics and/or interventions from the field of power produce a version of the synchronic field that takes its place as the 'always itself'. The various versions of the habitus are the product both of the internal dynamics of the field and of relations with (and influences derived from) other cognate fields and the field of power; however, as long as these changes and effects are not incommensurate with the habitus-as-disposition, the field will remain relatively stable. In *An Invitation to Reflexive Sociology*, Bourdieu and Wacquant (1992: 135) refer to an example from the field of religion in France that demonstrates this relation between the habitus-as-disposition and the synchronic and diachronic versions of the field:

> Habitus reveals itself—remember that it consists of a system of dispositions . . . of virtualities, potentialities, eventualities—only in reference to a definite situation. It is only in relation to certain structures that habitus produces given discourses or practices . . . We must think of it as a sort of spring that needs a trigger and, depending on the stimuli and structure of the field, the very same habitus will generate different, even opposite, outcomes. I could take here an example of my work on bishops . . . Bishops live to be very old, and when I interviewed them in synchrony I found myself talking with men ranging anywhere from 35 to 80 years of age . . . and who had therefore been constituted in very different states of the religious field. The sons of nobles who, in the 1930s, would have been bishops in Meaux, and would have asked the worshippers of their parish to kiss their ring in a quasi-feudal aristocratic tradition, are today 'red bishops' in Saint Denis, that is, radical clergymen active in the defence of the downtrodden.

This example of the transformation of the habitus of the religious field in France raises a number of issues about how the habitus functions in times of change, instability, disruption and crisis. Bourdieu (1990b: 78) suggests that when a field is characterized by indeterminacy, 'One can formulate the general rule that the more dangerous the situation is, the more the practice tends to be codified.' When, by extension, a field-as-habitus is going through perpetual diachronic adjustments—for instance, when it is colonized or being transformed by the field of power—then the safest and most straightforward course of action is to cite, and perform in accordance with, the verities of the synchronic field, much like the soldier in Pasolini's *Salò* who, on being discovered acting in a manner contrary to the values and laws of Mussolini's Italian state, automatically responds in a manner that affirms his *bona fides*—that is, by giving a Fascist salute.

Contrary to the perception that the habitus constitutes destiny, Bourdieu insists that it has the capacity to adjust to or negotiate the changing world. The habitus 'is endlessly transformed, either in a direction that reinforces it . . . or in a direction that transforms it and, for instance, raises or lowers the level of expectations and aspirations . . . Habitus can, in certain instances, be built . . . upon contradiction, upon tension, even upon instability' (Bourdieu 1990b: 116). The example of the transition from aristocratic to socialist bishops in France, for instance, demonstrates how different versions of the habitus are produced and sustained without leading to the collapse of a field. Cultural fields have the capacity to produce, incorporate, allow for and deal with various versions of the habitus because they can be (and often are) spatially and chronologically differentiated while being sustained, as a socio-cultural identity, by and through a citation of or joint commitment to 'that which we share and which unites us', such as a belief in God (the field of religion), the ethos of fair play (sport), the welfare of patients (medicine and health) or the sanctity of justice (law).

The question of which version of the habitus predominates in any period, and in which spaces, is predicated upon the field's relation to the field of power, and by extension to the relevant regime of cultural capital in operation. To return to the example of the socialist bishops, it is likely that parishioners who have a left-leaning political orientation will welcome the bishops' initiatives, but they may be deplored by older, right-wing parishioners who insist upon the incompatibility of religion and politics. The habitus

> changes constantly in response to new experiences. Dispositions are subject to a kind of permanent revision, but one which is never radical, because it works on the basis of the premises established in the previous state. They are characterized by a combination of constancy and variation . . . If . . . accommodation has the upper hand, then one finds rigid, self-enclosed, overintegrated habitus (as in old people). (Bourdieu 2000: 161)

Conclusion

One of the main functions of Bourdieu's theoretical apparatus is to facilitate the identification and analysis of the principles and logics constitutive of social identity and socio-cultural practice: cultural field, along with habitus, from which it is more or less inseparable, carries the greatest weight in this work. While the imbrication of habitus and cultural field provides the dispositions that are manifested as both embodied subjectivities and their concomitant cultural trajectories and practices, the cultural field is also the primary context (the set of sites, spaces, moments, relations, genres, discourses, texts, rules, regulations and categories) within which subjects and their practices are constituted, monitored, tested, evaluated, refined and recalibrated. In the next chapter, we will provide an account of the role that cultural field plays in the relation between the habitus and subject formation, and in the production of the various forms and categories of identity and identification that characterize the practices and trajectory of the habitus.

6
Cultural field

Introduction

Bourdieu (1990b: 14) writes in *In Other Words* that 'the analysis of objective structures—those of different fields—is inseparable from the analysis of the genesis . . . of mental structures which are to some extent the product of the incorporation of social structures'. Paul Rabinow (2002: 34) is more succinct: 'God, Bourdieu insists, is nothing more or less than the field . . . God is the social field.' Bourdieu characterizes and defines the concept of cultural field in a number of ways, but he is consistent in emphasizing two points: first, the notion that a field is constituted out of, bound by and played out and maintained as a set of interests; and second, and by extension, that the relation between these interests, and the form they take, is analogous to that of a game, in a ludic, social and sporting rather than an economic sense (Bourdieu 1990b: 110). He explains this last point of emphasis in the following terms:

To highlight the difference between the interest socially constituted in and by the necessity of a field and the interest presupposed by economics, there is no instance better than the interest called forth by the artistic field. Inasmuch as this field, particularly in the most autonomous sectors, defines itself by eschewing or inverting the rules and regularities that constitute the economic field, one can say that the interest promoted by this field is an interest in disinterestedness ... an interest which proves irreducible to economic interest in the ordinary sense. This economically disinterested interest remains nonetheless an interest, and one which can enter into conflict or competition with others ... Thus we have different fields where different forms of interest are constituted and expressed. This does not imply that the different fields do not have invariant properties. Among the invariant properties is the very fact that they are the site of a struggle of interests, between agents or institutions unequally endowed in specific capital ... or the fact that these struggles presuppose a consensus on what is at stake in the struggle. (1990b: 110–11)

For Bourdieu, the work performed by the concept of cultural field has three main orientations. The first concerns his understanding that both subjectivity and cultural practice are only explicable if they are located and considered on a temporal-spatial continuum: this is predominantly a reaction against and an attempt to overcome the scholastic tendency to abstract practices from both the specific situations in which they are carried out, and from their relation to time as an embodied historical consciousness. The second is the need to account for and explain the enduring specificities and objectivities (the field-as-habitus) that characterize socio-cultural spaces and practices. What Bourdieu designates as the field of cultural production, for instance, covers a broad range of activities, texts, genres, forms of capital and categories of identity that have no over-reaching institutionalized or formalized socio-cultural status or identity;

at the same time, however, they have a discursive identity (institutions and subjects-of-the-field are literate with regard to, recognize and deploy specific discursive regimes) and a shared habitus, manifested in terms of identifiable objectivities (levels of educational attainment, patterns of cultural consumption, histories of political affiliations). Subjects who share and maintain positions within socio-cultural space are not just likely to share (versions of) a habitus; they are also potentially available to be interpellated by and identify with the field and its values, and to compete with each other for cultural capital and status within the field:

> The notion of field reminds us that the true object of social sciences is not the individual, even though one cannot construct a field if not through individuals, since the information necessary for statistical analysis is generally attached to individuals or institutions. It is the field which is primary and must be the focus of the research operations. This does not imply that individuals are mere 'illusions', that they do not exist: they exist as agents . . . who are socially constituted as active and acting in the field under consideration by the fact that they possess the necessary properties to be effective, to produce effects, in this field. And it is knowledge of the field itself in which they evolve that allows us best to grasp the roots of their singularity, their *point of view*, or position (in a field) from which their particular vision of the world (and of the field itself) is constructed. (Bourdieu & Wacquant 1992: 107)

A third issue was the need, as Bourdieu saw it, to move beyond subjectivist theories that both removed subjects from their material and discursive contexts, and explained their practices and achievements in terms of individual qualities and characteristics, such as creativity and genius. This tendency, which Bourdieu identified as a discursive cornerstone of the field of cultural production, had a particular theoretical significance with regard to the work he was carrying out in education and culture in the 1960s and 1970s. For Bourdieu, the field of cultural production played an important part in socio-cultural reproduction and, by extension, the naturalization and maintenance of dominant forms of symbolic power: this was done both by way of the choice of content (legitimized and canonized cultural texts) and through an emphasis on how authorized culture had to be approached, treated, read and understood (within an order of aestheticized abstraction). Culture, cultural texts and artists displayed and articulated a particular relation to the world: authorized culture, for Bourdieu, provided a kind of meta-commentary that was simultaneously both removed from and superior to the world. In Bourdieu's work on the relation between education, culture and symbolic power, the cultural politics of authorized culture functions as a mechanism for facilitating the naturalization of a style of relating to the world (disinterestedness, an ease, a sense of one's individuality and distinctiveness) that is derived from the family background of the dominant classes and inculcated within educational regimes as an exemplary dimension of subjectivity and identity. Within Bourdieu's theory of socio-cultural reproduction, the field of cultural production plays the role of a Trojan Horse: it is offered to the lower classes as a gift that promises improvement, advancement, individuality and the accumulation of capital (both material, in the form of qualifications, and more generally as the acquisition of a distinctive way of relating to the world); its function, however, is to enact a symbolic violence that is meant to be misrecognized as self-failure, a lack of worth and cultural illiteracy. The means by which it is equipped to fulfil this role are derived, in equal parts, from the relative autonomy of the field and its ethos of separation from the world.

The concept of cultural field, as was the case with habitus and cultural capital, was associated with and derived from the theoretical issues that arose in Bourdieu's Algerian work and his educational sociology, and by extension and more generally as part of his attempt to formulate a scientific sociology capable of objectifying socio-cultural practices. However, there were both specific theoretical antecedents and changes in emphasis that influenced how the concept was developed and refined. One clear influence was Weber's work on and treatment of the development of the institutions, discourses, activities and socio-cultural functions of religion. These were not considered on their own terms or as a set of symptoms of wider factors: rather, religion was treated as a cultural continuity explicable in terms of both its own logics and the history of the interrelationship between the field and historical factors and forces. Bourdieu (1990b: 49) characterizes the influence exerted by Weber as being both positive and negative: 'I constructed the notion of field against Weber and with Weber.' There are two significant additions that Bourdieu brings to Weber's use of field. The first is a focus on the cultural politics of the field, both internally and with regard to the socio-cultural roles and functions that a field takes on in relation to regimes of symbolic power and domination. The second is a willingness to apply the principles of the cultural field across social contexts, and to incorporate a consideration of relations between and across fields and with regard to the field of power (itself a concept that Bourdieu developed to account for the internal deformation and transformation of fields). To arrive at the concept of cultural field,

> it was necessary to go beyond the first attempt to analyze the 'intellectual field' as a relatively autonomous universe of specific relationships: in fact the immediately visible relationships between the agents involved in the intellectual life, especially the interactions among the authors or the authors and editors, had concealed the objective relationships between the positions occupied by the agents, positions which determined the form of these interactions. And the first rigorous elaboration of the notion came out of a reading of the chapter, in *Wirtschaft und Gesellschaft*, which is devoted to the sociology of religion . . . at the cost of a critique of the interactional view of the relationships between the religious agents proposed by Weber and which implied a retrospective critique of my first elaboration of the intellectual field, I proposed a construct of the religious

field as a structure of objective relationships permitting the accounting of the concrete form of the interactions that Max Weber described as a realist typology. There remained only the need to put to work this thinking tool . . . by applying it to different fields. (Bourdieu 1985: 18)

There was also a debt, as Robbins (2000: 37–8) points out, 'to the approach of modern science that Cassirer had made explicit', one that 'involves a "relational mode of thinking, rather than one that supposed that it was dealing with the interaction of substances"'. At a negative level, there was, as Bourdieu (1985) points out in an early article, an attempt to overcome the tendency of Marxist thought to underestimate the role of the field of cultural production in the exercising and naturalizing of power and domination. The notion of cultural field:

initially served to indicate a direction of research, defined negatively, as the rejection of the alternative of internal interpretation and of external explication, before which were placed all the sciences of cultural works, religious sciences, art history or literary history: in these matters the opposition between a formalism born of the theorizing of an art which achieved a high degree of autonomy and a reductionism intent on directly linking artistic forms to social forms, with which . . . Marxism, despite the notion of relative autonomy, tended to identify itself, hid the fact that both of these trends disregarded the field of production as a social space of objective relationships. (Bourdieu 1985: 16)

Bourdieu made use of the concept of field in a number of major case studies of the French educational (Bourdieu & Passeron 1990) and academic fields (1988), the field of cultural production (1993a), bureaucracy (1996), the state (2014), journalism (1998b), science (2004) and economics (2005c), and more generally across a range of shorter studies of what Thomson (2012: 67–8) refers to as the 'restructured social sites of globalized de-industrialization'. Each study contributed something to the development of a 'general laws of fields' (Bourdieu 1993b: 72), and by extension was used 'to question and interpret other fields' (1993b: 72). One example that stands out concerns the issue of the refinement, recalibration or transformation of regimes of value within a field. This is not something that is reducible to internal dynamics because, as Bourdieu (1998c) points out, to a large extent the subject's commitment to the field, which is part of the rite of passage of entry into a field, ensures a level of stability and durability. The dynamics of a field are unlikely to involve any reconsideration of its core elements; rather, they are more usually matters of interpretation, focus and emphasis, such as when, in the literary or artistic field, the canonical order is gradually readjusted to take a body of new research into account. To move, as a community-as-field, to a new regime of value would require subjecting the collective habitus to a considerable disruptive violence, and that is something that a cultural field tends to foreclose by way of the mechanism of *illusio*.

However, cultural fields are only stable up to a certain point: changes and recalibrations tend to be accretional, but over time they tend to open up a disassociation between synchronic and diachronic versions of the field. There are three main reasons for the disjunction: first, ongoing internal dynamics produce spatial fragmentation and differentiation; second, fields are always caught up, to some extent, in wider socio-cultural and historical changes; and third, fields necessarily interact with, and are influenced by, developments in cognate fields. In order 'to account for structural effects which are not otherwise easily understood' (Bourdieu 1998c: 33), Bourdieu introduces the concept of the field of power. At a general level, it provided a set of logics and frameworks for helping to make sense of internal developments within fields, and changes in their relation to other fields, and at a more specific level it was used to analyse changes to the autonomy of fields such as the field of cultural production.

Research into the characteristics, structures, economic regimes and discourses of different cultural fields played a significant role in

Bourdieu's theoretical and methodological apparatus: the analysis of the relation between the educational field, the field of cultural production and the field of power, for instance, was instrumental in establishing a theory of symbolic power and socio-cultural reproduction. The development of the concept of and methodologies associated with reflexivity was derived from a detailed analysis of the relationship between the dispositions and research methodologies of the field of science. Bourdieu's ongoing analysis of the field of cultural production was also particularly important in terms of theorizing the logics underpinning regimes of capital and the relation between cultural and symbolic capital.

Cultural field

A cultural field can be understood as an imagined community, in Benedict Anderson's (1991) sense of the term. It is predicated on a successful act of discursive articulation that disposes subjects and institutions to identify with the values and forms of work of the field; those shared values-as-identity produce the 'between us' that facilitates group identification and binds the community together. In this respect, the process by which cultural fields and their ontological status are generated is more or less commensurate with Bourdieu's explanation of the relation between positions in socio-cultural space, class consciousness and the production (and status) of classes (Bourdieu 1990b).

A field is a discursive regime or entity and a materiality: the field of cultural production, for instance, is distinguished by forms of dress and address, texts and technologies, and the production, organization and use of space and architecture. However, the material conditions of a field are necessarily an extension of, and take their significance from, the discursive regime of which they are a product: the field is not and never can be reducible to its built environments, institutions or formal organizations, rules and regulations. A field is everywhere but only recognizable in terms of what it brings about—that is, in its capacity to produce significance, identification and ways of seeing and categorizing the world. The issue of the limits of a cultural field is difficult to determine

> because it is always at stake in the field itself ... Participants in a field ... constantly work to differentiate themselves from their closest rivals in order to reduce competition and to establish a monopoly over a particular subsector of the field ... Thus the boundaries of the field can only be determined by an empirical investigation. (Bourdieu & Wacquant 1992: 100)

A cultural field comes into being by fulfilling at least five separate criteria. First, it must be able to articulate and manifest itself simultaneously as a singularity and a differentiated but cognate group of entities joined together by, and recognizable in terms of, certain core discourses, imperatives, values, functions, rules, categories and practices. Second, it must be recognized and accepted by, integrated into and function in compliance with the network of fields that comprise the field of power (Bourdieu 1998c). Third, it must demonstrate that its own ethos is commensurate with, and its work contributes to, the values and enhancement of the wider socio-cultural field. Fourth, there needs to be a demographic of potential members, occupying similar positions in the socio-cultural field and sharing certain dispositions. In order for this to happen, a field must have the material means, leverage, discursive techniques and content, as well as potential socio-cultural functions and values, to enable it to be imagined into existence. Finally, it must have the discursive and technical wherewithal to represent, manifest and valorize itself in a consistent manner to its own potential members and to other fields, and most importantly to the field of power. The viability of a cultural field is necessarily predicated, then, on some degree of bureaucratization of people, activities and events within a regime that is specific and universal, changeable and timeless, and above all else reproducible.

Institutions, bureaucracies, titles, rules and categories are, however, only the objective manifestation of a cultural field. Fields and their objectivities are simultaneously constituted through and constitutive of a habitus, manifested as a set of dispositions that are embodied by its members. These embodied dispositions are derived from and reproduce the habitus at an epistemological level: they animate and justify the practices of a field, and speak (through and for) the field as a discourse of belief in, identification with and commitment to the field-as-idea, a relation-as-process that Bourdieu refers to as *illusio*. The habitus of a field manifests itself as a series of values and dispositions-as-bodily-practices that appear to come naturally to the subject:

> There is every reason to think that the factors which are most influential in the formation of the habitus are transmitted without passing through ... consciousness, but through suggestions inscribed in the most apparently insignificant aspects of the things, situations and practices of everyday life. Thus the modalities of practices, the ways of looking, sitting, standing, keeping silent or even of speaking ... are full of injunctions that are powerful and hard to resist precisely because they are silent and insidious, insistent and insinuating. (Bourdieu 2005b: 51)

While the habitus is marked by its durability, every cultural field is inflected and recalibrated, to some extent, by both the field of power and those factors and contexts that are felt across the wider social field. This requires improvisations within the field, which gradually produce different ways of seeing and experiencing the same types of activities. The habitus has the capacity to maintain itself, and continues to be productive—sometimes even in contexts where its orientation is contrary to self-interest. In such situations (when a subject moves into a new field, or if the field has been transformed), the habitus either moves seamlessly across to accommodate the new set of discursive conditions, or it remains left behind and 'out of time'. With regard to the second case, Bourdieu points to the introduction of capitalism in

Algeria under French colonialism, and to other 'historical conjunctures of a revolutionary nature in which changes of objective structures are so swift that agents whose mental structures have been molded by these prior structures become obsolete and act inopportunely' (Bourdieu & Wacquant 1992: 130).

Inclusion in and membership of a cultural field is always predicated upon, and monitored in terms of, a number of authorized performatives (bodily, linguistic, affective, generic) that are tied to and vary depending upon a subject's position and identity in the field. These performatives are associated with the field's identity categories, and are subject to variables such as gender, age, education, race, ethnicity and social status. The relationship between subjectivity, socio-cultural performances and cultural fields (and the forms and categories of identity produced by this relationship) is effectively a circular process: cultural fields, institutions, techniques and mechanisms produce subjects who are inclined to see and understand the world in terms of recognizable and authorized categories and their commensurate performances. This produces iterations of compliant performances, in turn accentuating and legitimizing those original templates. These dispositions are manifested as technically explicable practices, and reinforced and complemented by authorized, iterative performances of normal subjectivity (Butler 1993). This evaluation and categorisation of each and every subject is 'neither a single act nor a causal process initiated by the subject . . . Construction not only takes place in time, but is itself a temporal process which operates through the reiteration of norms' (1993: 10). This process is both reproductive and potentially dynamic. There are sites and times in a culture where performances of subjectivity come to embody and play out the tensions, ambiguities and changes in what is understood as acceptable and normal, both within a specific cultural field and more generally across the social field and the field of power. We can monitor whether our subjectivity is 'on track' in terms of our body shape, clothes, mannerisms or ways of seeing and evaluating other people. These images, ideas and performances constitute a vast store of up-to-date templates for, or models of, a normal subject. The efficacy of this process can be observed in the way bodies perform belief, naturally and intuitively, in the field and their place within the field:

> What is comprehended in the world is a body for which there is a world, which is included in the world but in a mode of inclusion irreducible to simple material and spatial inclusion. *Illusio* is that way of being in the world, of being occupied by the world, which means that an agent can be affected by something very distant, even absent, if it participates in the game in which he is engaged . . . It is because of the *illusio* which constitutes the field as the space of a game that thoughts and actions can be affected and modified without any physical contact or even any symbolic interaction . . . (Bourdieu 2000: 135)

The body is the locus of an unconscious process whereby the perspectives, frameworks, categories of thought and values of and relations to the world are gradually learnt, integrated and made coherent in the form of a bodily hexis as the habitus. The literate and socially comfortable body moves fluidly and naturally with regard to the tempos, rhythms and physical demands of the moment at hand. It also manifests the values and principles of the field: it carries the field with(in) it, and consequently is able to negotiate the world in terms of the field because of the successful incorporation of the logics and forms of knowledge of that field:

> The world is comprehensible, immediately endowed with meaning, because the body, which, thanks to its senses and its brain, has the capacity to be present to what is outside itself, in the world, and to be impressed and durably modified by it, has been protractedly (from the beginning) exposed to its regularities. Having acquired from this exposure a system of dispositions attuned to these regularities, it is inclined and able to anticipate them practically in behaviours which engage

a corporeal knowledge that provides a practical comprehension of the world quite different from the intentional acts of conscious decoding that is normally designated by the idea of comprehension. (2000: 135)

The subject who has incorporated the ethos, values and logics of a cultural field has an entirely different relationship with the activities and events of the field than that of a visitor or passer by. Members become literate with regard to the field precisely because it is a condition of entry: as Bourdieu (1993b: 74) writes, 'Through the practical knowledge of the principles of the game that is tacitly required of new entrants, the whole history of the game, the whole past of the game, is present in each act of the game.' The visitor, on the other hand, can be differentiated both by a lack of technical expertise and literacy (discourses, bodily hexis, history, forms of capital) and because, perhaps even more importantly, they just can't see the point of the expenditure of time and effort. To view a field from the outside is to bring in an entirely different visual and evaluative regime with regard to the practices, categories and general economy. The visitor marks divergences from the social field as idiosyncratic, eccentric or irrational; the subject-of-the-field, on the other hand, takes the game 'at its word' and accepts, implicitly and unthinkingly, that 'it is worth the candle' (Bourdieu 2000: 42). For the subject-of-the-field, 'Belief, even the belief that is the basis of the universe of science, is in the order of the automaton, the body, which, as Pascal never ceases to remind us, "has its reasons, of which reason knows nothing"' (2000: 12).

The authorization, legitimation and evaluation of cultural capital are most at stake in the practices and dynamics of a cultural field. This is also one of the ways in which objectivities within the field can be identified. 'To say that the structure of a field . . . is defined by the structure of the distribution of the specific forms of capital that are active in it,' Bourdieu writes, 'means that when my knowledge of forms of capital is sound I can differentiate everything that there is to differentiate' (Bourdieu & Wacquant 1992: 108). The convertibility and exchangeability of cultural capital vary both from field to field and historically. The field of cultural production, and in particular the autonomous pole of that field, is the exemplary site of an economy of cultural capital that is not only incommensurate with, but largely antithetical to, economism and the market. As Randell Johnson (1993: 6) writes in his Introduction to *The Field of Cultural Production*,

> the interests and resources at stake in fields are not always material, and competition among agents—which Bourdieu sees as one universal invariant property of fields—is not always based on conscious calculation. In the cultural (e.g. literary) field, competition often concerns the authority inherent in recognition, consecration and prestige. This is especially so in what Bourdieu calls the sub-field of restricted production, that is, production not aimed at a large-scale market. Autonomy based on consecration or prestige is purely symbolic and may or may not imply possession of increased economic capital. Bourdieu thus developed, as an integral part of his theory of practice, the concept of symbolic power based on diverse forms of capital which are not reducible to economic capital. Academic capital, for example, derives from formal education and can be measured by degrees or diplomas held. Linguistic capital concerns an agent's linguistic competence measured in relation to a specific linguistic market where often unrecognized power relations are at stake.

Fields are usually able to determine their own regime of capital; however, the field of power exercises an influence—sometimes formally and explicitly—over both what constitutes capital within a field and regimes of exchangeability. By way of example, Bourdieu's work in the final stage of his career focuses on the ways in which relatively autonomous fields such as the academy, science, the field of cultural production and sport are increasingly subjected to capitalist logics that have been smuggled into, and sit uncomfortably within or beside inalienable discourses, ethics and imperatives. In the academy, the scholastic point of view-as-habitus, and the dispositions and practices derived from it, which were once aligned with and marked by a performance of disinterestedness and distance from the thing, are increasingly being replaced by a focus on outside sources of funding and applied research (which is oriented towards delivering profits by way of the development of government grants, business investment, patents and product enhancements). In this respect, we are dealing with a situation where 'mental structures have been molded by these prior structures [that have] become obsolete' (Bourdieu & Wacquant 1992: 130).

In his later research, Bourdieu was increasingly concerned with the interventionist role of the field of power, and its ability to influence, inform, inflect and on occasion determine the rules of the game operating between and within fields. From this perspective, it is not just a player, but the determinant and principle force, in the articulation, deployment and maintenance of symbolic power and violence; and it exercises this domination by monopolizing the right to determine rates and regimes of value. The field of power

> is not a field like the others. It is the space of the relations of force between the different kinds of capital or, more precisely, between the agents who possess a sufficient amount of one of the different kinds of capital to be in a position to dominate the corresponding field, whose struggles intensify whenever the relative value of the different kinds of capital is questioned (for example, the exchange rate between cultural capital and economic capital); that is, especially when the established equilibrium in the field of instances specifically charged with the reproduction of the field of power is threatened . . . One of the stakes of the struggles which oppose the set of agents or institutions which have in common the possession of a sufficient quantity of specific capital (especially economic or cultural) to occupy dominant positions within their respective fields is the conservation or transformation of the 'exchange

rate' between different kinds of capital and, along the same lines, control of the bureaucratic instances which are in a position to modify the exchange rate through administrative measures . . . Domination is not the direct and simple action exercised by a set of agents ('the dominant class') invested with powers of coercion. Rather, it is the indirect effect of a complex set of actions engendered within the network of intersecting constraints which each of the dominants, thus dominated by the structure of the field through which domination is exerted, endures on behalf of all the others. (Bourdieu 1998c: 34)

The history, trajectory and identity of a field, and its relation to the field of power, are manifested at the level of its discursive regime. Discourses are epistemologically determinant—they are the means by which a field comes to know, understand and articulate itself, since every change in the discursive practices of the field serves as a kind of archaeological record (in Foucault's sense of the expression) of the historical interactions and relationships both within the field and between the field and other important fields (business, media, government, education). Every field, from its inception, is inflected by other fields and their values, logics, imperatives, forms of capital, technologies, identities and discourses. If we want to know where a field has come from, where it is going and why, then we need to be able to identify and analyse those moments, sites, occasions and events when the field and its practitioners have, collectively yet more or less unconsciously, become something else—something that the field in its earlier incarnations might not recognize.

A contemporary example of this process can be seen in the way the field of television journalism has been subjected to the twin constraints of time and effect (Bourdieu 1998b) associated with the commercial media. In *On Television and Journalism*, Bourdieu makes the point that the very limited time available to 'do' a news story means that issues are pared back, decontextualized and explicated in terms of simple binaries (right/wrong, business/unions, men/women, citizens/foreigners); in a sense, the same is true of non-news genres, such as soap operas and sit-coms. News programs provide the best example of this process: stories that are connected to one another only in the sense that they happened at the same time (a famine in Africa, a celebrity divorce, the enactment of government policies, an outbreak of war) are thrown together in an order that is not so much arbitrary as interest-driven ('Are people tired of hearing about African famines?'), without explanations of contexts or antecedents. Moreover, because each event is dealt with in a minute or so, the explanation of the story has to be punchy and evoke human interest—for instance, a famine might be articulated in terms of the plight of one starving child or family, or a government policy might be reduced to the effects of the policy on a single shopkeeper. Of course, once that single child is fed or the shopkeeper's problem solved, the issue effectively 'disappears' (for an extended account and discussion of this phenomenon, see Boltanski 2004).

The twin imperatives of time and effect make it virtually impossible for television news programs to say anything that is not sensationalized or simplistic. In fact, it really doesn't make sense for them to say anything much at all, which is why the news is invariably dominated by visuals. A 30-second description of a massacre, famine, riot or war usually produces an immediate emotional effect—which is what the news is meant to accomplish. Footage of a person being beaten to death, of emaciated babies, of crowds rioting, of masked faces, and of bombs zeroing in on bridges or 'terrorists' can provoke an immediate, and strong, response (pity, anger, fear, revulsion, elation); however, this action of taking the viewer 'into the story' effectively dissolves the story, at least as far as any kind of contextual understanding is concerned. Viewers are disposed to sympathize or empathize with, or fear or hate, the objects of the representation, but not to think about them and their contexts. The imperative is not to think, consider or try to understand, but to feel, and then to transfer that affective engagement onto the next person, thing, situation or story. Baudrillard (2003) refers to this regime of attention as being akin to someone playing a pinball machine: the player is taken up by and immersed in the audio-visual moment (the noise, the lights, the emotional roller coaster of coups and losses), but this engagement is always being cut short and restarted when the old game is completed and a new game commenced.

Conclusion

Bourdieu's analysis of the relationship between the fields of education and cultural production was the catalyst for the development of the concepts of cultural field and cultural capital, which he 'proposed in the early sixties to account for the fact that, after controlling for economic position and social origin, students from more cultured families not only have higher rates of academic success but exhibit different modes and patterns of cultural consumption' (Bourdieu 1998c: 93). Bourdieu's study of the ways in which, within the education system, certain kinds of speech, cultural literacy, networks and connections, styles of self-presentation, bodily hexis and cultural preferences were recognized and functioned as forms of value demonstrated that, 'The economic universe is made up of several economic worlds' that presumed and required 'dispositions adjusted to the regularities inscribed in each of them, to the "practical reason" that characterizes them' (1998c: 93). In his work on the field of cultural production, Bourdieu developed and refined his theory of a general economy in order to account for the dynamics of and variations in position-taking, and the distribution and exchange rates of different forms of capital, within cultural fields. In the next chapter, we will provide an account of Bourdieu's notion of general economy and cultural capital, and of the role played by symbolic capital in the naturalization and maintenance of evaluative regimes.

7
Cultural capital

Introduction

Bourdieu (1986: 240) identifies three main forms or 'guises' of capital: it can be economic (convertible into money), cultural (educational qualifications, forms of artistic literacy) and social (connections, networks, titles, one's 'good name'). Cultural capital

> can exist in three forms: in the embodied state . . . in the form of long-lasting dispositions of the mind and body; in the objectified state, in the form of cultural goods (pictures, books, dictionaries, instruments, machines, etc.) . . . ; and in the institutionalized state, a form of objectification which must be set apart because, as . . . in the case of educational qualifications, it confers entirely original properties on the cultural capital which it is presumed to guarantee (1986: 240).

In his educational work, Bourdieu identifies how certain class-inflected forms of cultural literacy and styles of self-presentation (commensurate with the notions of ease and disinterestedness) were authorized and naturalized, and effectively functioned as universal capital, within the French education system. The dominated classes, who brought the 'wrong' forms of capital into the system, were simultaneously offered and denied the access to the 'universal rights' accorded to subjects with the appropriate kinds of capital.

The notion of cultural capital is equally central to an understanding of the dynamics of cultural fields at both the internal and external levels. For Bourdieu, subjects-of-the-field both commit to the validity of, and compete for, the acquisition of capital as part of the process of *illusio*. Subsequently, positions within a field are constituted, and maintained or challenged, by and through the accumulation of relevant capital. According to Bourdieu (1986: 241):

> It is . . . impossible to account for the structure and functioning of the social world unless one reintroduces capital in all its forms and not solely in the one form recognized by economic theory. Economic theory has allowed to be foisted upon it a definition of the economy of practices which is the historical invention of capitalism; and by reducing the universe of exchange to mercantile exchange, which is objectively and subjectively oriented toward the maximization of profit . . . it has implicitly defined the other forms of exchange as non-economic, and therefore as disinterested. In particular, it defines as disinterested those forms of exchange which ensure the transubstantiation whereby the most material types of capital—those which are economic in the restricted sense—can present themselves in the immaterial form of cultural capital or social capital and vice versa.

Bourdieu contends that power operates within a general economy, primarily by way of regimes and orders of symbolic and cultural capital, rather than through more direct methods such as the threat of physical force (via the state's monopoly of forms of violence) or via wholesale and explicit imposition of market imperatives and regimes of value. The notion of a general economy allows for the analysis, at the level of a spatial and chronological intersection, of socio-cultural practices, capital, processes and affiliations that, because of the discursive regimes specific to certain cultural fields, cannot be reduced to the status of straightforward economic logics of calculation and accumulation, or configured as non-tendentious (and abstracted) social procedures and relations. Bourdieu (1986: 249) argues that:

> The real logic of the functioning of capital, the conversions from one type to another, and the law of conservation which governs them cannot be understood unless two opposing but equally partial views are superseded: on the one hand, economism, which, on the grounds that every type of capital is reducible in the last analysis to economic capital, ignores what makes the specific efficacy of the other types of capital, and on the other hand, semiologism (nowadays represented by structuralism, symbolic interactionism, or ethnomethodology), which reduces social exchanges to phenomena of communication and ignores the brutal fact of universal reducibility to economics.

There is a recognition, on Bourdieu's part, from the earliest period of his scholarly career in Algeria up until and including his work on the cultural fields of science (Bourdieu 2004) and economics (Bourdieu 2005c), of the socio-cultural and political implications of the imposition of economism as a naturalized and dominant discourse and set of logics, with and through which socio-cultural interactions and issues can be understood, measured and evaluated. His argument is that since capitalism is oriented towards the alienation of every aspect of the social field (2005c), then the logical extension of this process is that the social will be replaced, at a level of political consideration and intervention, by the social-as-economics. The various socio-cultural categories and issues that claim to be or are usually treated, in the West, as being inalienable—such as the family, human bodies, and universal access to the universal resources and rights of a polity (education, medical care, a minimum standard of living, access to a functioning and autonomous legal system, protection from physical and symbolic violence)—are largely incompatible with regard to the discourses and logics of market economics:

> Contrary to economistic reductionism a la Gary Becker, who reduces to economic calculation that which by definition denies and defies calculation, the domestic unit manages to perpetuate in its core a quite particular economic logic . . . In the case of Algeria, I was able to show that the generalization of monetary exchanges and the correlative constitution of the 'economic' idea of work as paid labor . . . leads to the generalization of calculating dispositions, threatening the indivisibility of goods and tasks on which the family unit rested. In fact, in differentiated societies the spirit of calculation and the logic of markets undermine the spirit of solidarity and tend to substitute the individual decisions of the isolated individual for the collective decisions of the household. (Bourdieu 1998a: 106–7)

Bourdieu's work identifies and analyses a general regime of capital in which the relation of dominant/domination is inscribed, maintained and naturalized, and which facilitates and organizes forms and processes of socio-cultural recognition, status, mobility and access to rights and privileges. The political economy, which is played out within a great deal of the activities within a general economy (through the production and maintenance of various regimes of cultural capital), is written off by economic theory as a form of 'disinterested' investment, because these activities constitute a form of expenditure that is not oriented towards profit (in a commercial sense). The autonomous pole of the field of cultural production, for instance, is characterized by an evaluative regime that is incommensurate with, and largely antithetical to, capitalist logics and imperatives. At the same time, it cannot completely sequester itself from interactions with other cultural fields and the field of power, nor is it closed, at an implicit level, to the possibilities of an articulation and exchange of capital across fields. While this disinterested ethos often refuses an association with or involvement in the market economy, it simultaneously produces, enacts and sustains forms of cultural production and consumption as differentiation and distinction, and constitutes and authorizes forms of capital that can potentially be exchanged (depending on spatial-temporal junctions and the specificities of the field) for economic or symbolic capital. Even when there is no easy or obvious opportunity for the transformation of cultural capital into economic capital (for instance, a postgraduate degree leading to a highly paid job), general and specific regimes of capital function as forms of socio-cultural (and by extension, commercial) architecture that recognize, authorize, organize, naturalize, orient, facilitate and block the socio-cultural trajectories and opportunities of subjects. As Bourdieu (1986: 242) writes, 'priceless things have their price, and the extreme difficulty of converting certain practices and certain objects into money is only due to the fact that this conversion is refused in the very intention that produces them, which is nothing other than the denial ... of the economy'.

Cultural capital

Cultural capital can be defined as anything that a field identifies as having value, and that can be exchanged within that field. We can characterize forms of cultural capital as arbitrary but motivated: there is no natural reason why any one thing should be designated or valued as capital; on the other hand, the production of value—much like the production of meaning—is never an accidental or unmotivated occurrence. While Nietzsche (1956) denies that there is an unmediated articulation between substance and attribute, such articulations are continuously posited and discursively produced, usually as a consequence of the internal dynamics of a field. The production and naturalization of regimes of value are central to relationships and activities both within fields and between a cultural field and the field of power, and changes to the orders or exchange rates of capital are always brought about by flows of power-as-leverage.

Anything can go through a phase where it is associated with or can constitute cultural capital; however, the range of capital within a field is usually both limited and tied to specific and relatively predictable logics. Like the habitus of the cultural field from which they are derived, regimes of capital tend to be durable: the level and intensity of the work that the subject has to commit to in order to be integrated into, and perform in accordance with, the dictates of a field militate against abrupt or dramatic recalibrations of a field and its regime of capital. However, because cultural capital is the primary means through which positions within the field and the orientations of the field itself are modified or challenged, it is subject to fluctuations in exchange rates, both spatially/synchronically and diachronically. If we refer back to Bourdieu's example, cited in an earlier chapter, of the 'red bishops of Meaux', we could read into it a narrative of a variation in the field of religion in France of what constituted cultural capital at a specific time and place: on the one hand, aristocratic pretensions, bodily hexis, connections and orientations, and on the other hand a concern for and a performance of solidarity and empathy with 'the people'. To some extent, this change might be explained in terms of significant reorientations of the Catholic Church, either in France or the Vatican, as part of a wider endeavour to attract worshippers by appearing to be more up to date and relevant. We could go further and suggest that, like all fields, the field of religion in France has become increasingly sensitive to and dependent upon the field of the media: the behaviour of a bishop who fights for the rights and resources of his parishioners would produce a much more sympathetic or dramatic media story than the behaviour of traditional bishops.

Another point to take from this example is that immaterial forms of cultural capital are far more likely to be subject to variation and change than material things. The argument is that things that have been discursively and formally identified as capital (an educational qualification or a professional award, for instance) are less vulnerable to challenges than those forms of value that are implicitly recognized but never actually articulated, or that in some cases cannot be articulated. There are, however, situations where certain kinds of immaterial capital can attain a highly privileged status within a field, to the extent that they are considered synonymous with or manifestations of the field-as-ethos. In the field of sport, for example, to be considered to be a fair player (that is, someone with a strong and unshakeable commitment to the ethos of fair play) is to be regarded as exemplary, as a manifestation of what the field says it is and ought to be. On the other hand, to have one's integrity doubted or called into question vitiates a player's standing—sometimes regardless of their level of success. While the field of sport is more or less pervaded by practices that are little more than conventionalized or formalized forms of cheating (concerted appeals in cricket that are meant to pressure an umpire into giving a batsman out, football players automatically raising their hands to claim a throw or a corner kick whenever a ball goes out of play), when a sportsperson is generally regarded as having no respect for the rules of the game or the ethos of the field, their status (and by extension their level of capital) is diminished, as was the case with the drug allegations that blighted the careers of the American cyclist Lance Armstrong and the Russian tennis player Maria Sharapova. Similarly, a player who displays artistry, flair and a strong commitment to the aesthetics of the sport (for instance, a cricketer who plays fluent attacking shots regardless of the state of the game) is more likely to be admired and praised than the mere battler who perseveres and grinds out a game or event (the 'water carrier' or the '*domestiques*' of French football and cycling, respectively). The example *par excellence* can be found in contemporary tennis, where the fitness, power and determination of a player such as Novak Djokovic are never as admired, appreciated or valued (in the media and by crowds, and certainly by advertisers) as the qualities of Roger Federer, with his knowledge and appreciation of the history of the game, and commitment to playing 'the right way' (trying to hit winners rather than waiting for an opponent to make mistakes or collapse from exhaustion).

There are also cases where immaterial things constitute implicit rather than explicit capital, without in any way depreciating their value. Having powerful or influential connections, for instance, is not something that can usually be spoken about openly or formally (that would imply cronyism or corruption), but only identified and recognized; however when it is in fact recognized, it constitutes—more or less universally—an important form of capital. Then there are situations where a form of capital that is incommensurate, at a conventional level, with the ethos and values of a field 'has a place' in the field's evaluative regime, without necessarily being articulated as such. Examples of this phenomenon can be found in the autonomous pole of the field of cultural production, particularly with regard to economic capital. The disinterested ethos of the field means that commercial success can disqualify a work and constitute negative capital: the artistic and literary fields, for instance, are not oriented towards popular consumption, but rather towards recognition and acceptance by peers (fellow artists, critics). However, the increasing level of penetration of the field of cultural production by capitalism and its logics means that cultural producers and associated institutions (publishers, agents, galleries, journals) play something of a double game: they have to maintain a discursive commitment to the 'purity' of the field-as-art, while cautiously and carefully commoditizing artistic work in the hope of attaining commercial success.

The difficult situation that the novelist Jonathan Franzen encountered in 2001 is a case in point: he had been critical and dismissive of popular television culture, only to have the television personality Oprah Winfrey praise his book. To have a cultural work singled out by Winfrey would usually constitute cultural capital in the media and help with sales, but from Franzen's position in the field, it potentially constituted negative capital: Winfrey praised books that he thought were trite and superficial, so her imprimatur more or less associated him with non-literary literature. However, his response, which openly lamented Winfrey's recognition, was interpreted (in both the media and the literary field) as a display of elitism and literary snobbery, and he eventually apologized to her (Kirkpatrick 2001).

This example indicates some of the complexities surrounding, and the difficulties in determining, the rates of exchange for different forms of cultural capital both within and across fields. With regard to the autonomous pole of the field of cultural production, it could be argued that, historically, economic capital and popular recognition did not translate into cultural capital—something of which Franzen was acutely aware, and which explains why he quickly distanced himself both from Winfrey and the consequence he foresaw (commercial success, popular media attention, looming celebrity status). The reaction of certain members of the field, however, demonstrated that his understanding of the field (and more specifically, its regime of capital) was out of date: in practice, the field had 'come to an arrangement', implicitly, with capitalism and the commercial media whereby the kind of publicity associated with Winfrey's book club was no longer likely to disqualify the recipient as a serious writer. This 'turn' towards celebrity culture in the literary field was already well advanced: the actress Jerry Hall and the composer Tim Rice, for instance, had served as judges on the British Whitbread Prize panel. However, even here the situation was anything but straightforward: while the organizers of the Whitbread Prize clearly felt that celebrity status constituted significant capital in the literary field, the rival Booker Prize organization took the opposite view, presumably in order to demonstrate its greater seriousness and superiority to the Whitbread Prize (Yates 2001).

What is played out here in the literary field—and doubtless in other areas of the field of cultural production—is a separation of the areas and institutions within the field, a process predicated upon different understandings of the exchange rates and viability of forms of capital. While the Whitbread Prize embraces celebrities and the publicity that goes with them, the capital that it accrues is predominantly exchangeable outside the field (within the popular media, for instance).

However, by refusing the capital that goes with appointing celebrity panellists, the Booker Prize turns its rejection of commercialism into a form of cultural capital recognized by and eminently exchangeable within the literary field. Both approaches, and the capital they acquire, are legitimate, but only in specific spaces within the field.

The struggle over what constitutes legitimate cultural capital, and the exchange rates between forms of capital, is informed by and eventually subject to what Bourdieu (1990c: 122) calls the effects of symbolic capital, which he characterizes as '"material" capital misrecognized and thus recognized'. Bourdieu uses this concept in order to provide a more 'rigorous meaning to what Max Weber designated with the term charisma . . . and an equivalent to what the Durkheim school called *mana*' (Bourdieu 1998c: 102). Symbolic capital operates 'like a veritable magical power: a property which . . . exercises a sort of action from a distance, without physical contact' (1998c: 102). Subjects, groups, institutions and names that have acquired symbolic capital are usually associated, in a particularly profound and intense manner, with the verities, capitalized ideas and sacred discourses and values of the field, a process that is often derived from historical continuity. In the English-speaking academic field, the venerable institutions of Cambridge and Oxford University are cases in point. If subjects commit to a field by accepting that its perspectives, conventions, work and practices are 'worth the candle'—that is, worth the investment of time and energy—then the holders of symbolic capital are the 'keepers of the flame' of the candle in question; accordingly, institutions such as Cambridge and Oxford stand in, both at a popular level and within academe, for the field and its core values (the disinterested pursuit and production of knowledge, scholastic autonomy and the separation of the scholarly world from the capitalist market). This requires an intensive and continuous performance, at a micro level, of their status as sequestered and even magical spaces, an effect delivered by and through, and manifested in, their medieval architecture with its spires and towers, robes and processions, stylishly languid student body, anachronistic and archaic conventions and rituals, and celebrated and long-observed sporting contests (the boat race, the cricket match). These 'primary texts', in turn, are rewritten as secondary and tertiary texts, in the form of television series (*Morse*, *Lewis*) and films and novels that reinscribe, disseminate and help to naturalize to a wide popular audience the association of those universities with symbolic capital.

Cambridge and Oxford do not constitute the academic field, even in the limited context of English tertiary education; however, they do stand in for and exemplify, at an almost universal level in the English-speaking academic world, what the field should be and to what it should aspire. In this sense, cultural capital is recognized as symbolic capital, which in turn engenders more capital for itself by setting the standard of what constitutes the appropriate performatives and indicators of a genuine university. The contestation and valorization of forms and exchange rates of capital within the academic field will thus be subject to the symbolic capital wielded by Cambridge and Oxford, and even if and when the logics and evaluative regimes of the field are challenged and gradually reformulated (for instance, by government funding policies that dispose lesser universities to run themselves 'as businesses'), this will not impinge on or apply to universities with symbolic capital. This process by which capital begets capital leads to a deepening of the division between those universities that can afford to be 'true to the field' and those that cannot. This is played out in a variety of ways, but it is particularly marked by different kinds of discursive performances and relations with regard to the potential student population: universities without symbolic capital are required to promote themselves and their qualities to a range of demographics, whereas Cambridge and Oxford can presume universal recognition of their name and value, and the quality of their applicants.

The range and force of the power of holders of symbolic capital extends beyond their immediate field: Bourdieu (1990c: 119) points out that, 'Symbolic capital is valid even in the market', and it is also usually recognized across, and functions as capital within, the wider social field. To be recognized and valued within the social field is both dependent upon but also slightly separated from position and place within a specific cultural field. Symbolic capital is exchangeable for social capital partly because a position of pre-eminence within a field more or less automatically creates and extends the set of networks and relationships within which a subject or institution is located. Social capital, for Bourdieu, is largely predicated on the production and maintenance of social connections and networks. He defines it (1986: 246) as

> the aggregate of the actual or potential resources which are linked to possession of a durable network of more or less institutionalized relationships of mutual acquaintance and recognition—or in other words to membership of a group—which provides each of its members with the backing of the collectively owned capital, a 'credential' which entitles them to credit, in the various senses of the word. These relationships may exist only in the practical state, in material and/or symbolic exchanges which help to maintain them. They may also be socially instituted and guaranteed by the application of a common name (the name of a family, a class, or a tribe or of a school, a party, etc.) and by a whole set of instituting acts designed simultaneously to form and inform those who undergo them; in this case, they are more or less really enacted and so maintained and reinforced, in exchanges.

Material and symbolic exchanges, reinforced over time, constitute the glue that binds social networks together: to offer a birthday or Christmas gift, supply information, provide an introduction to a club or society, or even to pick up the bill for a round of drinks or a meal is to introduce a sense of the 'between us' that can gradually move from individual to group associations and social networks. These networks are constituted by and through 'indissolubly material and symbolic exchanges, the establishment and maintenance of which pre-suppose reacknowledgement of proximity' (Bourdieu 1986: 246). The question of what is understood or implied by 'proximity' here is complex. While social networks are 'partially irreducible to objective relations of proximity in physical (geographical) space or even in economic and social space' (1986: 246), at the same time it follows that, just as social classes are more likely to be successfully interpellated if the demographics being targeted occupy similar positions in the social field, and share versions of the same habitus, social networks are to some extent dependent, and are built, on a commensurability of socio-cultural trajectories. The graduates of universities with symbolic capital, for instance, will not only be identified as valuable by, and be invited into, social networks (a case of capital attracting capital); they also have a high chance of integrating easily and naturally into social networks characterized by high levels of capital.

In *An Invitation to Reflexive Sociology*, Bourdieu and Wacquant (1992: 114–15) argue that one of the functions of the field of power, and in particular of the state, is to

> wield power over the different fields and over the various forms of capital that circulate in them. This kind of meta-capital capable of exercising a power over the species of power, and particularly over their rate of exchange ... defines the specific power of the state. It follows that the construction of the state goes hand in hand with the constitution of the field of power understood as the space of play in which holders of various forms of capital struggle in particular for power over the state, that is, over the statist capital that grants power over the different species of capital and over their reproduction.

Bourdieu (2014) suggests, however, that since the 1980s the state—at least in the West—has to some extent both formally and informally ceded ('outsourced') some of its roles and functions to global capitalism. The widespread deregulation of the field of cultural production, the privatization of government utilities and services, the introduction of 'user pays' policies for various public services (education, health, law) and the retreat from governmental commitments to public service culture means that sections of the field of cultural production, along with other relatively autonomous fields such as academe, science and the field of sport, are increasingly operating under two conflicting regimes of value: one formal and discursively recognized; the other disguised or euphemized, and usually implicit. Bourdieu addresses this issue with regard to the field of science in *Science of Science and Reflexivity* (2004). He argues that the modification and even transformation of culture and practices within the scientific field are a consequence of threats to, and the undermining of, the explicit evaluative regime that designates what is capital and how, when and for what it can be exchanged within the field. This issue is further complicated, first, by its connection with the character and orientation of the field-as-ethos (articulated in discourse such as 'knowledge for knowledge's sake', 'objectivity', 'disinterestedness' and 'theoretical research'); second, as a consequence of the imbrication of the scientific ethos, capital and methodology; and third, because the field-as-habitus disposes its members to take a position of critical reflexivity with regard to the work, knowledge, theories and methodologies of the field. What comes to be constituted as knowledge attracts cultural capital, but for research to be recognized as and attain the status of knowledge, it requires an undisputed adherence on the part of all the members involved to a variety of field-specific performances and procedures, including the justification of methodological frames, the careful recording and checking of experimental results and the vetting of the results, arguments and conclusions by and through a process of peer review. In other words, the scientific regime of cultural capital is, at least theoretically, entirely commensurate with the discourses and accounts that the field uses to characterize itself. However, once other regimes of capital are established and begin to inform, contextualize and orient practices, science starts to become something other than itself:

> There is every reason to think that the pressures of the economy are growing more intense with each day that passes,

especially in areas where the products of research are highly profitable, such as medicine, bio-technology (in agriculture in particular) and, more generally, genetics—not to mention military research. Many research scientists or research teams are falling under the control of large industrial companies seeking to secure a monopoly on commercially very profitable products, through patents; and the boundary, which has long been blurred, between fundamental research, in university laboratories, and applied research, is tending to disappear completely. Disinterested scientists, who have no programme other than the one that springs from the logic of their research and who know how to make the strict minimum of concessions to 'commercial' demands to secure the funding they need for their work, risk being gradually marginalized, in some areas at least . . . in favour of vast quasi-industrial teams working to satisfy demands subordinated to the imperatives of profit. (Bourdieu 2004: viii)

This often takes the form of competition for economic capital provided by or derived from sources that have no interest in and don't recognize the necessary relationship between the field and its methodologies-as-ethos and knowledge. This situation provides a challenge to, and can exert a potentially profound reorientation of, the scientific habitus-as-field and concomitant set of practices:

Industry and research are now so closely intertwined that not a day passes without new cases of conflict between researchers and commercial interests (for example, at the end of last year, a Californian company well known for producing a vaccine for increasing defences against the AIDS virus tried to prevent publication of a scholarly paper showing that the vaccine was not effective). There is reason to fear that the logic of competition, which, as we have seen in other times in the field of physics, can lead the purest of researchers to forget the economic, political or social uses that may be made of the products of their work, will combine and conjugate with more or less constrained or willing submission to the interests of firms to let whole areas of research drift little by little in the direction of heteronomy. (Bourdieu 2004: viii)

Conclusion

The examples we have considered in the field of cultural production, the academic field and the social field demonstrate how regimes of capital are caught between the internal dynamics of the field-as-habitus and the extent to which a field is susceptible to the influence of the field of power—in particular, the state, capitalism and the commercial media. For Bourdieu, the operations of power are not carried out within, or manifested in terms of, the conventional regimes of political economy, such as the ownership of the means of production. Nor are they explicable in terms of the Marxist notion of ideology, which largely subordinates the socio-cultural play of class-inflected discourses, meanings, narratives and genres to a secondary role in the class struggle, to the extent where it operates as a reflection (and to some extent a discursive justification) of the real political struggles carried out at the level of political economy. Bourdieu rejects the position, adopted by both Marxism and capitalist-inflected economic theory, whereby economic analysis of the forms of exchange, the regimes of value, the politics of economic relations and the distribution of resources only recognizes and refers to a specific form of capital and its concomitant economic discourses, categories and genres. He argues (1986: 242) that 'a science of mercantile relationships which ... takes for granted the very foundation of the order it claims to analyze ... private property, profit, wage labor' has foreclosed the possibility of a 'general science of the economy of practices, which would treat mercantile exchange as a particular case of exchange in all its forms'. In the next chapter, we will provide an account of Bourdieu's development of a theory of capital-as-symbolic power, which he uses to explain how the dominant class is able to naturalize and sustain its position by and through a (non-economic) dissimulation of the operations of power.

8
Symbolic power

Introduction

The earliest systematic analysis of symbolic power was carried out in Bourdieu's sociology of education period, but he also produced a number of case studies that described and analysed how the mechanisms of symbolic power played out with regard to the acquisition of cultural capital—*Distinction* (1989), *The State Nobility* (1996)—language—*Language and Symbolic Power* (2005b)—the state—the 1989–92 Collège de France lecture series collected together and published as *On the State* (2014)—gender—*Masculine Domination* (2001)—race, class and ethnicity—*The Weight of the World* (1999)—the media—*On Television and Journalism* (1998b)—politics—*Acts of Resistance* (1998a)—and economics—*The Social Structures of the Economy* (2005c). One aspect of Bourdieu's theory of symbolic violence that underwent refinement after the publication of *Distinction* was his understanding and development of the process of class formation.

In *Distinction*, class is understood not in the Marxist sense of a substantive demographic predicated on its relation to ownership of the means of production, but as a set of relations and positions within and across socio-cultural space, determined by and predicated upon a shared habitus and set of dispositions, forms of socio-cultural literacy and, by extension, levels and kinds of capital. In texts such as *In Other Words* (1990b), *Language and Symbolic Power* (2005b) and *Practical Reason* (1998c), Bourdieu provides a more refined and developed account of this relation-as-process: he argues that the shared dispositions and perspectives of the habitus constitute the basis for social proximities that are accessible and available to interpellation, most obviously from parties and institutions within the political field, but more generally and whenever it is in the interest of a group or organization to associate itself with, take it upon itself to speak for or mobilize in some way (demonstrations, voting, forms of cultural consumption) a group-as-class. Bourdieu (1990b: 75) writes:

> The theoretical classes drawn up by sociological science to explain modes of practice are ... not always concretely constituted classes. In both cases, we are dealing only with what appear to be groups on paper ... In short, groups ... are things you have to keep going at the cost of a permanent effort of maintenance ... And the same applies to classes, when they exist, even in a tenuous state ... belonging to a group is something you build up ... and play for ... Class is never something immanent; it is also will and representations, but it has no chance of incarnating itself in things unless it brings closer that which is objectively close and distances what is objectively distant.

The main studies in which Bourdieu develops and refines his theory of symbolic power are *Distinction* (1989), *Language and Symbolic Power* (2005b), *Masculine Domination* (2001) and *On the State* (2014). The first three of these have been dealt with, and their theoretical contributions and significance explained, in earlier chapters. *On the*

State constitutes Bourdieu's most thorough, detailed and theoretically sophisticated account of the roles and functions taken on by the state, and of the processes and mechanisms whereby it came to acquire a monopoly not just over physical forms of violence (the police, the army), but over many forms and procedures of socio-cultural naming, categorization and articulation. Bourdieu argues that the state has become, if not exactly synonymous or co-substantive with regard to the field of power, then its most significant and powerful component. Its relation to and place within his theory of symbolic power is tied partly to the influence it exerts on exchange rates between different forms of capital, and its role in constituting, authorizing and conventionalizing the procedures, genres and processes that characterize both the public and private spheres of communication. For Bourdieu, the state has effected a kind of self-apotheosis whereby its history as an arbitrary and self-interested player in the field of power has been transformed into an ontotheology: like God, the state is—and in the mind of most of its members has always been—everywhere.

One aspect of symbolic power that Bourdieu emphasizes across his work is the role played by the dominated in the process of their domination. The complicity of dominated groups in the maintenance, to their own detriment, of regimes of power is a central part of Bourdieu's explanation of socio-cultural reproduction in his sociology of education texts, and in his theorizing of class and the process of class formation in *Distinction* and *The State Nobility*. However, from his early work on gender and symbolic violence—for example, in *The Inheritors* (Bourdieu & Passeron 1979b)—Bourdieu was both struck by and unable to account for the process whereby women could largely be excluded from access to networks of power, consistently denied the possibility of acquiring the kind of educational capital open to men and systematically delimited in terms of their social and professional roles, functions and responsibilities. The sheer scope and historical continuity of the condition of masculine domination required a rethinking of compliance not as a dimension, but rather as a necessary and central component, of the operations of power. In the

Introduction to *Masculine Domination* Bourdieu (2001: 1–2) writes, 'I would probably not have embarked on such a difficult subject' had not he been compelled to do so

> by the whole logic of my research. I have always been astonished by what might be called the *paradox of doxa*—the fact that the order of the world as we find it, with its one-way streets and its no-entry signs, whether literal or figurative, its obligations and its penalties, is broadly respected; that there are not more transgressions and subversions, contraventions and 'follies' (just think of the extraordinary concordance of thousands of dispositions—or wills—implied in five minutes' movement of traffic around the Place de la Bastille or Place de la Concorde...); or, still more surprisingly, that the established order, with its relations of domination, its rights and prerogatives, privileges and injustices, ultimately perpetuates itself so easily, apart from a few historical accidents, and that the most intolerable conditions of existence can so often be perceived as acceptable and even natural. And I have also seen masculine domination, and the way it is imposed and suffered as the prime example of this paradoxical submission, an effect of what I call symbolic violence, a gentle violence, imperceptible and invisible even to its victims, exerted for the most part through the purely symbolic channels of communication and cognition (more precisely, misrecognition), recognition, or even feeling.

In the final stage of his career, Bourdieu didn't so much refine or develop his theory of symbolic power as provide it with a different point of focus: specifically, the situation in which the potential production and dissemination of oppositional and alternative accounts of contemporary cultural politics, emanating from the autonomous pole of the field of cultural production, was increasingly subject to intervention, interruption, displacement, scrutiny and censorship by way of both the activities and policies of the state and its apparatuses, and as a consequence of the colonization of important sub-fields (such as journalism) by global capitalism and its institutions, technologies, discourses, logics and imperatives. In a sense, Bourdieu's work on symbolic violence turns full circle: the kind of analysis he undertook with regard to the perpetration and euphemizing of state and capitalist symbolic violence in Algeria and Béarn is carried out, in later texts such as *Masculine Domination* (2001) and *The Weight of the World* (1999), by way of a much more extensive, developed and refined theoretical apparatus.

Symbolic power

Bourdieu (1978) argues that societies and cultures that pre-date the advent of capitalism were characterized predominantly by a system of symbolic exchange whereby access to power, forms of dependence and affiliation, hierarchical structures, and socio-cultural relations and obligations were determined by, played out within and explicable in terms of a regime of reciprocity that was largely unacknowledged and misrecognized. This symbolic system functioned to allocate and differentiate subjects in time and space, and to organize the set of relations that bound them together: it was simultaneously a generalized natural order, 'the way of the world', and the specific social fabric that constituted the 'between us' of the community. The need to maintain the fiction that the symbolic order was predominantly non-tendentious—a manifestation of nature-as-society—meant that it usually articulated itself 'in other words'—that is, in orders of discourse that called upon some external authority (religion, tradition, mythology as history) as the origin of or point of departure for, and as constitutive of, social conventions, hierarchies and relations of power. An example of how symbolic regimes foreclose their economic status can be seen in Bourdieu's story, taken from his work in Kabylia (Bourdieu 1978), of the decision taken by a mason to ask that his work be remunerated financially. Under normal circumstances, his time and labour would be subsumed in socio-cultural and familial conventions—for instance, in the provision of food by the recipient of the mason's time and work—and confirmed as a gift. By asking for money, the mason lays bare the economic dimension that underlies gift exchange, and in the process scandalizes the community by articulating what is necessarily suppressed if the system is to be maintained. As Bourdieu writes, apropos of the transformation of Kabylia society through the introduction of market capitalism, 'the generalization of monetary exchange, which exposes the objective workings of the economy, also brings to light the institutional mechanisms . . . which have the function of limiting and disguising the play of economic interests and calculations' (1978: 172).

A gift usually takes a generic and discursive form and status that is not reducible to the logic of the commodity or of exchange. When a gift is given, it is—at least theoretically—not put into circulation with the intention of producing a profit, constituting an obligation or initiating a relationship of reciprocity: in other words, it is a socio-cultural practice with no economic aspect or dimension. At the level of genre, the gift can either be followed or simultaneously accompanied by a gift returning in the opposite direction, which serves to cancel out any potential economic dimension, but it can also be accepted without return, which more or less performs the same function. Theoretically, a gift is discursively timeless: it is never marked as an asset to be realized down the track, nor can it be seen or said to arise out of a history of obligation or exchange. However, in actuality, every gift remains inscribed in time and has a history, which means that an apparently non-economic practice can set in train a series of ostensibly random practices that can function as a form of unspoken and unacknowledged general economy. Bourdieu argues that the fiction of a non-economic dimension to gift culture is exposed when such activities are contextualized, and by extension recognized, within and over time: an action can appear to have no reciprocal aspect until it is integrated into a wider socio-cultural pattern and chronology. The bestowing of gifts is an action that is always oriented towards the future, but done without any specific or recognizable performance of calculation; instead, the offering and acceptance of the gift produce a sense of the 'between us', which translates, at some place and time, as an implicit obligation.

Bourdieu insists that the defining characteristic of systems of symbolic exchange is that everything is potentially meaningful even, or perhaps most particularly, when nothing appears to be at stake and no discernible profit is accrued. The example *par excellence* is that of potlatch: for Bourdieu's French sociological predecessor Marcel Mauss (1967), the systematic destruction, wastage or giving away of material goods on a large scale is the opposite of play. Whereas play brings no benefit to the person involved, the point about potlatch is that it potentially accrues benefit by demonstrating that the person sacrificing goods has no need of them; the message and meaning of potlatch is that 'while others have to be careful about their expenditure, I don't'. As Bourdieu (1978: 194) writes, potlatch

> might seem to suspend the universal law of interest . . . whereby nothing is ever given for nothing . . . But in reality such denials of interest are never more than practical disclaimers . . . they satisfy interest in a (disinterested) manner designed to show that they are not satisfying interest.

Symbolic power, for Bourdieu, can be understood as the mechanism through which a symbolic system disguises, reinforces, sustains and naturalizes established orders and relations of economic capital, networks of power and, by extension, regimes of socio-cultural, political and economic domination. The most notable feature of symbolic power is the inverse relation between the amount of work it does and the extent to which it is recognized in relation to that work. On the one hand, it informs each and every practice and act of communication, is central to the ways in which cultural fields are organized, is the most significant factor in the formation of subjects and categories of socio-cultural identity, and is responsible for, and facilitates and authorizes, most forms of violence—both non-physical and otherwise. On the other hand, despite or perhaps because it operates at an everyday micro level, and is experienced by and through the habitus, it is not recognized for what it is—it is misrecognized as the way of the world, the natural order of things, human nature or, most ironically, the condition of freedom. As John Thompson (2005: 23) writes in his Introduction to *Language and Symbolic Power*:

> Bourdieu uses the term 'symbolic power' to refer to ... forms of power as they are routinely deployed in social life. For in ... day-to-day life, power is seldom exercised as overt physical force: instead, it is transmuted into a symbolic form, and thereby endowed with a kind of legitimacy that it would not otherwise have ... symbolic power is an 'invisible' power which is 'misrecognized' as such and thereby 'recognized' as legitimate.

For Bourdieu, symbolic power is exercised predominantly by and through the valorization, acquisition, evaluation and exchange of cultural capital, which reflects and perpetuates socio-cultural hierarchies and helps to determine the allocation of positions in socio-cultural space. Symbolic power is more or less continuous with regard to what Bourdieu calls symbolic capital, which he characterizes as a form of meta-capital that equates to cultural capital recognized as such and, by extension, a form of status that helps establish and determine regimes of capital within cultural fields. The example Bourdieu often cites as exemplary in this regard is the state (Bourdieu 2014), which in its modern incarnation has attained a monopoly over the exercising of violence in a polity, and determines everything from the ways in which countries, cities, towns and suburbs are organized into discrete units, to the definition and differentiation of night and day, trading and working hours, holidays and the ages at which people can leave school, vote and legally have sexual relations. To capture the extent of the state's domination over the everyday epistemological categories and mechanisms used by subjects to negotiate and make sense of the world, Bourdieu refers to the example of anarchists who, while discursively and politically opposed to systems of power, reset their watch to account for the introduction of daylight saving (Bourdieu 2014); we can extend this to include their use of toilet facilities that bear the name of the gender category to which they were assigned at birth, or their observation of 'No Smoking' signs in cafes, on public transport and other public places. Bourdieu points out that the state has infiltrated, and exercises control or influence over, every aspect of contemporary life—both personal and professional—in a manner that exceeds what might be expected from the most rigorous and unrelenting theocratic regime. State apparatuses and institutions produce authorized discourses, which effectively bring into existence what they purport to describe, such as gender and age categories, definitions of illegal acts, chronologies and geographical boundaries.

The symbolic capital accrued by the state and by certain cultural fields (law, science, business) and religious, educational, political, media, military and cultural institutions, is both historically contingent and a consequence of struggles played out within the field of power. The acquisition of symbolic capital helps groups and institutions to make the world over in their own image: the example we used in the previous chapter of the idea of Oxbridge determining, to a large extent, how the English-speaking academic field articulates itself and the forms of capital that it valorizes is a case in point. At the same time, forms of capital—symbolic and otherwise—and by extension the ability to impose evaluative regimes, disseminate discourses and interpellate socio-cultural groups (citizens, taxpayers, Americans), is always both the stake in and constitutive of the game that is the field of power. For a political party, pressure group or movement to win out in the struggle over symbolic capital, it must be in a position to appeal to a significant sector of the population who occupy similar positions to each other in the social field, more or less share a habitus and have similar responses to socio-economic issues (the loss of jobs, an inability to afford to buy or rent a house, a polluted local environment):

> To change the world, one has to change the ways of making the world, that is, the vision of the world and the practical operations by which groups are produced and reproduced. Symbolic power, whose most exemplary form is seen in the power to produce groups ... is based on two conditions. Firstly, like every form of performative discourse, symbolic power has to be based on the possession of symbolic capital ... Symbolic capital is a credit, it is the power granted to those who have obtained sufficient recognition to be in a position to impose recognition: in this way, the power of constitution, a power of making a new group ... can be obtained only at the end of a long process of institutionalization ... Secondly, symbolic effectiveness depends on the degree to which the vision proposed is based on reality. Evidently, the construction of a group ... has all the more chance of succeeding the more it is founded on reality: that is ... in the objective affinities between people who have to be brought together. (Bourdieu 1990b: 138)

Bourdieu refers to the effects of the deployment and utilization of symbolic power to effect and maintain socio-cultural (and by extension, political and economic) domination as forms of symbolic violence. Bourdieu's theory of symbolic power informs all his immediate post-Algerian work, including *Outline of a Theory of Practice* (1978), his sociology of education work and, at a particular level of socio-cultural detail, his studies of peasant society in his native Béarn. In the work collected together in the book *The Bachelors' Ball* (2008a), Bourdieu studies the ways in which a newly introduced social formation, resulting from wider economic trends and their concomitant policy regimes, produced localized 'situations' and contexts which effectively marginalized or rendered redundant a considerable number of the population. He shows how under the statist 'colonization' of the Béarnaise peasantry, all were 'divided against themselves' (Bourdieu & Wacquant 1992: 165–6): the imposition and integration of imperatives of market capitalism effectively destabilized social networks, conventions and relationships, and substituted a regime of competition and economic logic for a more generalized market (in this case, with regard to the acquisition of brides by bachelors). As Bourdieu explains in *An Invitation to Reflexive Sociology*:

> I tried to rethink this case as a particular case of a general theory ... of symbolic violence ... the ball is a concrete incarnation of a matrimonial market ... What I had seen was the matrimonial market in a practical state, the locus of the new, emerging form of exchange, the concrete realization of the 'open market' which had only a few years before replaced the protected market of the past ... here I could cite Polanyi. The bachelors who stood like so many wallflowers around the dance floor were the victims of the replacement of a closed market by an open market where everyone must manage on his own and can count only on his assets, on his own symbolic capital ... This transition from a protected matrimonial regime to a matrimonial regime of 'free exchange' has made victims, and these victims are not randomly distributed. (Bourdieu & Wacquant 1992: 164–5)

Bourdieu is referring to the actualities and scope of the violence carried out by way of state policies that doubtlessly were discursively represented as the modernization and development of a backward region, and that further involved its integration, at the national and global levels, into what were presented, characterized and euphemized as more effective and efficient forms of social, cultural and above all economic organization. The socio-cultural institution of the bachelors' ball functions as a 'concrete and visible realization of the market in symbolic goods, which, as it became unified at the national level ... had thrust a sudden, brutal devaluation on those who were bound up with the protected market of the old-style matrimonial exchanges' (Bourdieu 2008a: 4). As Bourdieu observes: 'France has eliminated a large chunk of its peasantry in the space of three decades without any state violence ... In other words, under definite conditions and at a definite cost, symbolic violence can do what political violence can do, but more efficiently' (Bourdieu & Wacquant 1992: 166).

A second, and more generalized, form of the imposition of symbolic power-as-violence with which Bourdieu deals around this time was the role that the education system, and more specifically curricula and forms of pedagogic action, played out in the reproduction of regimes of cultural capital, by and through which dominant groups maintained and naturalized their domination. We have covered Bourdieu's sociology of education work, and his formulation of the concept of cultural capital as a mechanism of symbolic power, in detail in a previous chapter. Here it is useful to add that, taken together, the two concepts provide a convincing and consistent technical account of how power-as-symbolic system produces and sustains at levels of subjectivity and socio-cultural identity and practices, and more specifically in terms of class, gender, ethnicity and language use, a situation whereby dominated groups recognize, accept, resign themselves to and are complicit in their own domination.

Bourdieu's educational work, along with his later work on class and cultural consumption (1989), gender (2001) and ethnicity (1999), is particularly useful for demonstrating how the compliance of dominated groups is tied in with the forms in which symbolic violence is enacted. In order to ensure that systems and acts of symbolic violence are accepted and misrecognized as just, inevitable or natural, they usually are produced through highly conventionalized and formalized procedures and discursive performances. Bourdieu (2005b) cites and makes use of Austin's (1975) theory of language performativity to analyse the relation between communication practices and the valorization and accumulation of cultural capital, and how linguistic and socio-cultural performances require either a tacit or formal manifestation of authority if they are to be accepted as felicitous. The theoretical weight of this analysis is to be found in a lengthy, worked-through and detailed critique that Bourdieu directs towards Austin's theorizing of language use and conventions, specifically with regard to Austin's failure to recognize the theoretical and socio-political implications of language being authorized 'from the outside' (Bourdieu & Wacquant 1992: 147).

The felicity of a speech act is partly predicated on the performance of appropriate cultural literacy: to launch a ship or a book, the person performing the act needs to be literate in the sense that they are familiar with the discursive and other meaning systems relevant to the occasion, and that they understand the requirements of the task (tone of voice, pace of speaking, forms of address, background and contextual information, knowledge of procedures and protocols). However, in order for the performance to be truly felicitous, the person also requires some marker of authority or valorization (anything from a bureaucratic or governmental identity to the possession of a literary name and a mandate from the publisher or author of the book). Symbolic acts always require both the form (an adherence to established generic procedures, the right kind of manner) and the substance (a government identity card, the uniform that attests to the person's *bona fides*, or an invitation from the ship's owners to launch the ship) in order for a speech act to be accepted and effected.

This is also true of acts of symbolic violence carried out by the state and its apparatuses: when a judge pronounces the accused guilty and imposes a punishment, the same kinds of procedures and performances of authority are enacted, regardless of the severity of the sentence (a prison term, a fine, the death penalty). The symbols of office (the wig, the gown), the bodily hexis (the slow, dignified walk, the featureless expression) and the forms of 'between us' (the court rises when the judge enters and departs, the judge determines who speaks and when) all attest to a performance 'without regard to' (personal connections, class affiliations, racial or ethnic identity, wealth) on the part of both the judge and the legal system more generally. Like the state, the legal system can only carry out its sanctioned violence by dissociating itself from its history, network of connections, exclusive character of membership and vested interest in maintaining its own privileges, and it does this by way of an adherence to a discursive regime that 'speaks for itself'. As Bourdieu (1990b: 84–5) writes, 'form, formalization and formalism do not merely act through their specific and properly technical effectiveness of clarification and rationalization'. Also necessary is

> a properly symbolic effectiveness of form. Symbolic violence, of which the realization *par excellence* is probably law, is a violence exercised . . . in formal terms, and paying due respect to form. Paying due respect to form means giving an action or a discourse the form which is recognized as suitable, legitimate, approved . . . a form of a kind that allows the open production, in public view, of a wish or a practice that, if presented in any other way, would be unacceptable . . . this is the function of the euphemism . . . The force of this form . . . allows force to be fully exercised while disguising its true nature as force and gaining recognition, approval and acceptance by dint of the fact that it can present itself under the appearance of universality.

Bourdieu's citation and use of Austin's theory of language performativity is accompanied by the caveat that speech act theory never follows through and inquires about how the magic of socio-cultural valorization, which turns pointless and empty utterances into felicitous symbolic acts, is tied into a socio-cultural politics whereby symbolic power and capital discursively make over and maintain the world in their own image. Starting from the position that language use is always informed by cultural politics, Bourdieu sets this against the tendency of linguistic theory 'to neglect the social-historical conditions underlying the formation of the language which they take, in an idealized form, as their object domain' (Thompson 2005: 7); from here, he directs his attention to what is at stake—both theoretically and in terms of a wider cultural politics—in the playing out of this tendency across the work of Saussure, Chomsky and Austin. As Thompson (2005: 7) writes, for Bourdieu the 'practical sense' that informs every speech utterance 'cannot be derived from or reduced to the competence of Chomsky's ideal speaker'. Moreover, the notion of 'practical competence' ignores the contextual and political issue that 'the capacity to produce grammatical utterances' is linked to 'the capacity to make oneself heard, believed, obeyed' (2005: 7–8). Bourdieu argues that Austin does not follow through on the implications that the conditions of felicity are primarily social conditions,

> hence there is a tendency in the literature on speech acts to resort to analyses of a purely linguistic ... kind ... Austin refers, rather vaguely, to 'conventional procedures' which must be followed for the felicitous utterance of a performative ... But never does Austin examine in detail the nature of these conventions ... never does he consider carefully what it might mean to treat these conventions as social phenomena, implicated in sets of social relations, imbued with power and authority, embroiled in conflict and struggle. (Thompson 2005: 9)

There are two main questions that need to be posed here. First, to what extent is the hard and fast distinction that Bourdieu and Austin make between authorized and unauthorized performances necessarily valid? Second, and by implication, is the separation that they presume between discursive utterances and institutionalized authority theoretically sustainable? With regard to the relation between authorization, social magic and the felicity of speech acts, we can point to the example we referred to in an earlier paragraph of 'the uniform that attests to the person's *bona fides*' as an indication that the symbols, markers and signs of authority (a uniform, bodily hexis, a historical text) are basically discursive performances valorized by other discursive performances. In the classic 1960s Hong Kong film version of the Chinese folk tale *The Butterfly Lovers*, which involves a young upper class woman disguising herself as a man in order to receive a scholarly education, the impersonation succeeds because the woman is much more of a culturally literate, confident and convincing man than any of her fellow (male) students.

The possibility of her being anything other than a man is effectively foreclosed precisely because of the ideological naturalization, internalized by both men and women, of attribute-as-substance; in other words, her culturally literate performance ensures that her physiology is misrecognized. In a sense, the denouement of the story, in which the heroine steps out of her impersonation to demonstrate that her qualities are not gender specific, and is subsequently returned to her proper place (that is, exchanged in marriage to facilitate her family's socio-cultural connections) by masculine power, constitutes both a critique and a validation of Bourdieu's position—and, by extension, Butler's (1999) argument. In the film, power speaks when it is spoken to—that is, the public articulation of a disjunction between socio-cultural doxa and reality attracts a response that invalidates that original articulation as infelicitous. At the same time, it is made clear that authority rests on performativity, and each and every performance is potentially available for impersonation. As Butler (1999) argues, the institutions that guarantee or sign off on speech acts are themselves constituted by and through a set of discursive performances that, while more or less self-valorizing, are not beyond challenge or appropriation.

Conclusion

In her critical analysis of Bourdieu's use of Austin (1975), Judith Butler (1999: 23) extends his consideration of the relation between symbolic power, performativity and the felicity or otherwise of speech acts by asking whether a speech act 'must compel collective recognition in order to work', and whether 'the misappropriation or expropriation of the performative might not be the very occasion for the exposure of prevailing forms of authority and the exclusions by which they proceed?' (1999: 123–4). Butler counters Bourdieu's theory of the relation between subjects, the habitus and the spatial/temporal configuration of cultural fields by arguing that cultural literacies engender practices simultaneously congruent with, but never reducible to, the discursive regimes of symbolic power. Using this opposition as a departure point, in our final chapter we will provide an account of Bourdieu's theories of the relationship between the habitus, symbolic power and cultural literacy, and consider how the logics and imperatives of the habitus inform and dispose cultural practices.

9

The logic of practice

Introduction

For Bourdieu, the extent to which a subject can mediate and negotiate the world is predicated upon the relationship between the sociocultural trajectory that constitutes the habitus and the cultural field in which the subject is situated: the conjunction of these two factors is constitutive of what he refers to as the logic of practice. Just as the habitus is history misrecognized as nature, so too the logic of practice is produced by and largely congruent with regard to the epistemological and evaluative categories derived from the habitus and immersion in a cultural field.

Bourdieu identifies two main forms of the logic of practice, which he designates as practical and reflexive knowledge. We can characterize practical knowledge as a 'feel for the game'—that is, as an ability to simultaneously and more or less non-reflexively comprehend and negotiate the rules, discourses, imperatives, regimes of value and contexts of both specific cultural fields and the socio-cultural field in general. Reflexivity, on the other hand, is manifested in the form of an interrogation of the habitus set in train by the dispositions of the habitus and the imperatives of the relevant cultural field.

The theoretical techniques and concepts Bourdieu develops and utilizes in his analysis of the imbrication of practice, culture and context provide an often empirically-driven counter to the tendency, often associated with but not confined to cultural studies, for theorists to under-estimate the extent to which a subject's practices are derived from a set of dispositions, acquired and naturalized across their socio-cultural trajectory and thus tend to be reproductive of the field. These techniques and concepts also help to identify, explain and demonstrate the processes and conditions that allow for the possibility of what we can call non-reproductive practices—practices that are both commensurate with the habitus and the logics of a cultural field, while simultaneously creatively negotiating across and among, and sometimes contrary to, the rules and imperatives of that field. Bourdieu argues that while practical logic does not operate outside the socio-cultural conditions and contexts out of which the habitus is constituted and deployed, there is nothing deterministic about this contention. He insists that the 'Habitus is not the fate that some people read into it . . . Being the product of history, it is an open system of dispositions that is constantly subjected to experience . . . It is durable but not eternal' (Bourdieu & Wacquant 1992: 133).

Bourdieu (1978) argues that theories of practice are disposed to abstract their objects of study: this is because the cultural frameworks that are employed to describe, identify, categorize, evaluate, and more generally see and read the relation between practices and contexts are derived from places and perspectives (the academy, science, anthropology, ethnology) that are removed from any specific time and place. In Bourdieu's terms, the production of supposedly objective knowledge is characterized by a tendency, associated with the scholarly habitus, to overlook the need to objectify the process of objectification-as-abstraction:

> The knowing subject . . . inflicts on practice a much more fundamental and pernicious alteration which, being a constitutive condition of the cognitive operation, is bound to pass unnoticed: in taking up a point of view on the action, withdrawing from it in order to observe it from a distance, he constitutes practical activity as an object of observation and analysis, a representation. (1978: 2)

What distinguishes Bourdieu's approach from disciplines such as anthropology and ethnology is a research apparatus that is both reflexive (that is, committed to incorporating the presumptions and techniques of scholarship into the field of study) and oriented towards an understanding and analysis of practice as the product of a spatial and chronological continuum. The generative function of the habitus is the theoretical means by which Bourdieu plots a path between objectivist and subjectivist accounts of the logic of practice. He argues (1990b: 53) that practices are explicable neither with regard to the institutional and authorized logics, narratives and rules of a cultural field, nor in terms of any form of agency that allows the subject to step out of the world. Rather, the principles, values, perspectives and dispositions of the habitus-as-field

> generate and organize practices and representations that can be objectively adapted to their outcomes without presupposing a conscious aiming at ends or an express mastery of the operations necessary in order to attain them. Objectively 'regulated' and 'regular' without being in any way the product of obedience to rules, they can be collectively orchestrated without being the product of the organizing action of a conductor.

The discourses, orientations and values of the habitus are usually compliant with regard to the epistemological categories of the field, a conjuncture that is constitutive of a set of dispositions-as-practices misrecognised as normal and natural, while the 'most improbable practices are therefore excluded, as unthinkable, by a kind of immediate submission to order that inclines agents to make a virtue of necessity' (1990b: 54). Practices, and the negotiations, deliberations and option-taking that produce them, are misrecognized by subjects as congruent with the order of things (and thus in a sense, natural and inevitable), or as arising out of individual decision-making and agency (via a process of self-abstraction whereby the subject steps 'out of the world'). Both positions, however, are a consequence of processes of immersion in which the habitus and the subject-of-the-field imagine themselves into existence by way of the epistemological categories acquired across the course of their socio-cultural trajectory.

We have already pointed out that Bourdieu's Algerian research and experiences were crucial to the development of his major theoretical concepts: as Yacine (2013) observes, by the end of his Algerian period Bourdieu had formulated, at least in incipient forms, modes and mechanisms of thought that would develop into concepts such as habitus and cultural capital. However, an argument can be made that the aspect of Bourdieu's theoretical apparatus that is most clearly and closely derived from and indebted to his work in Algeria is that of reflexivity: 'The critical vigilance that I engaged in my later works originates from these first experiences of research situations where nothing is self-evident and everything is constantly called into question' (Bourdieu 2007: 51). This was a consequence of being drawn into a world marked by continuous physical and symbolic violence, which left Bourdieu without recourse to either the familiarity and ease afforded by everyday cultural literacy or the sense of distance, mastery and control—seeing and surveying from a 'bird's eye view'—characteristic of the habitus of the colonial anthropologist and ethnologist. In a section of *Sketch for a Self-Analysis* (2007), Bourdieu makes clear the extent of the irrelevance and impracticality of the rules of the academic game, and most particularly of the scholarly disposition, to matters at hand in Algeria. He was forced to conduct fieldwork in a situation where he was compelled 'to reflect on everything, to monitor everything, and in particular all that is taken for granted in the ordinary relation between the observer and the informant, the interviewer and the interviewee' (2007: 50).

In his writing on the influence of his Algerian work and experiences, for instance, what is emphasized is both the way in which certain things (physical violence, suspicion, the difficulty of identifying and confirming who is what) interrupt and problematize the smooth operation of the scholarly disposition, and how this situation, where every activity and decision seems to have a political dimension, calls into question the status of both the researcher and the research. It would be wrong to universalize or even generalize from this situation to that of the French academic field as it operated in Algeria: as Bourdieu (1990b: 70) makes clear, the disciplines of anthropology and ethnology continued to function without any major sense of concern or disquiet precisely because they were equipped with a particularly durable scholarly habitus that made a virtue and necessity of maintaining a distance from both their objects of study and their own research culture:

> There is something unhealthy about the way ethnology can exist as a separate science, and that we risk, through this division, accepting all that was written into the initial division out of which it came and which is perpetuated ... in its methods (for example, why should there be this resistance to statistics?) and especially in its modes of thought: for example, the rejection of ethnocentrism which prevents the ethnologist from relating what he observes to his own experience ... leads, behind the facade of respect, to the setting up of an unbridgeable distance ... And this can be just as much the case when one carries out the 'ethnology' of peasants or workers.

The situation in Algeria had the potential to inflect or engage a scholarly habitus either where there was already a disposition—for instance, derived tangentially or otherwise from Marxism—to think of research as having a political dimension, or alternatively where the status of the relation between the subject and the relevant academic context and habitus (in Bourdieu's case, involving the fields of philosophy, anthropology and ethnology) was incipient rather than fully formed. Both characterizations could be applied to Bourdieu's situation: while he was effectively committed to the academic field, how this commitment manifested itself at a disciplinary level was still being played out. It is apparent from Bourdieu's own writing (Bourdieu 2007) that his sense of being an outsider in the academic game—particularly when confronted by the distanced and distancing cultures of philosophy, anthropology and ethnology—was accentuated by his Algerian experiences.

The influence exerted by the more scientific, reflexive and historicizing work of Durkheim, Weber, Bachelard and Canguilhem, on the other hand, would have seemed entirely to the point. What they emphasized, in their different ways, was that epistemology was necessarily tied to, dependent upon and inflected by the theoretical and methodological apparatus in question, and they insisted that good scholarly practice should, in Bourdieu's terms, objectify the means of objectification. Applying this imperative to his Algerian research, where situations and socio-cultural realities, the link between rules and practices, and the strategic elements of cultural interactions all remained more or less opaque to the culturally illiterate outsider, was predominantly a practical rather than a theoretical or ethical consideration.

Bourdieu (1990b, 1998c, 2000) insists that the disposition to take a reflexive relation to the operation of research is both derived from the habitus and, by extension, oriented towards the accumulation of capital. The explanation that Bourdieu provides on this point, in *Practical Reason* (1998c: 132), could be applied to his theoretical, methodological and disciplinary trajectory in Algeria:

> The conversion in theoretical approach provoked by theoretical reflection on the theoretical point of view and on the practical point of view, and on their profound differences, is not purely

speculative: it is accompanied by a drastic change in the practical operations of research and by quite tangible scientific profits. For instance, one is led to pay attention to properties of ritual practice that structuralist logicism would tend to push aside . . . the ambiguities, the polysemic realities, underdetermined or indeterminate, not to speak of partial contradictions and fuzziness that pervades the whole system and accounts for its flexibility . . . in short everything that makes it 'practical'.

The complex of factors and dispositions that characterized the relationship between Bourdieu's research and the situation in Algeria (and later in Béarn) put him on a course that would culminate in 'reflexive sociology'. Bourdieu was, in Pascalian terms, 'launched' in Algeria (Bourdieu 2000). 'If there is a single feature that makes Bourdieu stand out in the landscape of contemporary social theory', writes Wacquant (in Bourdieu & Wacquant 1992: 36),

> it is his . . . obsession with reflexivity. From his early investigations of marriage practices in the isolated villages of the Pyrenees mountains where he was raised . . . to the hunt for the *Homo academicus gallicus* . . . the tribe he joined as a result of his upward social climb, Bourdieu has continually turned the instruments of his science upon himself.

This obsession was deliberately put into practice, and developed and refined, in 'test cases' where Bourdieu's affiliations and dispositions could be identified, monitored and evaluated in terms of the extent to which they informed his research (Bourdieu 2007). *The Logic of Practice* (1990c) is an important work in this regard: it provides a rigorous account of how the theoretical issues that feature in his transition from anthropologist and ethnologist to sociologist were being worked through. It looks back to and learns from his research in Algeria and Béarn, and more specifically the material collected in *Outline of a Theory of Practice* (1978), to both move beyond structuralism and, by extension, to develop a non-subjectivist account of the generative capacity of the habitus and the logic that underpinned and produced cultural practices. 'I was forced constantly,' he writes (1990c: 15),

> to question both the generic and the particular aspects of my relationship to the object . . . And it may be the objectification of the generic relationship of the observer to the observed which I endeavoured to perform, through a series of 'tests' that increasingly tended to become experiments, is the most significant product of my whole undertaking.

One of the features of Bourdieu's ongoing presentation of reflexivity is that, while it is associated with the sciences in general, at times it takes on a disciplinary-specific orientation. Bourdieu (1993b) suggests that sociology's peripheral and relatively minor status within the academy means it is more strongly disposed than more prestigious disciplines, such as philosophy, anthropology and psychology, to incorporate and accentuate reflexivity within the habitus. He contends that sociology constantly calls other sciences 'into question' (1993b: 8), and that consequently its own status is always subject to scrutiny:

> The more advanced a science is, the greater is the capital of knowledge accumulated within it and the greater the quantity of knowledge that subversive and critical strategies . . . need to mobilize in order to be effective. In physics, it is difficult to triumph over an adversary . . . by denouncing the political content of his theory. There, the weapons of criticism have to be scientific in order to be effective. In sociology, on the other hand, every proposition that contradicts received ideas is open to the suspicion of ideological bias . . . It clashes with social interests: the interests of the dominant groups, which are bound up with silence and 'common sense' . . . That is why sociology is asked to provide infinitely more proof . . . than is asked of the spokesmen of 'common sense' . . . and every discovery of

science triggers off an immense labour of conservative 'critique', which has the whole social order working for it . . . aimed at re-covering what has been dis-covered. (1993b: 11).

Sociological reflexivity is derived, then, from the double sense of its 'critical' identity: 'If sociology is a critical science', Bourdieu writes, 'that's perhaps because it is itself in a critical position' (1993b: 8). In this regard, sociology is opposed to the culture of the field of philosophy, where, 'Paradoxically, this critical and reflexive disposition is not at all self-evident', and which is led 'by the social definition of their function, and by the logic of competition with the social sciences, to refuse as something scandalous the historicization of their concepts or their theoretical inheritance' (Bourdieu 1990b: 16).

Bourdieu's understanding of reflexivity is re-examined and re-evaluated in his work on the socio-cultural roles, functions, status and value of the autonomous pole of the field of cultural production. The key element is Bourdieu's reappraisal of the notion of disinterestedness. In his sociology of education work, he argues that in scholarly culture disinterestedness both enables and enacts a distancing from and an abstraction of the object of study, and is a component and manifestation of the embodiment, on the part of the dominant class, of a naturalized, aristocratic ease. However, in *The Field of Cultural Production* (1993a) and *The Rules of Art* (1995), disinterestedness is cast in an altogether different and more generative form: the distance it facilitates is reconsidered as potentially facilitating the production of alternative sets of perspectives and accounts of the socio-cultural world that are not necessarily compliant with the meanings and narratives associated with symbolic power. In *Practical Reason* (1998c), disinterestedness is put forward as the means by which the scientific field and the autonomous pole of the field of cultural production are able—in fact are disposed—to take a critical and reflexive position with regard to both their own discourses and forms of social doxa. In the end, for Bourdieu, the relation between disinterestedness and the acquisition of a critical socio-cultural disposition is a matter of the logics and imperatives of the cultural field, and how this plays out at the level of the habitus. 'If disinterestedness is sociologically possible,' he writes (1998c: 88),

> it can only be through the encounter between the habitus predisposed to disinterestedness and the universes in which disinterestedness is rewarded. Among these universes, the most typical are . . . the different fields of cultural production . . . [and] the scientific field, microcosms which are constituted on the basis of an inversion of the fundamental law of the economic world and in which the law of economic interest is suspended. This does not mean that they do not know other forms of interest: the sociology of art or literature unveils . . . and analyzes the specific interests which are constituted by the field's functioning . . . and for which one is ready to die.

The main criticism directed at Bourdieu's notion of reflexivity is that he limits it to sociology. In fact, Bourdieu associates a disposition towards reflexivity with a variety of cultural fields, including that of intellectuals (Bourdieu 1993b: 44), literature and the sciences (Bourdieu & Wacquant 1992: 175), history (Bourdieu & Wacquant 1992: 90) and art, and more generally the autonomous pole of the field of cultural production (Bourdieu & Haacke 1995: 1). Reflexivity is potentially available within any field that systematically disposes its subjects towards 'the systematic exploration of the unthought categories of thought which delimit the thinkable and predetermine the thought' (Bourdieu & Wacquant 1992: 40).

Practical logic

Practical sense or logic can be defined as the ability to comprehend and negotiate cultural fields, and by extension to participate, in a literate manner, in the game that is played out between subjects and the dynamics of those fields. Playing the game requires and involves literacy with regard to the various discourses, genres, codes, narratives, forms of cultural capital, written and unwritten rules, values and imperatives that are both constitutive of, and things that are at stake in, the cultural field-as-game. Cultural literacy, which is developed via the habitus, allows subjects to determine which practices, discourses, moves or deployment of forms of cultural capital are appropriate to the moment.

While the habitus is incorporated by the subject (is constitutive, in fact, of the subject) as a set of values, epistemological categories and bodily dispositions, the process by which a subject is incorporated into a cultural field necessarily requires an adjustment to its logics, values and discursive regimes, and accordingly this process of adaptation constitutes part of the ongoing (re)formation of the habitus. Incorporation requires that the subject accept the game on its own terms, relatively unquestioningly—a condition Bourdieu designates as *illusio*, or 'the fact of being caught up in and by the game, of believing . . . that playing is worth the effort' (Bourdieu 1998c: 76). However, while the field as a discursive regime is generally stable (how the field articulates itself and its core values and ethos is resistant to change), the dynamics that make up the field—for instance, in terms of competition for the acquisition of cultural capital—mean that the game is simultaneously always and never exactly itself. Given this situation, the logic of practice is neither bound by objectified rules and procedures, nor able to step out of the world and abandon the epistemological categories derived from the habitus and the field.

A subject comes into being and functions within a cultural field, but only to the extent that they incorporate the world at a level of tacit and more or less automatic literacy and compliance. This is, for Bourdieu, essentially a regulatory process, one that is ongoing and largely a matter of unconscious bodily recognition:

> The world is comprehensible, immediately endowed with meaning, because the body, which, thanks to its sense and its

brain, has the capacity to be present to what is outside itself, in the world, and to be impressed and durably modified by it, has been protractedly (from the beginning) exposed to its regularities. (Bourdieu 2000: 135)

For Bourdieu, congruence between habitus and field constitutes the subject-in-the-world: the world is rendered comprehensible because it has written the subject into existence by way of its discourses, evaluative categories, perspectives, dispositions and logics. Because 'the world encompasses me':

> I, as a thing for which there are things, comprehend this world. And I do so ... because it encompasses me and comprehends me, it is through this material inclusion—often unnoticed and repressed—and what follows from it, the incorporation of social structures in the form of dispositional structures ... that I acquire a practical knowledge and control of the encompassing space. (Bourdieu 2000: 130)

Subjects incorporate the history of the game/cultural field, but that incorporation functions, simultaneously, as a delimitation. They know what the field knows, but not what it has foreclosed. This 'enchanted' relation to the game not only (re)produces knowledge as the 'vision and division' of the world; it also brings about a (tacit) self-interested ignorance or illiteracy:

> Once one has accepted the viewpoint that is constitutive of a field, one can no longer take an external viewpoint on it. The 'nomos', a thesis which, because it is never put forward as such, cannot be contradicted, has no antithesis. As a legitimate principle of division which can be applied to all the fundamental aspects of experience, defining the thinkable and the unthinkable, the prescribed and the proscribed, it must remain unthought. Being the matrix of all the pertinent questions,

it cannot produce the questions that call it into question. (2000: 97)

Even where socio-cultural contexts and developments outstrip or contradict the habitus, this does not lead to the production of a reflexive disposition: the habitus is characterized by both a durability and a generative capacity over and across cultural trajectories and time and space, and even when a disconnection between the habitus and the objectivities of the field encourages subjects to revise their ideas and perspectives, in most fields there is little or nothing to be gained from reflexivity and reflexive knowledge.

Variations in and across a cultural field arise from both chronological and spatial dynamics. Because a cultural field is the consequence of an ongoing discursive set of relations, interpellations and recognitions, it is continually reimagined and manifested at a micro level, not only on the part of new members, but also within existing subjects and spaces. Variations are not likely to be much removed from the official discursive articulations of and about the field (an authoritative pronouncement, the formulation of rules or policies), but they are never quite the same either. This production of difference-as-the-same is subject to a number of factors, such as proximity to the field of power or another powerful field (the state, capitalism, the legal field), and changes to the nature, exchange rate or convertibility of cultural capital. Whatever the reason, these differences and variations constitute gaps in the field, which can cause uncertainties or ambiguities; or again, they produce a disjunction between those who identify with and embody what the field was, and those who anticipate where it is going. Competition for capital, status, position and access to power can engender sets of practices that are tactical, rather than strategic, in Certeau's (1988) sense of the terms. Knowledge about and familiarity with the objectivities of a field (formal and tacit), including rules, genres, forms of capital, history, categories, discourses and values, constitute a central factor in the refinement of the 'feel for the game' that constitutes practical sense:

> The lines of action suggested by habitus may very well be accompanied by a strategic calculation of costs and benefits which tends to carry out at a conscious level the operations that habitus carries out in its own way. Times of crisis ... constitute a class of circumstances when indeed 'rational choice' may take over. (Bourdieu & Wacquant 1992: 131)

Bourdieu makes the point that a feel for the game involves, first and foremost, a sense of anticipation, and more specifically an understanding of the relation between chronology (past, present and future) and objectivities. This aspect of the practical sense does not negate or conflict with the habitus, but it does allow subjects (more or less unconsciously) to recalibrate the relation between the habitus and the field. Moreover, whenever a field specifically interpellates subjects-as-members, there is always a level of symbolic violence that is involved: to be designated, characterized, located, narrated and evaluated is to be inscribed by power in a process that has its residues and infelicities, and this is particularly accentuated when the interpellation has a negative dimension (for instance, when forms of capital, status and identity are associated with or predicated upon gender). What this means is that subjects can negotiate around the rules, regulations and normative apparatuses of a field because the conditions under which fields operate dispose them to do so, even if this is not done in a conscious or deliberate manner.

For Bourdieu, the habitus is necessarily unconscious of itself because a meta-relation to the habitus-as-field would be interruptive and render it more or less dysfunctional. The logic is that in order for the habitus to smooth the progress of the subject in the world, it needs to function as an epistemological facility that is consistent, continuous, at hand and of the moment. The logic of practice follows closely from the habitus in that the latter provides the dispositions that are used to sift through, evaluate and negotiate the options and possibilities that present themselves both of the moment and across various durations. However, while subjects tend to perform in accordance with the doxa of a field, they will also be aware that at some level situations are often contingent and open to negotiation:

> Notions which Bourdieu attempts to restore to their rightful place, like those of innovation, invention, improvisation ... come into play in two quite different ways in the practice of obedience to a rule. Invention may be necessary, if the relevant rule has left a reasonably large margin of indeterminacy, or because the application of the rule in a particular case may raise a problem of interpretation which one cannot hope to resolve by invoking a supplementary rule to cover the correct fashion in which the rule is to be interpreted. In many cases, knowing how to apply a rule correctly means ... in certain cases knowing how to ignore it or break it intelligently. Musil's remark about moral rules spring to mind here, where he compares them to a sieve, where the holes are at least as important as the solid parts. (Bouveresse 1999: 55)

The fact that a field is always subject to both internal and external pressures means that the literacy Bourdieu associates with practical knowledge is informed, at least potentially, by a tacit awareness of the game that goes into making the game. Practice-as-cultural literacy, from this perspective, can only be identified as the traces of variations to the relation between the habitus and the objectivities of a field. However, while cultural practices are derived from the epistemological schema of habitus and the field, they are also inextricably linked to time and place. What Bourdieu identifies in Kabylia (and the practices that characterize the house as cultural space) and Béarn (and its matrimonial strategies), for instance, are the objective traces of use that appear to obey logics that aren't inscribed anywhere, but that at the same time clearly exist as a flexible ensemble.

Reflexivity

Reflexivity—or reflexive knowledge—is both an extension and development of, but also different from, practical logic: while it is also acquired via immersion in a cultural field, it manifests itself as an awareness and evaluative understanding of both the relationship between the subject and the world, and how this relationship disposes, informs and produces, on the part of the subject, an understanding of the world and a concomitant set of practices. The main difference between practical logic and reflexivity for Bourdieu is the extent to which a subject can mediate their acquired regime of the mediation of the world. Both epistemologies constitute an extension or facility of the habitus. However, with practical logic, the habitus is oriented towards a negotiation and accommodation of the world and its contexts, but without regard to the role played or the influence exerted by the habitus in the determination of how those forms of negotiation and accommodation take place. Bourdieu argues that reflexivity constitutes a meta-relation to the habitus, and is capable of being taught and learned (at the level of technique), and consciously incorporated into different levels of praxis. The epistemological distance and the acuity it provides are produced through specific cultural fields and their evaluative regimes, and therefore we can say that it is derived from and consistent with regard to a field- or context-specific habitus—one that Bourdieu locates within and associates with the cultural field of science and, more generally, with certain areas of the autonomous pole of the field of cultural production.

Reflexivity involves a reflexive relation to the habitus, to demands and influences exerted by cultural fields, and to one's own practices within those fields. For Bourdieu, the issue of reflexivity is not simply a scholastic or philosophical question abstracted from the world; rather, it is a problem that informs his own practices as a sociologist and academic. The production of reflexive knowledge is tied to two main contexts and their concomitant theoretical questions or concerns. The first involves the process of socio-cultural change, and the question of how and why subjects break with their incorporation and naturalization of the habitus. The second is more specific, and relates to the process whereby subjects are able to incorporate and naturalize, as part of the habitus, a critical and analytical relation to the dispositions, logics and perspectives acquired and employed within a cultural field. Both issues involve a confrontation with, and a negotiation of, the dictum that a subject is in the world because the world is in the subject: in other words, what needs to be considered is how is it possible that subjects can, metaphorically speaking, step out of the world and take up a position that gives them a privileged and seemingly objectified perspective on objectifying practices and contexts. We can ask, for example—and using Bourdieu's own terms—how a subject's misrecognition is recognized, how *illusio* is to be seen, and how it is possible to critically analyse the flows of power that constitute, authorize and facilitate the methodologies and values of critical analysis. David Swartz (1997: 270) writes that:

> Since Bourdieu argues that his theory of symbolic power and violence applies to all forms of symbolic representation, he faces a critical dilemma in developing a sociological practice designed to expose the hidden forms of symbolic power: how can one practice a social science—itself a symbolic enterprise—and yet not reproduce the effects of social distinction Bourdieu so vigorously denounces? If, as he argues, all symbolic systems—including science itself—embody power relations, and all practices—including intellectual practices—are interested, how is it possible to construct a social science that will not be yet another form of symbolic violence?

For Bourdieu, reflexivity can be understood as a set of dispositions, processes and mechanisms that interrogate the epistemological frameworks that are constitutive of thought. It is oriented towards the limitations of the habitus, which arise, first, from social and cultural origins, trajectories and categories (generation, class, religion, gender, ethnicity); second, from positions within cultural fields from which a subject is located (as an anthropologist, journalist, politician); and third, from an intellectual bias—that is, a tendency for subjects from certain fields to abstract practices from their contexts, and see them as ideas to be contemplated, rather than problems to be addressed or solved (Bourdieu & Wacquant 1992: 39).

It needs to be emphasized that, for Bourdieu, reflexivity is something that is produced by and through a collective habitus: it is not a facility that can be acquired at the level of individual agency on the part of the subject. Moreover, and by extension, a reflexive disposition should not be understood as the effect of some kind of Pauline conversion: reflexivity is developed, incorporated and naturalized systematically, in the same way and via the same set of processes as any other aspect of the habitus; consequently, a critical relation to the doxa of the field must be a constitutive part of any field that is characterized by a reflexive disposition. Subjects are shaped, constrained and disposed towards thoughts and actions through their immersion in, and their incorporation of, the procedures, mechanisms, capital, explicit and implicit rules and values of the field. In the fields that Bourdieu identifies or associates generally with a larger scientific field, the rules, procedures and capital are (at least theoretically) oriented towards reflexivity; consequently, in the scientific field, it is incumbent upon subjects to think and act in a reflexive manner. One of the difficulties this produces, in sociology and other forms of science, 'lies in the fact that we believe we're already imbued with science; we believe we understand immediately, and one of the obstacles to understanding is this illusion of immediate comprehension. One of the ways to break with this illusion is to objectivize it' (Bourdieu & Chartier 2015: 39).

Every field is characterized by competition for recognition, status, position and capital. In the sciences, the main means of achieving these aims is through the production of what is marked and recognized as knowledge. Unlike most other fields, the sciences are relatively autonomous, and the truth or validity claims of what is produced as knowledge are subject to a variety of supposedly objective and objectifying procedures, such as peer review and the utilization of authorized methodological procedures, and adherence to a scholarly and methodological ethos. Authorization and recognition of knowledge are predicated upon agreed procedures of evaluation (such as blind refereeing) and means of verification (forms of legitimated analysis, rules for carrying out quantitative and qualitative research). These procedures and principles have no natural or abiding value in themselves; their value lies only in their being accepted, at any one moment, by the field.

Bourdieu (2000: 113) points out that while various non-scientific fields (he cites religion and politics) are similarly characterized by a tacit agreement between subjects as to what constitutes the objective reality of the field, subjects in those fields do not necessarily agree on the principles, procedures and means of verification. What is unique to the sciences, Bourdieu writes, is that competition for the accumulation of capital is predicated upon the production of knowledge that is disposed to interrogate its own claims to truth and objectivity, both individually and with regard to the field as a whole. This rationale and disinterested 'interestedness' is only possible, he argues, because the scientific field is relatively autonomous, and therefore not subject to domination by the fields of power, the state or business (2000: 111). If this were not the case, then criteria for success would shift from the production of knowledge acknowledged, sanctioned and legitimated by peers, and authorized and verifiable procedures, to other criteria (such as commercial possibilities, or the extent to which the work was politically useful) determined both outside the field and without regard to peer evaluation.

Bourdieu defines reflexivity as an interrogation of the three types of limitations—of social position, of field and of the scholastic point of view—that are constitutive of knowledge itself. For example, I can ask certain questions of people only because it is 'self-evident' (at least to, say, a male anthropologist) that these questions (about cultural rituals, or the genesis of social classificatory systems) are important; and I can only follow up these questions, and turn this research into knowledge if I accept, tacitly, that the instruments being used (observation, surveys, focus groups) are legitimate mechanisms for the production of objectivities.

An exemplary case of science attempting to account for and negotiate its involvement in the production of knowledge is to be found and demonstrated in Bourdieu's *The Weight of the World* (1999). Under Bourdieu's direction, a team of researchers spent three years interviewing predominantly lower class and/or migrant men and women in France about the conditions of their everyday lives. The interviews were then transcribed and written up more or less as a series of short stories. The main point of the research was to achieve and articulate an understanding of the conditions and factors that produced the 'pain and misery' of everyday life, but Bourdieu was also attempting to communicate more generally 'the simultaneously practical and theoretical problems that emerge from the particular interaction between the interviewer and the person being questioned' (1999: 607).

The Weight of the World constitutes an attempt to both interrogate the presuppositions of, and to address and overcome the problems associated with, empiricism and its methodologies, such as accounting for how the genesis and basis of interviewers' questions, and the situation of the interview itself (location, time, differences of understanding), work to construct rather than elicit the responses of those being interviewed. According to Bourdieu, the care and rigor evident in the interviewing process allowed the researchers to be more sensitive, sympathetic and empathic interviewers; this, along with offering the interviewees an 'absolutely exceptional situation for communication, free from the usual constraints (particularly of time)' (1999: 614), also enabled them to 'grasp this situation as an exceptional opportunity offered to them to testify, to make themselves heard, to carry their experience over from the private to the public sphere' (1999: 615).

This transformation of private testimony into public knowledge constitutes an example of scientific reflexivity, precisely because what was both considered and included in the textual (re)production of oral testimony was the process of that reproduction. *The Weight of the World* put into circulation narratives about the everyday lives of dominated groups, but a central part of the research was an attempt to free those narratives from the predispositions, mechanisms, discourses and points of view of the researchers themselves. The process of scientific reflexivity hardly stops there: the field itself (sociology specifically, but the social sciences more generally) is necessarily disposed both to take on board the issues and problems identified in *The Weight of the World,* and to subject the research and the methods employed in it to critique. Even when the field—or at least sections of it—is completely given over to the reproductive and largely non-reflexive tendencies that Bourdieu (1993b) associates with what he calls 'instrumental positivism', the fact that the mediation of social knowledge has been placed on the table means that it can't be ignored by researchers; more importantly, it becomes—at least potentially—the focus for future research and competition among researchers within the field. Such research is potentially available to be taken up by the field because, despite what Bourdieu writes about the interconnectedness between knowledge and competition within a field that disposes its subjects towards reflexivity, in practice reflexivity does not necessarily occur. Bourdieu's description of the scientific field as a site of the institutionalizing of a reflexive disposition does not mean that it informs all the practices within the field; rather, it constitutes an account of what the field says it is, and how it articulates itself (and its values) to other fields.

If, as Bourdieu suggests, subjects generally pave over the gaps between habitus and practice that might otherwise generate reflexive thought, then how does reflexive knowledge emerge? Two conditions are necessary for fields to produce such a culture: first, a degree of autonomy (because the field cannot be completely dominated by the field of power, say, or fields of politics or business); and second, and as a corollary, a disposition to produce knowledge that does not necessarily serve, or act in the interests of, hegemonic fields. These criteria are often associated with fields that are informed by a scholastic point of view (*skhole*); however, Bourdieu identifies *skhole* as a potential impediment to reflexive knowledge, partly because of the tendency of academics to abstract issues and treat them as if they had no consequences or practical dimension, and also because it replaces the point of view of practitioners in the field with that of scholars: 'ignoring everything that is implied in the "scholastic point of view" leads to the most serious epistemological mistakes in the human sciences, that which consists in putting "a scholar inside the machine", in picturing all social agents in the image of a scientist' (Bourdieu 1998c: 133).

It can be argued that this is the case with economic forecasting, which tends to model its outcomes on the ideal practice of an ideal economist (thereby ignoring the possibility of random approaches to economic choices on the part of consumers). At the same time, it is precisely their distancing both from hegemonic fields and from the practices they research that allows scholars to reflect on the 'unthought categories of thought' (Bourdieu & Wacquant 1992: 40)—that is, to reflect beyond the immediate concerns associated with any praxis. They are able, therefore, 'to accede to meta-discourse on the practice of discourse' (Bourdieu 1998c: 131), which Bourdieu argues is the fallacy of scholarly culture, but also provides the reason for the field to develop and make use of the mechanisms of 'training, dialogue and critical evaluation' that work to institutionalize reflexivity. Fields that are informed by the scholastic point of view are likely to be characterized by the set of conditions constitutive of reflexive knowledge, and the scholastic point of view is therefore simultaneously both a potential impediment to and a condition of the production of a reflexive disposition. In the study of history, for instance, it is the immanent tendency of the field to subject everything, including the texts of history and historiography, to a historicizing analysis that targets both 'the privilege of a knowing subject arbitrarily excluded from the effect of objectification' (Bourdieu 2000: 119), and the conditions (dispositions and values, including the scholastic point of view) that produce the subject and knowledge itself. But this is only possible because, as Bourdieu points out, the distanced and disinterested ethos of (at least parts of) the field are reproduced through the interested, competitive ethos that capitalizes the production of reflexive knowledge.

There is another reason why fields characterized by the scholastic point of view, and the conditions associated with it, tend to produce subjects disposed towards reflexivity. Autonomy (with regard to the field of power, and more specifically to capitalism) is a sign that there is no significant economic benefit to be gained from the alienation of the field or, alternatively, that it is possessed of enough symbolic capital to maintain itself against colonization. The autonomy of the sciences is increasingly subject to the intrusion of state and capitalist logics, imperatives and regimes of value, which threaten to undermine it; however, the scholarly disposition to bracket off the world can and still does lead to a reciprocity whereby the field of power brackets off 'pure' scientific and other forms of scholarly research. This apparent irrelevance of some scholarly research to the field of power works to increase the likelihood of a reflexive disposition: this is because the process of misrecognition that characterizes the scientific and other autonomous and reflexive fields (which involves a commitment to and identification with the things of scholarship, including disinterestedness) is necessarily and consistently turned against itself, and subject to interrogation and analysis. As long as there is a perception, on the part of the field of power and capitalism, that there is nothing at stake in the scholarly game, there is also no particular reason to intervene in or limit the scholarly game of critical self-analysis.

Bourdieu's notion of reflexivity is a practical tool (of research, analysis, critique) that can be taught and learned. The specific ground—the methodologies, logics, imperatives, conventions and cultural ethos—that disposes subjects to reflect on and critique their practices provides two distinct epistemological advantages. First, it enhances a subject's practical literacy: it allows the subject to map the limits of the game that characterizes cultural fields, and to adjust their practices accordingly; as a corollary, it provides them with a certain amount of distance from the process (and the consequences) of being produced and spoken 'by the field'. The second advantage is that reflexivity, as a transposable set of methodologies and dispositions, provides subjects with the basis for negotiating across societies, cultures and cultural fields. If reflexivity takes away some of the comforts associated with a naturalized habitus and practical knowledge, at the same time it provides a means of moving beyond what the subject already knows on a practical level, and offers the advantages of the application of a transposable relation to the mechanisms, processes and practices of socio-cultural domination.

There are six main aspects to reflexivity. First, it can be understood as the 'systematic exploration' of dispositions and epistemologies 'which delimit the thinkable and predetermine the thought' (Bourdieu & Wacquant 1992: 36). Second, reflexivity is a collective rather than an individual process: it is incorporated at the level of the 'social and intellectual unconscious embedded in analytical tools and agents' (1992: 36). Third, it is largely specific to those fields that have institutionalized, through the mechanisms of training and discursive interpellation, a disposition for subjects to turn those mechanisms against themselves. Fourth, the reflexive disposition is tied to specific regimes of cultural capital: again, because subjects misrecognize their relation to the field, they are able to engage with reflexivity, simultaneously, as both principle and lure. Fifth, only fields that are relatively autonomous—that is to say, they are not dominated by the field of power or capitalism—are able and inclined to invest reflexivity with cultural capital. Finally, the disinterested disposition associated with the scholastic point of view (and, more generally, with the autonomous pole of the field of cultural production) is one of the preconditions of, as well as an impediment to, the production of reflexive knowledge.

Conclusion

Bourdieu's work, and the scholarly apparatus that he produced and developed to deal with theoretical and methodological issues and problems arising out of that work, could be characterized as having two points of focus: the identification and analysis of the relationship between education, culture, class formation and socio-cultural politics; and an attempt to go beyond the limitations of objectivist, subjectivist and Marxist theories of cultural practice. There were a number of specific questions and issues tied to this work, such as how power operates in socio-cultural contexts and spaces; the status of class as an epistemological and political category; the relations between specific and general regimes of economy; and the validity or otherwise of substantive and relational forms of analysis. Bourdieu's response was to develop, refine and deploy concepts such as habitus, cultural capital, cultural field and socio-cultural reproduction in order to analyse, identify and evaluate the mechanisms that allowed dominant groups to inscribe, naturalize and maintain their pre-eminence, on both the everyday and bodily levels, without recourse to physical violence or intimidation, and in a manner that was neither direct nor substantive (for instance, by way of ownership of the means of production, and the accumulation and deployment of economic capital for the purposes of exercising political leverage).

While Bourdieu's theories have proven to be influential across a wide range of discipline areas—most obviously education and sociology, but also anthropology, ethnology, critical theory, cultural studies, media studies, gender studies, sport and even unlikely areas such as business, sports management and public relations—they have attracted not inconsiderable criticism, outlined in earlier chapters, regarding his supposed unwillingness to allow for what he has termed 'subjectivist' explanations of cultural practices. As a corollary, his work has been charged with extending the narrative that it purports to be challenging, which is that symbolic power and domination are natural and inevitable phenomena. This can be read as a concern with Bourdieu's refusal of subjectivity-as-agency, exemplified in Reed-Danahay's (2009: 157) comment that 'many North Americans are uncomfortable with theories that deny individual autonomy and free choice'. However, it is also consequent on partial readings of his work and ideas, as in the case of the statement that, 'There is no way out of the game of culture' being considered without regard to the qualifier 'and that one's only chance of objectifying the true nature of the game is to objectify as fully as possible the very operations which one is obliged to use in order to achieve that objectification' (Bourdieu 1989: 12).

Where more telling theoretical issues and problems can be identified is in Bourdieu's theorizing of the relationship between the habitus and socio-cultural practices, and the extent to which the epistemological facility of the habitus is able to turn acquired cultural literacies into what we can call, for want of a better term, strategic considerations. As Butler (1999: 125) asks:

> Although Bourdieu understands himself to reject the Marxian notion of class in its substantializing form through embracing a notion of 'class position', is it not the case that the spatial metaphorics of 'position' can be equally reifying as the monolithic conception of class itself? For 'positions' are not merely spatial locations, but temporarily produced effects and, hence, as subject to the logic of iteration, dependent on unstable forms of rearticulation. Although Bourdieu underscores the temporal dimension of the habitus and of social practice as ritual, it seems that the focus on temporality disappears when he shifts into the 'objective' domain of the social field, a field described almost exclusively in spatialized terms. Left unaccounted for within this topography is the critical question of how 'positions' achieve their spatial status within the current political imaginary . . . If a 'social position' is produced in part through a repeated process of interpellation, and such interpellations do not take place exclusively through 'official' means, could this reiterated 'being hailed into social existence' not become the very occasion for a reappropriation of discursive power, a further articulation of the habitus, a 'regulated improvisation', to use Bourdieu's terms.

Butler's questions have constituted the departure points for the accounts and evaluations articulated in this book. We have considered a variety of issues that emerge from Bourdieu's analysis of the ongoing relation between subjects, objective structures, and time and place, all of which can be collected, considered and contextualized under the notion of 'cultural literacy'. These issues are also to be found in Certeau's (1988) evaluation of the theoretical apparatus used in *Outline of a Theory of Practice*, which played a formative role in the development of the continuity of habitus, field and practice. Certeau argues that Bourdieu's analysis of the cultural practices of the peasants of Kabylia and Béarn presents us with a catalogue of moves, techniques and tricks, as well as certain 'essential procedures' (1988: 54), all of which are dominated by 'an economy of the proper place' (1988: 55). This attachment to the notion of an economy of place, however, is informed by another economy: a theoretical economy of gain and loss. The theoretical investment in the primacy of place pays off in the sense that Bourdieu is able, through his own familiarity with and ability to extrapolate from the combinations and conditions of the rules, logics and values of the contexts in question (house and family), to 'outwit' practice ('I know what you know, therefore I know what you do'). Certeau argues, however, that in presupposing a link between 'practices and a proper place (a patrimony), on the one hand, and a collective principle of administration (the family, the group), on the other' (1988: 55), Bourdieu loses the ability to trace or even consider the possibility of the same kind of practices outside his purview. He notes that in his later, sociological work situated in urban France:

> When Bourdieu encounters the same type of practices among today's 'petit bourgeois', or housewives, they are merely 'short term and short sighted strategies', 'anarchical responses' relative to 'a disparate ensemble of semi-knowledges' . . . A mere 'bric-à-brac of decontextualized concepts'. A single practical logic is nevertheless at work, but independently of the place

that controls its functioning in traditional societies ... in ... *Outline* the problematic of the place seems to win out over the problematic of practices. (1988: 55)

Bourdieu's notion of practice-as-literacy incorporated three key elements: an awareness of the objective structures, sets of interests, and contexts of the field, and of one's place in it; an understanding of the laws, regulations, conventions, history and precedents that constitute the rules of the game; and finally, and by extension, a feel 'for the game' at hand. This is one of the pay-offs of Bourdieu's theorizing of practice: he is aware that subjects are capable of responding to and altering their activities in the face of complex and variable external conditions, and this means that he can follow their practices and procedures (in Kabylia and Béarn, if not necessarily in French supermarkets) because he remains (theoretically) open to all possibilities, regardless of whether they are inscribed in institutional rules or sociological discourse.

What is more complicated, however, is the process of negotiation whereby subjects, in the form of the habitus that disposes, guides and virtually produces them, adjust to and act within the constraints, imperatives and economies of a field. Because Bourdieu's work has been at pains to set itself against subjectivist notions of practice—particularly with regard to those fields dominated by artists and intellectuals, which garner much of their capital and sense of worth precisely through reference to qualities such as individuality and creative genius—he is loath to accept that the relation between habitus and practice, on the one hand, and practice-as-literacy, on the other, is anything but unconscious. There is an insistence in Bourdieu's writing in *Outline of a Theory of Practice* (1978) and *The Logic of Practice* (1990c)—his two most 'worked through' versions of the relationship between habitus and practice—that models of practice 'are only valid as long as they are taken for ... logical models giving an account of the observed facts in the most coherent and economical way; and they become false and dangerous as soon as they are treated as the real principle of practices' (1990c: 11). For Bourdieu (1991b: 2), the articulation of any 'other' logic of practice is always first subordinated to an unconscious subtraction and denial of the 'place' from where (supposedly) objectivist knowledge is produced:

> The knowing subject . . . inflicts on practice a much more fundamental and pernicious alteration which, being a constitutive condition of the cognitive operation, is bound to pass unnoticed: in taking up a point of view on the action, withdrawing from it in order to observe it from above, from a distance, he constitutes practical activity as an object of observation and analysis, a representation.

There is a remarkable consistency on this matter, not just between *Outline of a Theory of Practice* and *The Logic of Practice*, but across Bourdieu's work as a whole: practices are in no way reducible to or explicable in terms of the scientific logics that bring them back to scientific inquiry. Yet Bourdieu's own attempts (primarily through the notion of habitus) to account for practices are themselves informed by certain theoretical moves in which, as Certeau (1988: 51) writes, the 'particularity of the originary experience is lost in its power of reorganizing the general discourse'.

Outline of a Theory of Practice not only provides an interesting account of the pitfalls and politics of anthropological objectifications of practice; it also contains one of his more often quoted definitions of habitus, that 'durably installed generative principle of regulated improvisations' that

> produces practices which tend to reproduce their regularities immanent in the objective conditions of the production of their generative principle, while adjusting to the demands inscribed as objective potentialities in the situations, as defined by the cognitive and motivating structures making up the habitus. (Bourdieu 1978: 78)

Practices-as-habitus are explicable neither in terms of the institutional logics, narratives, rules, values, discourses and ideologies of a field (the objective conditions of practice), nor in terms of individual, unmediated decision-making (subjectivity); rather, a subject acquires a habitus and is in turn produced as a subject. The habitus is made up of a number of dispositions, modes of operation, inclinations, values and forms of bodily hexis that:

> Even when they appear as the realization of the explicit, and explicitly stated, purposes of a project or plan, the practices produced by the habitus, as the strategy-generating principle enabling agents to cope with unforeseen and ever-changing situations, are only apparently determined by the future. If they seem determined by anticipation of their own consequences, thereby encouraging the finalist illusion, the fact is that, always tending to reproduce the objective structures of which they are the product, they are determined by the past conditions which have produced the principle of their production. (Bourdieu 1978: 72)

Practices are the result, then, of the conjuncture—always slightly 'out of sync'—between the formative dispositions of the habitus and the objective conditions that are themselves produced out of these conjunctures. The crucial point here is Bourdieu's assertion that habitus, and the ways in which the habitus negotiates the objective structures of a society, in no way function as a conscious adherence to a set of rules or imperatives. For example, Bourdieu (1990c: 112) refers to the process whereby certain economies of social or cultural capital are normalized and naturalized within a field: 'Capital (or power) becomes symbolic capital only when it is misrecognized in its arbitrary truth as capital and recognized as legitimate... this act of (false) knowledge and recognition is an act of practical knowledge.' Similarly, the dispositions, orientations and values of the habitus obey the same (unconscious) logic of 'practical knowledge':

> In reality, the dispositions durably inculcated by the possibilities . . . inscribed in the objective conditions . . . generate dispositions objectively compatible with these conditions and in a sense pre-adapted to their demands. The most improbable practices are therefore excluded, as unthinkable, by a kind of immediate submission to order that inclines agents to make a virtue of necessity. (Bourdieu 1990c: 54)

'Knowledge' and 'the unconscious' are two terms that are largely ironized in Bourdieu's work: both are used, in a sense, to indicate the opposite of their conventional meanings. Knowledge, for Bourdieu, is understood as a kind of necessary misrecognition, and this also stands as a more than adequate definition of how he understands and uses the term 'unconscious', which is 'never anything other than the forgetting of history which history itself produces by incorporating the objective structures it produces into the second nature of habitus' (Bourdieu 1991b: 78–9). Bourdieu insists that practices, and the negotiations, deliberations and option-taking that produce them, are simultaneously misrecognized—paradoxically—as both natural (and thus in a sense, inevitable), and the consequence of individual decision-making:

> Each agent . . . is a producer and reproducer of objective meaning. Because his acts and works are the product of a Modus Operandi of which he is not the producer and has no conscious mastery, they contain an 'objective intention' . . . which always outruns his conscious intentions. The schemes of thought and expression he has acquired are the basis for the intentionless invention of regulated improvisations. (Bourdieu 1978: 79)

In this context, various forms of what we might understand as knowledge—such as arriving at and taking up a position of self-reflexivity with regard to one's own practices and habitus—are the ultimate examples of misrecognition. Bourdieu has written that, 'The individual is always, whether he likes it or not, trapped—save to the extent that he becomes aware of it' (Bourdieu & Wacquant 1992: 126), but this kind of self-reflexivity is itself effectively circumscribed by, and a product of, habitus:

> One can ... say that social agents are determined only to the extent that they determine themselves. But the categories of perception and appreciation which provide the principles of this (self-)determination are themselves largely determined by the social and economic conditions of their constitution. (Bourdieu & Wacquant 1992: 136)

Bourdieu is not unaware of the problems involved in reducing practice to a logic of misrecognition: after all, this is precisely what he takes structuralism and anthropology to task for in *Outline of a Theory of Practice* and *The Logic of Practice*. As he explains in an interview in *An Invitation to Reflexive Sociology*, 'Habitus is not the fate that some people read into it' (Bourdieu & Wacquant 1992: 133). Bourdieu's theory of the habitus-as-practice allows that the gap between habitus and cultural field can be productive to the extent that their lack of synchronicity can be the basis for their denaturalization; in other words, where two strongly naturalized systems or logics confront one another, a subject's 'unconscious belief' must be challenged at some level. What we have referred to as cultural literacy is more than an understanding of or familiarity with the rules and forms of knowledge operating in a field: it is based on the presumption that any developed knowledge of a field is predicated on what Butler would call 'the contingent nature' of the field and its regimes of capital. However, Bourdieu's position is that while subjects can negotiate both objective social structures and the delimitations imposed by their own habitus, socio-cultural resistance remains 'more or less invisible to the cultivated eye' (Bourdieu 1990a: 155).

ACKNOWLEDGEMENTS

We'd like to acknowledge the value of the feedback and suggestions contributed by our two readers, Professor John Frow of Sydney University and Associate Professor Tony Moore of Monash University: this is a significantly better work because of their input. John was also instrumental in determining how we approached the task of writing a book on Bourdieu, and has been a very generous mentor and influence for over 25 years.

The following people were helpful and supportive in one way or another: Barbara Chin, Madeleine Collinge, Rachel Gamby, Jenny Lou, Beverley and Susan Price, Kirsten Reid, Belinda and Harry Ricketts, Hugh Roberts and Jan Stewart.

The University of Macau provided Tony Schirato with sabbatical leave during the first half of 2017. The staff of the National Library of Ireland were, on a daily basis, friendly and helpful.

We would like to extend our thanks to Rebecca Allen, the in-house editor at Allen & Unwin, and Susan Jarvis, the freelance copyeditor. Finally, Elizabeth Weiss has been—and remains—a wonderful publisher and a good friend.

BIBLIOGRAPHY

Note: FFP—first French publication; FEP—first English publication.

Bourdieu's works

Bourdieu, P. (1978). *Outline of a Theory of Practice*, trans. R. Nice. Cambridge: Cambridge University Press (FFP 1972, FEP 1977).
—— (1979a). *Algeria 1960*, trans. R. Nice. Cambridge: Cambridge University Press (FFP 1963, FEP 1979).
—— (1979b). 'Preface to the American Edition', in P. Bourdieu & J.-C. Passeron, *The Inheritors: French Students and Their Relation to Culture*, trans. R. Nice. Chicago: University of Chicago Press (FEP 1979).
—— (1985). 'The Genesis of the Concepts of "Habitus" and of "Field"'. *Sociocriticism*, 2(2): 11–24 (FEP 1985).
—— (1986). 'The Forms of Capital', trans. R. Nice. In J. Richardson (ed.), *Handbook of Theory and Research for the Sociology of Education*. New York: Greenwood Press (FFP 1983, FEP 1986).

—— (1988). *Homo Academicus*, trans. P. Comer. Cambridge: Polity Press (FFP 1984, FEP 1988).

—— (1989). *Distinction: A Social Critique of the Judgment of Taste*, trans. R. Nice. London: Routledge (FFP 1979, FEP 1984).

—— (1990a). 'Academic Order and Social Order: Preface to the 1990 Edition', in P. Bourdieu & J.-C. Passeron, *Reproduction in Education, Society and Culture*, trans. R. Nice. London: Sage (FEP 1990).

—— (1990b). *In Other Words: Essays Towards a Reflexive Sociology*, trans. various. Cambridge: Polity Press (FFP 1982/1987, FEP 1990).

—— (1990c). *The Logic of Practice*, trans. R. Nice. Cambridge: Polity Press (FFP 1980, FEP 1990).

—— (1991a). *The Political Ontology of Martin Heidegger*, trans. P. Collier. Cambridge: Polity Press (FFP 1988, FEP 1991).

—— (1991b). 'Sport and Social Class', in C. Mukerji & E. Schudson (eds), *Rethinking Popular Culture*, Berkeley, CA: University of California Press (FEP 1991).

—— (1993a). *The Field of Cultural Production: Essays on Art and Literature*, trans. various. New York: Columbia University Press (FFP 1968–87, FEP 1993).

—— (1993b). *Sociology in Question,* trans. R. Nice. London: Sage (FFP 1984, FEP 1993).

—— (1995). *The Rules of Art: Genesis and Structure of the Literary Field*, trans. S. Emanuel. Stanford, CA: Stanford University Press (FFP 1992, FEP 1995).

—— (1996). *The State Nobility: Elite Schools in the Field of Power*, trans. L. Clough. Cambridge: Polity Press (FFP 1989, FEP 1996).

—— (1998a). *Acts of Resistance: Against the New Myths of Our Time*, trans. R. Nice, Cambridge: Polity Press (FFP 1998, FEP 1998).

—— (1998b). *On Television and Journalism*, trans. P. Ferguson. London: Pluto Press (FFP 1996, FEP 1998).

—— (1998c). *Practical Reason: On the Theory of Action*, trans. various. Stanford, CA: Stanford University Press (FFP 1994, FEP 1998).

—— (1999). *The Weight of the World: Social Suffering in Contemporary Society*, trans. various. Stanford, CA: Stanford University Press (FFP 1993, FEP 1999).

—— (2000). *Pascalian Meditations*, trans. R. Nice. Cambridge: Polity Press (FFP 1997, FEP 2000).

—— (2001). *Masculine Domination*, trans. R. Nice. Cambridge: Polity Press (FFP 1998, FEP 2001).

—— (2003). *Firing Back: Against the Tyranny of the Market 2*, trans L. Wacquant. London: Verso (FFP 2001, FEP 2003).

—— (2004). *Science of Science and Reflexivity*, trans. R. Nice. Cambridge: Polity Press (FFP 2001, FEP 2004).

—— (2005a). 'From the King's House to the Reason of State: A Model of the Genesis of the Bureaucratic Field'. In L. Wacquant (ed.), *Bourdieu and Democratic Politics*. Cambridge: Polity Press (FEP 2005).

—— (2005b). *Language and Symbolic Power*, trans. G. Raymond & M. Adamson. Cambridge: Polity Press (FFP 1982–84, FEP 1991).

—— (2005c). *The Social Structures of the Economy*, trans. C. Turner. Cambridge: Polity Press (FFP 2000, FEP 2005).

—— (2007). *Sketch for a Self-Analysis*, trans. R. Nice. Cambridge: Polity Press (FFP 2004, FEP 2007).

—— (2008a). *The Bachelors' Ball*, trans. various. Cambridge: Polity Press (FFP 2002, FEP 2008).

—— (2008b). *Political Interventions: Social Science and Political Action*, trans. D. Fernbach. London: Verso (FFP 2002, FEP 2008).

—— (2010). *Sociology is a Martial Art: Political Writings by Pierre Bourdieu*, trans. various. London: The New Press (FEP 2010).

—— (2012). *Picturing Algeria*, trans. various. New York: Columbia University Press (FFP 2003, FEP 2012).

—— (2013). *Algerian Sketches*, trans. various. Cambridge: Polity Press (FFP 2008, FEP 2013).

—— (2014). *On the State: Lectures at the Collège de France 1989–1992*, trans. various. Cambridge: Polity Press (FFP 2012, FEP 2014).

Bourdieu, P., Boltanski, P., Castel, R. & Chamboredon, J.-C. (1990). *Photography: A Middle-brow Art*, trans. S. Whiteside. Cambridge: Polity Press (FFP 1965, FEP 1990).

Bourdieu, P., Chamboredon, J.-C. & Passeron, J.-C. (1991). *The Craft of Sociology: Epistemological Preliminaries*, trans. R. Nice. New York: Walter de Gruyter (FFP 1968, FEP 1991).

Bourdieu, P. & Chartier, R. (2015). *The Sociologist & the Historian*, trans. D. Fernbach. Cambridge: Polity Press (FFP 2010, FEP 2015).

Bourdieu, P., Darbel, A. & Schnapper, D. (1990). *The Love of Art: European Art Museums and Their Public*, trans. C. Beattie & N. Merriman. Cambridge: Polity Press (FFP 1966, FEP 1990).

Bourdieu, P. & Haacke, H. (1995). *Free Exchange*, trans. various. Cambridge: Polity Press (FFP 1994, FEP 1995).

Bourdieu, P. & Passeron, J.-C. (1979a). 'Epilogue'. In P. Bourdieu & J.-C. Passeron, *The Inheritors: French Students and Their Relation to Culture*, trans. R. Nice. Chicago: University of Chicago Press (FEP 1979).

—— (1979b). *The Inheritors: French Students and Their Relation to Culture*, trans. R. Nice. Chicago: University of Chicago Press (FFP 1964, FEP 1979).

—— (1990) *Reproduction in Education, Society and Culture*, trans. R. Nice. London: Sage (FFP 1970, FEP 1977).

Bourdieu, P., Passeron, J.-C. & Saint Martin, M. (1994). *Academic Discourse: Linguistic Misunderstanding and Professorial Power*, trans. R. Teese. Cambridge: Polity Press (FFP 1965, FEP 1994).

Bourdieu, P. & Wacquant, L. (1992). *An Invitation to Reflexive Sociology*. Chicago: University of Chicago Press (FEP 1992).

Secondary sources

Abish, W. (1974). *Alphabetical Africa*. New York: New Directions.

Aboulafia, M. (1999). 'A (Neo)American in Paris: Bourdieu, Mead, and Pragmatism'. In R. Shusterman (ed.), *Bourdieu: A Critical Reader*. Oxford: Blackwell.

Anderson, B. (1991). *Imagined Communities*. London: Verso.

Appadurai, A. (1988). 'Introduction: Commodities and the Politics of Value'. In A. Appadurai (ed.), *The Social Life of Things*. Cambridge: Cambridge University Press.

—— (1997). *Modernity at Large*. Minneapolis, MN: University of Minnesota Press.

Archer, M. (1983). 'Process Without System'. *European Journal of Sociology*, 24(1): 196–221.

Austin, J. (1975). *How to Do Things with Words*. Oxford: Clarendon Press.

Barnard, H. (1990). 'Bourdieu and Ethnography: Reflexivity, Politics and Praxis'. In R. Harker, C. Mahar & C. Wilkes (eds), *An Introduction to the Work of Pierre Bourdieu*. London: Macmillan.

Baudrillard, J. (2003). *The Consumer Society*, trans. G. Ritzer. London: Sage.

Blanchot, M. (1986). *The Writing of the Disaster*, trans. A. Smock. Lincoln, NE: University of Nebraska Press.

Boltanski, L. (2004). *Distant Suffering*, trans. G. Burchell. Cambridge: Cambridge University Press.

Bottomore, T. (1990). 'Foreword', in P. Bourdieu & J.-C. Passeron, *Reproduction in Education, Society and Culture*. London: Sage.

Bouveresse, J. (1999). 'Rules, Dispositions and the Habitus'. In R. Shusterman (ed.), *Bourdieu: A Critical Reader*. Oxford: Blackwell.

Brown, N. & Szeman, I. (2000). 'Introduction: Fieldwork and Culture'. In N. Brown & I. Szeman (eds), *Pierre Bourdieu: Fieldwork in Culture*. New York: Rowman & Littlefield.

Butler, J. (1993). *Bodies That Matter.* New York: Routledge.
—— (1999). 'Performativity's Social Magic'. In R. Shusterman (ed.), *Bourdieu: A Critical Reader.* Oxford: Blackwell.
Calhoun, C. (1993). 'Habitus, Field, and Capital: The Question of Historical Specificity'. In C. Calhoun, E. LiPuma & M. Postone (eds), *Bourdieu: Critical Perspectives.* Cambridge: Polity Press.
Cause, L. (2010). 'Bernstein's Code Theory and the Educational Researcher'. *Asian Social Science,* 6(5): 3–9.
Certeau, M. (1988). *The Practice of Everyday Life,* trans. S. Rendall. Berkeley, CA: University of California Press.
Collins, J. (2000). 'Bernstein, Bourdieu and the New Literacy Studies'. *Linguistics and Education,* 11(1): 65–78.
Crary, J. (2013). *Late Capitalism and the Ends of Sleep.* London: Verso.
Crossley, N. (2008). 'Social Class'. In M.J. Grenfell (ed.), *Pierre Bourdieu: Key Concepts.* New York: Routledge.
Danto, A. (1999). 'Bourdieu on Art: Field and Individual'. In R. Shusterman (ed.), *Bourdieu: A Critical Reader.* Oxford: Blackwell.
Derrida, J. (1976). *Of Grammatology,* trans. G. Spivak. Baltimore, MD: Johns Hopkins University Press.
Frow, J. (1995). *Cultural Studies and Cultural Value.* Oxford: Clarendon Press.
Goodman, J. (2009). 'The Proverbial Bourdieu: *Habitus* and the Politics of Representation in the Ethnography of Kabylia'. In J. Goodman & P. Silverstein (eds), *Bourdieu in Algeria: Colonial Politics, Ethnographic Practices, Theoretical Developments.* Lincoln, NE: University of Nebraska Press.
Goodman, J. & Silverstein, P. (eds) (2009a). *Bourdieu in Algeria: Colonial Politics, Ethnographic Practices, Theoretical Developments.* Lincoln, NE: University of Nebraska Press.
—— (2009b). 'Introduction: Bourdieu in Algeria'. In J. Goodman & P. Silverstein (eds), *Bourdieu in Algeria: Colonial Politics, Ethnographic Practices, Theoretical Developments.* Lincoln, NE: University of Nebraska Press.
Grenfell, M. (ed.) (2012). *Bourdieu: Key Concepts,* 2nd ed. Jaipur: Rawat.
The Guardian Online (2001). 'Booker Judges Announced', 15 February, www.theguardian.com/books/2001/feb/15/bookerprize2001.thebookerprize, accessed 18 April 2017.
—— (2002). 'Pierre Bourdieu: Obituary', 28 January, www.theguardian.com/news/2002/jan/28/guardianobituaries.books, accessed 4 September 2017.

Guillory, J. (2000). 'Bourdieu's Refusal'. In N. Brown & I. Szeman (eds), *Pierre Bourdieu: Fieldwork in Culture*. New York: Rowman & Littlefield.
Hammoudi, A. (2009). 'Phenomenology and Ethnography: On Kabyle *Habitus* in the Work of Pierre Bourdieu'. In J. Goodman & P. Silverstein (eds), *Bourdieu in Algeria: Colonial Politics, Ethnographic Practices, Theoretical Developments*. Lincoln, NE: University of Nebraska Press.
Harker, R. (1990). 'Bourdieu: Education and Reproduction'. In R. Harker, C. Mahar & C. Wilkes (eds), *An Introduction to the Work of Pierre Bourdieu*. London: Macmillan.
Harker, R., Mahar, C. & Wilkes, C. (eds) (1990). *An Introduction to the Work of Pierre Bourdieu*. London: Macmillan.
Harker, R. & May, S. (1993). 'Code and Habitus: Comparing the Accounts of Bernstein and Bourdieu'. *British Journal of Sociology of Education*, 14(2): 169–78.
Jenkins, R. (1992). *Pierre Bourdieu*. London: Routledge.
Johnson, R. (1993). 'Editor's Introduction'. In P. Bourdieu, *The Field of Cultural Production*. Cambridge: Polity Press.
Kirkpatrick, D.D. (2001). '*Oprah* Gaffe by Franzen Draws Ire and Sales', *The New York Times*, 21 October, www.nytimes.com/2001/10/29/books/oprah-gaffe-by-franzen-draws-ire-and-sales.html, accessed 17 April 2017.
Kuhn, T. (1970). *The Structures of Scientific Revolutions*. Chicago, IL: University of Chicago Press.
Lefort, C. (1986). *The Political Forms of Modern Society*, trans. various. Cambridge, MA: MIT Press.
Mahar, C., Harker, R. & Wilkes, C. (1990). 'The Basic Theoretical Positions'. In R. Harker, C. Mahar & C. Wilkes (eds), *An Introduction to the Work of Pierre Bourdieu*. London: Macmillan.
Mangan, J.A. (1981). *Athleticism in the Victorian and Edwardian Public School*. London: Routledge.
Marx, K. (1969). 'Theses on Feuerbach'. In K. Marx & F. Engels, *Marx/Engels Selected Works Volume One*, trans. W. Lough. Moscow: Progress Publishers.
Mauss, M. (1967). *The Gift: Forms and Functions of Exchange in Archaic Societies*, trans. L. Cunnison. New York: W.W. Norton.
Nietzsche, F. (1956). *The Birth of Tragedy* and *The Genealogy of Morals*, trans. F. Golffing. New York: Doubleday.
Polanyi, K. (1957). *The Great Transformation*. Boston, MA: Beacon Press.
Poupeau, F. & Discepolo, T. (2005). 'Scholarship with Commitment: on the Political Engagements of Pierre Bourdieu'. In L. Wacquant (ed.), *Bourdieu and Democratic Politics*. Cambridge: Polity Press.

Rabinow, P. (2002). 'The Pathos of Absolute Illusion'. *Iichiko*, 75: n.p.
Rancière, J. (2004). *The Philosopher and His Poor*, trans. various. Durham, NC: Duke University Press.
Reed-Danahay, D. (2005). *Locating Bourdieu*. Bloomington, IN: Indiana University Press.
—— (2009). 'Bourdieu's Ethnography in Béarn and Kabylia: The Peasant Habitus'. In J. Goodman & P. Silverstein (eds), *Bourdieu in Algeria: Colonial Politics, Ethnographic Practices, Theoretical Developments*. Lincoln, NE: University of Nebraska Press.
Robbins, D. (2000). *Bourdieu & Culture*. London: Sage.
Sapiro, G. (2010). 'Introduction'. In P. Bourdieu, *Sociology is a Martial Art: Political Writings by Pierre Bourdieu*, trans. various. London: The New Press.
Snook, I. (1990). 'Language, Truth and Power: Bourdieu's Ministerium'. In R. Harker, C. Mahar & C. Wilkes (eds), *An Introduction to the Work of Pierre Bourdieu*. London: Macmillan.
Swartz, D. (1997). *Culture and Power: The Sociology of Pierre Bourdieu*. Chicago, IL: University of Chicago Press.
Thompson, J. (2005). 'Editor's Introduction'. In P. Bourdieu, *Language and Symbolic Power*, trans. G. Raymond & M. Adamson. Cambridge: Polity Press.
Thomson, P. (2012). 'Field'. In M. Grenfell (ed.), *Bourdieu: Key Concepts*. Jaipur: Rawat.
Wacquant, L. (1996). 'Foreword'. In P. Bourdieu, *The State Nobility: Elite Schools in the Field of Power,* trans L. Clough. Cambridge: Polity Press.
—— (2013). 'Bourdieu 1993: A Case Study in Scientific Consecration'. *Sociology*, 47(1): 15–29.
Webb, J., Schirato, T. & Danaher, G. (2002). *Understanding Bourdieu*. Sydney: Allen & Unwin.
Wellek, R. (1981). *A History of Modern Criticism, 1750–1950*. Cambridge: Cambridge University Press.
Wittgenstein, L. (1983). *Philosophical Investigations*. Oxford: Blackwell.
Yacine, T. (2013). 'Presentation'. In P. Bourdieu, *Algerian Sketches*. Cambridge: Polity Press.
Yates, E. (2001). 'Booker Judges Announced'. *The Guardian*, 16 February, www.theguardian.com/books/2001/feb/15/bookerprize2001.thebookerprize, accessed 18 April 2017.

INDEX

Abish, Walter 32
Aboulafia, Mitchell 41
aesthetics, aesthetic disposition 56, 115–18, 124, 127, 129–31, 141, 159, 180
Althusser, Louis 28
Anderson, Benedict 163
Appadurai, Arjun 131, 149
Archer, Margaret 95
Aron, Raymond 4
Austin, J.L. 202–6

Bachelard, Gaston 15, 20, 24, 33, 35–6, 46, 59–60, 213
Barnard, Henry 63
Barthes, Roland 2, 32
Becker, Gary 177
Bernstein, Basil 95–6
Blanchot, Maurice 7
Boltanski, Luc 172

Bottomore, Tom 98
Bourdieu, Pierre
    and Algeria 3–4, 8–9, 15–17, 24–5, 32, 42, 44, 50, 54–66, 98, 134, 139, 159, 166, 176–7, 195, 200, 211–14
    and anthropology 2, 9, 16, 21, 24–5, 32, 45–6, 49–50, 54, 56, 58, 63, 65–6, 116, 209–10, 212–13, 232, 239
    and Béarn 16, 61–6, 98, 139, 195, 200, 214, 222, 234–5
    and cultural turn 71, 84, 87, 140
    and educational work 9, 17–22, 43–51 passim, 66–75, 82, 87, 89–115 passim, 119, 124, 139, 142, 159, 161, 163, 173, 175, 193, 200, 202, 216
    and empiricism 2, 14–16, 18, 20, 34, 42, 45, 58–9, 63, 68, 71, 81, 117–21, 135, 164, 209, 227

Bourdieu, Pierre *continued*
  and ethnology, ethnography 9, 22, 45, 49–50, 54, 56, 58–63, 65–7, 211–14
  and existentialism 8, 24, 30, 36–7, 134
  and history and philosophy of science 33, 37, 56, 60
  and Kabyle, Kabylia 67, 195–6, 222, 234–5
  and linguistics 21, 33, 50, 56
  and Marx, Marxism 6, 8–9, 23, 25, 27–30, 33, 37, 39, 43, 50–1, 56, 63, 161, 189, 192, 212, 232–3
  and objectivism 23, 30, 33, 39–40, 61, 80, 134–5, 148
  and phenomenology 8, 30–1, 50, 134
  and philosophy 2–3, 8, 22–7, 34–5, 37–40, 45, 50, 54, 56, 59, 63, 81, 213, 215–16
  and political activism 1, 6, 9, 27, 34, 37, 45, 50, 54–5, 61, 64, 85
  as public intellectual 5, 84–5
  and scholarly apparatus 42, 68, 87, 231
  and scholarly trajectory 11, 21, 23, 42–3
  and social sciences 9, 11–13, 15, 21–5, 27, 32, 40, 45, 56, 107, 117, 134, 142, 158, 216, 228
  and sociology 2, 22–5, 33–4, 38, 40, 43, 45–6, 50–1, 54–66 passim, 71–2, 81, 90–3, 117, 141–4, 159, 214–17, 228, 232
    as reflexive science 15–16, 45–6, 54–5, 60–2, 67, 80, 82, 90, 94, 112, 123, 141, 143, 163, 187, 227–8
  and structuralism 13, 30, 32, 43, 49, 56, 58, 63, 65, 110, 134, 176, 214, 239
  and subjectivism 23, 30, 33, 39–40, 80, 134-5, 148

works
  Academic Discourse 50, 68–9, 87, 91–101 passim, 104
  Acts of Resistance 22, 83–4, 191
  Algeria 1960 41, 65
  Algerian Sketches 65
  Bachelors' Ball, The 200–1
  Craft of Sociology, The 41, 48, 60, 68, 74
  Distinction 28, 41, 46, 51–4, 63, 66, 68, 71, 73–6, 78, 90, 113–25 passim, 128, 191–3
  Field of Cultural Production, The 41, 68, 71, 76–7, 82, 140, 143, 169, 216
  Firing Back 6, 22, 83
  Free Exchange 71, 76, 80, 82
  Homo Academicus 16, 41, 72, 90, 139
  Inheritors, The 18, 50, 68–9, 71, 87, 89, 91–4, 99, 101, 103–5, 193
  In Other Words 20, 28, 41, 66, 72, 80–2, 123, 135, 156, 192
  Invitation to Reflexive Sociology, An 20, 28, 35, 38, 41–2, 46, 52, 72, 78, 80, 82, 123, 135, 152, 186, 201, 203, 239
  Language and Symbolic Power 20, 28, 41, 50, 68, 72, 80–2, 119, 140, 191–2, 198
  Logic of Practice, The 39, 41, 54, 58, 65, 72, 79–80, 82, 107, 131, 135, 214, 235–6
  Love of Art, The 68, 113, 118–19, 124
  Masculine Domination 29, 51, 69, 123, 191–2, 194–5
  On Television and Journalism 5, 20, 45, 71, 76, 80, 82, 171, 191
  On the State 81, 90, 191–3
  Outline of a Theory of Practice 32, 39, 41, 63, 65, 72, 80, 131, 134, 200, 214, 234–6, 239

INDEX

Pascalian Meditations 20, 37–8, 41, 65, 72, 80–2, 86, 135–6, 139–40, 214
Photography 68, 113, 117, 119, 124
Picturing Algeria 54
Political Interventions 55, 57, 83
Political Ontology of Martin Heidegger, The 26, 41, 72, 115
Practical Reason 29, 39, 41, 53, 65, 72, 80–2, 123, 135, 140, 143, 192, 213, 216
Reproduction in Education, Society and Culture 18, 50, 68–71, 87–92, 97–9, 101, 104–5, 108–11, 119
Rules of Art, The 41, 65, 71, 76–7, 82, 143, 216
Science of Science and Reflexivity 13, 22, 82–3, 187
Sketch for a Self-Analysis 3–4, 23, 32, 55, 59, 61, 211
Social Structures of the Economy, The 22, 82–3, 191
Sociology in Question 14, 18, 20, 41, 58, 68, 72, 80, 82
Sociology is a Martial Art 83–4
State Nobility, The 14, 65–6, 68, 90, 121, 125, 191, 193
Weight of the World, The 16, 45, 63, 66, 72, 82, 112, 191, 195, 227–8
Bouveresse, Jacques 135–6, 144–5, 222
Bové, José 2
Brown, Nicholas 2–3, 86
Butler, Judith 166, 206, 233–4, 239

Calhoun, Craig 10, 73
Canguilhem, Georges 15, 20, 24, 33, 35–6, 46, 60, 213
capital
 cultural 6, 8, 10–11, 13, 23, 28, 50, 61, 64, 68–72, 76, 79, 86–7, 97, 99–101, 103, 116, 119–23, 125–6, 128–9, 139, 149, 154, 157–9, 163, 168–71, 173–90 passim, 192–3, 198–9, 211, 213, 215, 218, 220–1, 225–6, 230–2, 237, 239
 economic 10, 122–3, 169–70, 174, 176, 178, 181–2, 188, 197, 232
 linguistic 70, 93, 97, 101–3, 122, 169
 social 122, 185
 symbolic 11, 64, 68, 85–6, 122–3, 128, 163, 173, 178, 183–6, 190, 198–201, 204, 230, 237
capitalism 7–10, 12–13, 22, 44, 64, 72, 83, 86, 128, 148, 165, 169, 175–6, 178, 181–3, 186, 189, 195, 200, 202, 220, 230–1
Cassirer, Ernst 161
Cause, Leanne 95
Certeau, Michel de 62, 70, 220, 234, 236
Champagne, Patrick 5
Chartier, Roger 134, 225
Chomsky, Noam 204
class 9, 13, 16–20, 28–30, 36, 46, 51–4, 58, 62, 64, 68–70, 73–6, 89–97, 99–113 passim, 114–20, 122–31, 135, 139, 143, 148, 159, 163, 171, 175, 185–6, 189, 191–3, 202–3, 205, 216, 224, 226–7, 232–3
Collins, James 95
Comte, Auguste 47
Crary, Jonathan 7
Crossley, Nick 121
cultural arbitrary 90, 99–100
culture 4, 8, 19, 22, 34, 46, 48, 61–2, 64, 68–75, 82, 88, 90, 95, 105, 109, 111, 113–19, 122–31, 134, 141–2, 159, 166, 181–2, 187, 195, 209, 228, 231–3

Danto, Arthur 79
Darbel, Alain 68, 113, 118
Derrida, Jacques 139
Discepolo, Thierry 50

253

discourse 9, 11–14, 22, 26, 34, 38, 45, 62, 64, 68, 71–3, 75–6, 78–9, 83–6, 88, 102, 115–16, 120, 124, 128, 137, 143, 146, 148, 150–1, 153, 155, 160, 162, 164–5, 168, 170–1, 176–7, 183, 187, 189, 195, 199–200, 204, 208, 210, 216, 218–20, 228–9, 235–7
distinction 49, 78, 113, 116, 123, 125, 127, 130–1, 178, 124
 and aesthetics 56, 115–18, 124, 129–31, 141, 159, 180
 and disinterestedness 115–16, 124, 130, 142–3, 157, 159, 170, 175, 187, 216–17, 230
 and taste 91, 116–17, 119, 124–5, 128–30
doxa 51, 103, 141, 151, 194, 206, 216, 221, 225
Durkheim, Emile 15, 27, 33–5, 45, 60, 64, 67–8, 90, 137, 183, 213

Elias, Norbert 35
epistemology 11, 36, 87, 118, 213

Fanon, Franz 9, 63, 65
field 7, 11, 15, 19–20, 23, 26, 28–30, 37, 40, 42, 50, 64, 70–3, 76–9, 82, 87, 93, 109–10, 120–1, 123, 126, 129, 134, 138–9, 141, 143–4, 147, 152, 154–73 passim, 175–6, 178–9, 185, 197–9, 206, 208–10, 217–20, 223–5, 230–2, 239
 academic 11, 22, 37, 45, 66, 72, 85, 161, 183–4, 189, 199, 212, 214
 artistic 157, 162
 of cultural production 10, 13, 20, 43–4, 46, 50, 71–2, 76–7, 80, 82–3, 87, 123–4, 128, 143, 157–9, 161–3, 169, 173, 177
 economic 83, 157
 and economism 83, 169, 176
 of education 8, 45, 92, 96, 100, 126
 and French educational system 17, 68, 89–90, 98, 105, 161, 175
 and language 18, 41, 88, 94–6, 99, 100–2, 114, 202
 and learning 18–19, 106, 127
 and pedagogic action 98–100, 202
 and pedagogic work 99–100, 104, 51, 62, 66, 68, 70, 73, 87–92, 95–99, 103, 109, 113, 124
 and rational pedagogy 88, 103–5
 and reproduction in 51, 62, 66, 68, 70, 73, 87–92
 and teachers 17, 71, 96–7, 100–1, 104–5, 126
 of intellectuals 2, 73, 76, 87, 122, 217, 235
 literary 16, 43, 76–7, 79, 126, 141–3, 151, 162, 169, 181–2
 of journalism 50, 64, 72, 80, 171, 195
 of the media 12, 14, 76, 83–5, 95, 148–9, 171, 179, 181–3, 189, 199
 political 76, 83, 192
 of power 10–13, 18–20, 72, 76–7, 79, 120, 122–4, 126, 142–3, 152–4, 160, 162–6, 169–71, 178–9, 186, 189, 193, 199, 220, 228, 230–1
 of science 4, 11, 30, 82, 142–4, 187–8, 216–7, 225, 228
 of sport 64, 80, 82, 125, 127, 146–7, 154, 156, 169, 180, 184, 187, 232
Flaubert, Gustave 43, 77–8, 141
Foucault, Michel 2, 29, 81, 85, 148, 171
Franzen, Johnathan 181–2
Frow, John 53, 73–4, 115–16, 122

gender 50, 69, 92–3, 120, 123–4, 127, 135, 148, 166, 171, 191, 193–4, 199, 202, 206, 221, 224
 and masculine domination 29, 193–4
general economy, theory of 10, 150, 168, 173, 175–7, 196

254

INDEX

gift 196–7
Goodman, Jane 9, 16–17, 20, 63–4
Grenfell, Michael 3–5, 68
Guillory, John 10

Haacke, Hans 71, 76, 80, 217
habitus 3, 5, 15–21, 23, 28–30, 37, 40, 42, 45–7, 49–50, 54–5, 61, 64, 70, 73, 76, 78–9, 82, 87, 94, 99–100, 103, 109–11, 116, 119, 121, 127, 131–62 passim, 165, 167, 170, 179, 186–9, 192, 198–9, 206–13, 215, 217–25, 228, 231–9
  and bodily hexis 31, 39, 70, 86, 125, 127, 136, 140, 147, 149, 152, 165, 167–8, 173, 179, 203, 205, 218, 232, 237
  and socio-cultural trajectory 88, 133, 138, 146, 149, 208–9, 211
  as disposition 19, 21, 23, 25–6, 29, 31, 47–8, 50, 54–6, 60–4, 69, 75–6, 86, 107, 109–10, 116, 119–20, 124, 127, 129–30, 132–3, 137–8, 143, 145–8, 150, 152–5, 163–7, 170, 173–4, 177, 192, 194, 209–14, 216–21, 224–5, 228–31, 237–8
  scholarly 15, 22–3, 25, 38, 47, 55, 109, 138, 157, 170, 209, 211–13, 223, 226, 228–31
Hammoudi, Abdellah 21
Harker, Richard 17, 30, 63, 68, 70–1, 90, 95–6
Heidegger, Martin 26–7, 34, 37, 40, 56, 115

ideology 11, 29, 57, 73, 94, 189
illusio 28, 35, 141–2, 162, 165, 167, 175, 218, 224

Jenkins, Richard 17, 20, 41, 68, 70, 73, 133
Johnson, Randell 169

Kant, Emmanuel 114–16
Kuhn, Thomas 37, 152

Lacan, Jacques 2
Lazarsfeld, Paul 60
Lefort, Claude 11–13
Leiris, Michel 57
Levi-Strauss, Claude 4, 21, 32, 56
literacy, cultural 20, 79, 115, 119, 123, 140, 145, 173, 175, 192, 203, 207, 211, 218, 222, 234, 239

Mahar, Cheleen 30, 63, 68, 70–1
Mangan, J.A. 128
Mauss, Marcel 137, 197
May, Stephen 95–6
Merleau-Ponty, Maurice 26, 31
misrecognition 21, 28, 35, 98, 107, 194, 224, 230, 238–9
multiple correspondence analysis 121
museums 50, 116, 118

Nietzsche, Friedrich 23, 33, 40–1, 81, 178

Panofsky, Erwin 138
Pascal, Blaise 33, 38–9, 81, 136–7, 168, 214
Passeron, Jean-Claude 4, 18, 35, 41, 47, 50, 60, 68–70, 74, 87, 89–99, 101–12, 117, 119, 161, 193
photography 50, 66, 117–19
Polanyi, Karl 7, 201
potlatch 197
Poupeau, Franck 50
practice, logic of 17, 21, 39, 61, 65, 73, 75, 87, 132, 136, 138, 146, 208, 210, 218, 221, 236
  and reflexivity 7, 20, 23, 37, 47, 62, 72, 74, 79, 142–3, 208–17 passim, 220, 223–5, 228–31, 238–9

Rabinow, Paul 156
Rancière, Jacques 18–19, 71
Reed-Danahay, Deborah 71, 232

reproduction, socio-cultural 9, 20, 45, 51, 62, 66, 68, 70, 73, 87–92, 95, 98–9, 103, 109, 113, 124, 131, 137, 139, 141, 146–7, 159, 163, 170, 186, 193, 202, 227, 232
Robbins, Derek 3–5, 46, 48–9, 71, 74–7, 161

Saint Martin, Monique de 5, 50, 68–70, 87, 91–7, 102, 104
Sapiro, Gisele 6, 84–5
Sartre, Jean-Paul 1, 9, 30, 35, 56, 77, 85
Saussure, Ferdinand de 33, 50, 135, 204
Silverstein, Paul 9, 16, 20, 63–4
Snook, Ivan 41
state, the 82–3, 161, 176, 186, 189, 191, 193–5, 198–9, 201, 203, 220, 230
subjectivity 87, 126, 148, 157, 159, 166, 202, 232, 237
symbolic power 10, 14, 19–22, 28–30, 39, 41, 50, 59, 68, 72, 81–2, 90, 92, 113, 115–16, 119, 123–5, 131, 137, 139, 143, 159–60, 163, 169–70, 191–5, 197–8, 200, 202, 204, 206–7, 216, 224, 232
  and language 41, 202–4

as violence 22, 28, 30, 35, 41, 43–4, 51, 59, 68, 71–2, 81–2, 87, 90, 92, 96, 98–9, 111, 151, 159, 170, 177, 191, 193–5, 200–4, 211, 221, 224
Szeman, Imre 2–3, 86

Thompson, John 198, 204–5

Wacquant, Loïc 4–6, 15–16, 18, 20, 28, 30–1, 33, 35–6, 38, 40–2, 46–9, 51–2, 60, 63, 65, 72, 78, 80, 123, 126, 135, 143, 152, 158, 164, 166, 168, 170, 186, 200–3, 209, 214, 217–21, 225, 229, 231, 239
Weber, Max 15, 20, 27, 33, 35, 45–6, 60, 64, 67–8, 90, 125, 137, 160–1, 183, 213
Wellek, René 115
Wilkes, Chris 30, 63, 68, 70–1
Winfrey, Oprah 181–2
Wittgenstein, Ludwig 7, 16, 24, 33, 37–40, 43, 50, 80–1, 145

Yacine, Tassadit 9, 56, 61, 63–5, 211

Zola, Emile 1, 85